Erotic Morality

EROTIC MORALITY

The Role of Touch in Moral Agency

LINDA HOLLER

RUTGERS UNIVERSITY PRESS
New Brunswick, New Jersey, and London

#46872274

Library of Congress Cataloging-in-Publication Data

Holler, Linda, 1952–
    Erotic morality : the role of touch in moral agency / Linda Holler.
        p.   cm.
    Includes bibliographical references and index.
    ISBN 0-8135-3044-X (cloth: alk. paper)—ISBN 0-8135-3045-8 (pbk. : alk. paper)
    1. Ethics.   2. Touch.   I. Title.

BJ1031.H753 2002
176—dc21
                                                                    2001031784
British Cataloging-in-Publication data for this book is available from the British
Library

Manufactured in the United States of America

*To my mother, Edith Holler,
and in memory of my father,
Dean Holler (1919–1995)*

Contents

Acknowledgments

My thanks to family, friends, and colleagues for their guidance and their patience with me over the years I have worked on this project. In the end, my resolve to complete the work came from my respect for those who have found ways to stay in touch with the world even when that is painful.

I am grateful to Alan Sparks, my former department chair at San Diego State University, for giving me a reduced teaching load and funds to hire research assistants. Many thanks to Matt Calarco, Vince Biondo, and David Bailey, who found resources, summarized materials, and took copious notes. Renee Carson also provided invaluable assistance, checking sources, helping with software, and fixing computer glitches. Administrative Coordinators Elaine Rother and Marge Thompson have done whatever was necessary to help me stay afloat, especially since I became department chair. I am also grateful to students who helped me sort through difficult literatures during the two semesters I taught courses on religion and the body.

I received advice on a variety of research topics from colleagues Susan Cayleff, Laurie Baron, Sandra Wawrykto, and Roberta Hobson. Ruth Denison and Treelight (Lucinda) Green answered questions on mindfulness for me at Ruth's Vipassana retreat center, Dhamma Dena, in Joshua Tree, California. Charlene Spretnak and Mary Clark made detailed and immensely helpful suggestions for revisions based on careful readings of a complete draft. Their hard work produced a much stronger argument. Kathy Jones introduced my book proposal to Marlie Wasserman, my editor at Rutgers, whose support for the project has never wavered.

I would never have completed the book without the help of Mary Kelly who read every draft. Mary helped me to think through the arguments and to achieve a clarity of language that I am rarely capable of on my own. I also need to thank my mother, Edith, for her steadfast encouragement and her patience with me when this project seemed to consume all of my time and energy. I dedicate the work to her and to my late father, without whose love and kindness my own capacity for eros would be sorely diminished.

Erotic Morality

INTRODUCTION

> All power emerges from erotic power either, in
> life-giving form, from our acknowledgement
> of it and our ability to live in that understand-
> ing or, in destructive form, from the broken-
> heartedness that refuses to understand it.
> —Rita Nakashima Brock, *Journeys of the Heart*

For more than two decades feminist and other ethicists concerned
with social justice and ecology have called for and worked toward
an understanding of morality that is body-affirming rather than
body-denying. Just as dualistic, disembodied philosophy inevitably
gave rise to an ethic based on *logos*—on rules, authorities, and duties—so embodied awareness is giving rise to an ethic based on
eros, a somatic, intuitive form of agency in which empathy, compassion, and care are the central moral qualities. This book seeks to
be part of the transformation, within ethics, that hopes to reshape
understandings of the moral life by teaching us to value our senses
and our experiences as sentient beings.

In this text, touch is used as the primary sense around which to
compose a discourse about moral agency. Touch is the first sense
given to us in evolutionary and individual biological history, and in
its physiological and psychological dimensions touch may be our
most foundational erotic sense. Erotic in poet Audre Lorde's use of
the term, touch unites sensory and emotional feeling. The ways
that we are physically touched help to determine our repulsions, attractions, and indifferences and our ability to respond emotionally
to what goes on around us, that is, to care passionately and compassionately about our own lives and the lives of others. Eros is this

passion for life, the embodied expression of the relational nature of existence in constructions of identity, awareness, and action. In her classic essay, "Uses of the Erotic: The Erotic as Power," Lorde describes eros as inclusive of all forms of love, joy, and shared feeling; it is "creative energy empowered" because one is touched from within and from without, both emotionally and physically.[1]

As the interweaving of the inner and outer dimensions of identity, eros is, as I see it, the home of Trinh Minh-ha's infinitely layered self: "I am not i can be you and me."[2] Because bodies define the conscious and unconscious boundaries of our interconnectedness, our senses act as seats of consciousness, places from which we construct identities and subjective relations. Touch is the sense by which our contact with the world is made most intimate, and it is therefore home to both our wisdom and our neuroses. Boundaries blur as self and not-self meet. In any touch, we both touch and are touched; we give and receive. Replete with pleasure and pain receptors, skin is the largest organ of the body. Studies have shown that premature infants gain almost 50 percent more weight when touched and that people who touch animals recover from illness more quickly than those who do not. Touch helps to lower blood pressure and slow the pulse; it relaxes as well as stimulates us. Primates have literally been driven to brain damage from being denied touch, and the abused become abusers through violent touch.

Compared to vision, our other senses of hearing, smelling, tasting, and touching—in that order—bring us increasingly into actual physical contact with the world and therefore can serve to prevent forms of denial, solipsism, and idealism.[3] We touch the world and are touched by it in all perception—for example, the eyes have been called the windows of the soul because when we make eye contact we touch each other very deeply. But the proximal senses—taste, smell, and touch—are the most direct means by which we take the world within us and leave our marks upon it. Besides our senses, other bodily functions, such as eating and breathing, provide important examples of the self-world intimacy represented by touching. Smell, taste, and touch warn us of potential dangers, but they also trigger some of our most powerful—and earliest—erotic memories. All of our senses help to compose boundaries for our protection, but the senses also determine how permeable the borders are that allow us to be nourished and come closer to each other. When I eat, breathe, or put clothes on my back, I am touched by means of the sensations in my mouth, lungs, and skin, but in each of these acts I also touch the material conditions of my existence—soil, plants, animals, photosynthetic processes, biosystems, and laborers. From this perspective, one's skin stretches as far back into our evolutionary history as the first cell and as far out into space as the energy that sustains life on this planet. Attention to embodiment reveals selves and worlds constructed out of their interrelations rather than an isolated self—as Diane Ackerman has suggested, in *A Natural History of the Senses*, perception is a form of grace.[4]

Daniel Goleman has called the process of coming to our senses "emotional intelligence," while Buddhists call it the practice of "mindfulness"—the simple, straightforward awareness of feeling as it happens, described by one Buddhist teacher as a ruthless, non-solipsistic form of realism.[5] Whatever we call sensual awareness, coming from non-sense to sense is a moral and political act because it restores our ties to the material world and to the consequences of our actions. Tactile forms of consciousness are forms of embodied wisdom that help us remain in touch with the extended network of our biological and economic lives. In so doing, erotic awareness creates a subjective life attuned to bodies, or—as Marx might have said—a materialism that takes subjectivity seriously.[6] Thus, in the phenomenology of touch that I am constructing, touch is a metaphor for the entire sensual gestalt and further assumes a relational ontology in which—to borrow another phrase from Buddhism—"This is like this because that is like that."

The extent to which the senses, particularly touch, form crucial links among self-awareness, world awareness, and emotional feeling became clarified for me by a source that initially seemed most unlikely: two women discussing their struggles with autism. Victims of Asperger syndrome, a form of autism linked to very high intelligence and linguistic proficiency, Temple Grandin and Donna Williams withdrew from touch because they were born experiencing almost all touch as painful. Because of their sensory disorders, each of these women in her own way knows that consciousness of the body and of the world are inseparable, that feeling makes the world ontologically present in ways that concepts alone never can, and that intersubjective life is lost when the body is experienced as an alien other. As articulate witnesses to the futility of solipsism and to the distortions of reality that attend a mind divorced from the body, both women have written eloquently about the ways that distorted sense experience affects the development of self-hood, intersubjective life, and world awareness.[7] Each of them emerged from sensory and emotional chaos by practicing a reflective kind of awareness about boundaries and attachments, barriers and openings, and prisons and sanctuaries that are associated with feelings. This practice of awareness made it possible for them to find ways to outwit their own defenses and fears and develop strategies allowing them to be physically and emotionally at home in the world—which is also, I will argue, what we need to do.

Grandin is a professor in the department of animal sciences at Colorado State University in Fort Collins and author of *Emergence: Labeled Autistic* and *Thinking in Pictures: And Other Reports from My Life with Autism*. She demonstrates remarkable rapport with animals and is known internationally for her design of feedlots, dip chutes, humane restraining devices, and slaughterhouses. Her "squeeze machine," a mechanically controlled hug device that she fashioned for herself from a cattle chute, particularly impressed me as a magnificent example of how touch can be used to connect us to each other. Grandin says that through the comfort and calm the machine's embrace provided, she came to learn empathy and the ability to comfort others. She credits the squeeze machine with giving her what other people could not give her due to her autism—comfortable tactile sensation. "When I was in the chute, I felt closer to people like Mother . . . it broke through my barrier of tactile defensiveness, and I felt the love and concern of these people."[8] A scientist by training, Grandin is secure in herself and her autism. "If I could snap my fingers and be non-autistic, I would not," she declares. "Autism is part of who I am."[9] Her knowledge of animal behavior and neurophysiology and her own experience of tactile deprivation are valuable resources for thinking about the erotic nature of morality. In this work, her squeeze machine is a central symbol of eros, that is, our ability to connect to the world in an empathetic way through comforting, loving touch.

Donna Williams was unable to tolerate touch or emotional

connection with others for most of her life without thereby experiencing a loss of selfhood. Alternatively hyposensitive and hypersensitive to external stimuli, Williams's senses are prone to either shut down or overload. Existing in what she calls the "all world, no self" or "all self, no world" condition, Williams can experience intense self-awareness or intense other-awareness, but never both self and other at the same time—and never the subjective life of the other.[10] Trained philosophers will be hard-pressed not to see in Williams's descriptions in her two autobiographies, *Nobody Nowhere: The Extraordinary Autobiography of an Autistic* and *Somebody Somewhere: Breaking Free from the World of Autism*, existential counterparts to many ideas in Western philosophy, such as Sartre's *en soi/pour soi* and Descartes's *res extensa/res cogitans*. At times she seems like the ultimate isolated and atomistic self, existing in a "self-made womb" and experiencing the world as if "under glass." She calls herself "a universe of one" and, with great wit, I think, a "culture looking for a place to happen."[11] At other times she seems like the ultimate soluble self, lost in the world as profoundly as any woman who ever loved too much or any aspiring mystic. As she reflects, "I learned eventually to lose myself in anything I desired—the patterns on the wallpaper or the carpet, the sound of something over and over again."[12]

Grandin's and Williams's struggles to experience their own bodies as less alien prompted my curiosity about the ways we, as individuals, as a society, and as a culture, ignore, denigrate, and destroy the feeling self, creating conditions that approximate organic feeling disorders such as autism. Thus, my initial attraction to this project was what seemed to me an exquisite irony, that these women who suffer from feeling disorders are perceptive enough about feeling to recognize and reflect back to us the ways we hide from our own feelings as individuals and as a society. Donna Williams suggests, for example, that emotions are central to our ability to *be* rather than merely to appear or to function: they allow communication between body and mind and are therefore central to the way subjectivity takes flesh. Her description of the importance of the emotions is very much like the argument made by philosopher Alison Jagger when she pointed out that traditional ethics had taken the "Dumb View of the emotions" by relegating emotions to "noncognitive responses to environmental stimuli."[13]

Reading these works in the context of my philosophical and theo-logical training, I knew that Grandin and Williams could help me understand the dualistic heritage of Western philosophy but also, and perhaps more importantly, the rapidly rising number of people in our society who suffer from some form of stress, trauma, or abuse or are otherwise alienated from their sensory and emo-tional lives.

On a more personal level, I was drawn to the life stories of these autistic women because they spoke to me about my own sen-sory and emotional life. Environments mold body chemistry and nervous systems, helping to determine how and to what extent we can touch the world and be touched by it; and the more stressful my own life becomes, the more I find that I, too, experience forms of hypersensitivity and shutdown to sensory overload. For example, I am barely able to tolerate the increasingly loud music played in restaurants and stores; one has to compete with it to speak or even to think. Once a source of pleasure, music has be-come for me just another irritating noise. In the urban area of southern California where I live, it is no longer possible to escape the cacophony emanating from cars, boom boxes, garden blowers, and construction machinery—even in the desert wilderness the military jets buzz the landscape so low that one's entire nervous system floods with adrenaline. For me—and I think many other people—this sensory overload results in escalating impatience with other drivers on the roads, or with slow lines at the grocery store, and it ultimately manifests itself in the stories of this or that form of rage so often featured in the news. Since I say this as a healthy and highly privileged person with many emotional, intellectual, and material resources at my disposal, I can only imagine what it takes to survive under much worse conditions, with no hope of es-caping the pressure cooker of poverty, violence, and substance abuse. Stress reinforces habitual conditioning and encourages ad-dictions and obsessive-compulsive rituals; it feeds withdrawal and aggression, and by compromising our ability to feel at home in the body, it compromises our capacity for empathy. Overstimulated lifestyles work like restricted environments to feed hypersensitivity and create states of vigilance not unlike those produced by As-perger syndrome or post-traumatic stress disorder. Those of us who feel too much find ways to shut down, and those of us who feel too little find ways to harm ourselves or others in an effort to feel anything at all. As I will argue, the fight-or-flight reactions provoked by stress and trauma may help us perceive immediate dangers, but they can also create dangers where there are none—and they will never give us the perceptual acuity needed to deal responsibly with chronic problems. Hypersensitive nervous systems leave us obsessing over small annoyances and engaging in escapes that provide temporary relief rather than attending to the larger warning signs and long-term consequences of maladaptive behavior—ozone depletion, deforestation, global warming, malnutrition, hate crimes, school shootings.

To be healthy morally and otherwise, we need protected yet porous relations that open and close as the membranes of cells do to create appropriate exchanges between inner and outer. Donna Haraway and Sharon Salzberg have therefore suggested using immune systems to model discourse about constructing responsible relations. For Haraway, the model of the immune system allows us to imaginatively "construct and maintain the boundaries for what may count as self and other in the crucial realms of the normal and the pathological." And Salzberg compares our inability to see ourselves in others with autoimmune diseases that make it impossible for the body to recognize its own cells as having integrity.[14] In immune system dysfunctions, some areas of the body may be left entirely unprotected while other areas may develop autoimmune reactions in which protective systems become so overactive that they attack perfectly healthy parts of the body.[15] Disorders of feeling can take on similar dynamics, leaving one insensitive to real dangers and hypersensitive to what is harmless. A healthy immune system, Haraway suggests, constructs borders responsibly in the critical areas where self and nonself meet. By means of the metaphor of touch, I want to examine these critical meetings, arguing that the numb and hypersensitive places on our individual and social bodies turn our capacities for sensuality and emotional connection against us by means of habitual conditioning and sadomasochistic responses.

For those who find the world too painful, the self develops a thick skin, often taking on forms of rigidity that are manifest in repeated, self-defeating actions. As Donna Williams might say, one's sanctuaries quickly turn into prisons, cutting off exchanges necessary for a healthy mind-body. Along with stress, trauma, and abuse, habitual conditioning is an important way that attractions and repulsions become pathogenic because habits leave us desensitized, closed to present experience, open to addiction, and therefore inwardly less free. The loss of plasticity leaves us out of touch with our inner lives and open to control by external authorities. When we live in non-sense, we tend to repeat the past and, particularly, to repeat the ways we have learned to shut ourselves off from pain (and pleasure), and thus we are shut off from the possibility of change and intimacy. Therefore, the question that drives this inquiry is how we can achieve healthy thresholds of sensory and emotional feeling, thresholds that will enhance rather than restrict empathetic, intersubjective life. How do we create responsible exchanges that hold onto the defenses we need while allowing us to remain open and compassionate?

From the point of view of mainstream ethics and culture, the title *Erotic Morality* may appear to be an oxymoron because our understanding of love, like our understanding of morality, has been privatized and sexualized. As such, too much moral attention has been placed on restrictions surrounding sexual pleasure and not enough attention has been given to the prevention of pain and suffering. Ideologies that view moral virtue as something won over and against the body have proven counterproductive by promoting fear of the body and fear of those tied to the body in our cultural imagination: traditionally, women, the mentally ill, children, people of color, Jews, and homosexuals. The association of the body with sin not only promotes fear of the body but psychic states of blame, guilt, or shame, conditions that are rarely empowering for moral action. Once we become caught up in punishing biopsychological feedback loops that reproduce guilt, shame, or violence, we become unable to engage in even the most minimal demands of healthy agency, such as performing actions in accord with enlightened self-interest. As a society, moreover, we prefer to read symptoms of the subversion of feeling as individual character flaws rather than as social issues.

While this is not a book about sexual morality, it is about moving the discussion of our capacity for intimacy and passion from the private to the public arena. In erotic forms of morality, the personal becomes political not through government legislation of intimacy, but by unmasking individual and social pathologies originating from our failure to take intimacy seriously. I see feeling disorders as symptoms of social and political illness—like the French feminists viewed Victorian hysteria—in a society completely out of touch with erotic life but fully immersed in pornography, that is, the cultivation of sensations divorced from emotional connections. In Lorde's words, "To refuse to be conscious of what we are feeling at any time, however comfortable that might seem, is to . . . allow ourselves to be reduced to the pornographic, the abused, the absurd."[16] In a similar fashion, Nel Noddings, in *Caring* and *Women and Evil,* reinterprets evil as anesthetization to pain. We cannot be moved to care about the pain or pleasure of others, she suggests, if we are numb to our own. To the contrary, the less we feel, the more detached, violent, and self-destructive we allow ourselves to be. Alienated from the seasons and rhythms of nature and our own bodies, as Charlene Spretnak has observed, we remain glued to our television and computer screens, devices that present the world and bodies to us merely as objects for consumption.[17]

Societies that fear eros cannot create morally adaptive somatic conditions because they care more about constructing impermeable boundaries than they do about the suffering created by those boundaries. Since there are no impermeable boundaries in living systems, our failed attempts to create them are reborn into the world as pollution, violence, poverty, and disease. Sensory and emotional isolation acts to perpetuate social injustices and shields us from the consequences of how we are living. It is therefore not surprising that we have been unable as a society to enact public policies to provide everyone with something as essential as health care. In subtle ways we continue to regard mental illness as a character defect and addiction as a failure of will power. And we continue to build prisons that research shows are little more than laboratories for the creation of crime and violence. Reclaiming the sentient awareness necessary for our physical, psychological, and moral well-being demands that we heal the places where we have become either numb or hypersensitive to touch and soften the rigidities of our bodies and ideologies.

When viewed as a source of moral truth, the body is released from being an object for legislation, punishment, and discipline and allowed to be what it has been in the history of our evolution—the core of our subjective life and consciousness, the central way we know and respond to what is going on around us. Somatic states provide direct evidence about the situations in which we find ourselves, and, like canaries in a mine, the alarms and beacons of our embodied lives are ignored or repressed at our peril. As early as 1976 Adrienne Rich described the body as "the corporeal ground of our intelligence."[18] However, as Pamela Moore complains in her introduction to *Building Bodies,* contemporary scholars writing about embodiment tend only to study the body in passing, on their way to subjectivity.[19] While, as an ethicist trained in philosophy and theology, I am certainly guilty of a concern with subjectivity, my intent is to study the subjective nature of the flesh rather than simply pass through it as if the subject lived somehow separately within it.[20] Methodologically, therefore, considering the body as central to moral agency has led me beyond my own field to research in evolutionary biology, neurophysiology, and psychology. Maxine Sheets-Johnstone similarly argues, in *The Roots of Thinking,* that if one wants to understand thought, one must first understand the physical foundations of sense experience. To Sheets-Johnstone, the body does not divide itself into the "mind" of philosophy and the "material" of science. Rather, one cannot separate what is thought from what is felt by the tactile-kinesthetic body. Epistemology arises from within the whole of our sentient being and is observable in physiognomies of the flesh. In her words, "A creature finding no connection between the felt impact of stone on stone . . . could hardly have been a tool-maker."[21]

In a parallel fashion, Ruth Ginzberg's essay "Philosophy Is Not a Luxury" proposes that we develop a moral philosophy around the conditions for survival, where survival is understood as the conditions necessary for bodily, psychological, and communal health, "that which infuses every aspect of well-being."[22] While Ginzberg is explicitly concerned with the survival of women living in conditions of poverty and violence, if "all forms of well-being are taken to be part of survival," then our evolutionary heritage and relationship to nature should be included as well.[23] If we view our evolutionary inheritance as tied to the well-being of all life-forms on this planet, then ethics needs to take biology, and the ways culture interacts with nature, seriously in an effort to determine ways of life commensurate with our physical and moral health. A moral theory that is body-affirming rather than body-denying would place the mind into the body and the body into nature. As Susan Griffin has observed, for us the question should not be whether a tree falling in the forest makes a sound if no one is there to hear it, but whether we would have ears if the world were silent.[24] Ethics would thereby be grounded in biology and psychology, both of which could be engaged in the process of social criticism.[25] Such a moral theory would respect what we share with animals: the environment, the ability to feel pain and pleasure, and the engagement in social relations. The senses would be recognized as providing an important foundation for moral authority, and discussions of moral agency would emphasize compassion for sentient beings and awareness of the consequences of our actions upon them. To paraphrase Zen master Dogon, it is not we who affirm the myriad of things, but the myriad of things that affirm us.

In trying to show how the senses and emotions interact to develop subjectivity, intersubjectivity, and self-world relations, chapter one describes the ways Donna Williams and Temple Grandin have been able to develop their own subjective and intersubjective lives in spite of the sensory difficulties caused by autism. Here I explain the respective strategies they have devised to move beyond ritualized behaviors as well as strategies that have enabled them to escape the solipsistic prison that defines the world of autism. In addition, this chapter examines the effects of touch deprivation on infants in orphanages and animals subjected to lab experiments, factory farming, and other kinds of restrictive environments. Grandin's and Williams's insights about the nature of perception, along with studies of the physiological and emotional consequences of sensory deprivation and abuse, thus provide experiential and biological foundations for further exploration of the value of eros for moral agency.

Chapter two reviews the problems that a philosophical model built on body-mind dualism presents for contemporary reflections on morality. Descartes and Kant provide examples of the dissociative ego, which Michel Foucault locates in the bourgeois body and which Freud calls the obsessive mind, that constructs the self around taboos on touch even though connection with others is precisely what it needs and craves. To establish the importance of emotions to cognitive and practical life, I turn to Antonio Damasio's neurological research, which shows how emotions are imprinted in somatic markers that have functioned in our evolutionary history to help us practically negotiate the world. Through the work of Damasio, we meet Gage and Elliot, two men with brain disorders that not only prevent them from feeling pain and from forming emotional attachments, but also prevent them from acting in their best interests. The chapter concludes, following the work of clinical psychologist Louis Sass, by drawing parallels between extreme cases of the divorce between mind and body, as found in some kinds of schizophrenia, and "the philosopher's disease," in which modern philosophies and technologies have turned bodies into objects.

The third chapter examines ethical systems aligned with an understanding of the body as provocative and dangerous. This chapter is concerned with feeling disorders and social pathologies induced by corporal punishment and other forms of child abuse. Particular attention is paid to Alice Miller's work on pedagogical practices in Germany in the nineteenth century, prior to the rise of the Third Reich. The denial of pain and fear of pleasure have tremendous moral consequences for society insofar as they are tied to the worship of authority and the hatred of weakness—understood primarily as feeling—in oneself and in those who represent weakness. Susan Griffin also reads pornography in this way, as an attack on feeling, an attack that strips the body of its subjective life. The dangers of coming to see the body as Other include cycles of sadomasochism (cycles that reproduce the initial acts of abuse) as well as assaults upon the subjectivity of the body by behaviorist and eugenic movements.

Having witnessed the impact of divorcing the senses and emotions from moral agency, the rest of this text examines ways of healing that breach. Chapter four explores the ways some ascetic and masochistic practices manipulate states of pain and pleasure to transform consciousness, the body in these practices serving as an instrument either to withdraw from or enhance erotic life. This chapter begins by discussing contemporary forms of hysteria deriving from chronically overstimulated and stressed nervous systems. I suggest that we view asceticism on a continuum of feeling, one that moves from Saint Augustine's and other Church Fathers' disciplining of the flesh to certain Christian desert ascetics, medieval mystics, and also Tibetan Tantrics, who use ascetic practices to affirm the flesh and reconnect with the world around them. On one end of the continuum, where the goal of asceticism is to feel nothing, addictive and compulsive disorders, such as anorexia, self-mutilation, and obsessive forms of bodybuilding, are understood as ways of disciplining the flesh and maintaining emotional detachment from others. On the other end of the continuum, contemporary representations of the body in performance art, in consensual sadomasochism, and in female saints are discussed as attempts to use pain and pleasure to reconnect with the feeling self.

Chapter five concludes the book by suggesting that practices of mindfulness such as vipassana or tonglen forms of Buddhist meditation represent ways for us to come to our senses and live fully aware in the present. These spiritual practices increase somatic, emotional, and mental awareness, reuniting mind and body in ways that counteract habitual conditioning and allow us to live in permeable space. Just as Grandin came to experience connections with others through the embrace of the squeeze machine, mindful attention to ordinary bodily acts such breathing and eating can lead us to feel the self's "emptiness" or fundamental interrelatedness with other selves. Mindful touch means that we can no longer shield ourselves from pain or suffering—either our own or that of others—and that we must face the consequences of our larger patterns of consumption for the sake of the networks of life that support and compose us.

1

AUTISTIC TOUCH
Body as Prison

> I think "my world's" end began at the outside
> of my body . . . now I am accepting that the
> outside of my body is attached to the rest, and
> it all belongs to me.
>
> —Donna Williams, *Somebody Somewhere*

Although the tendency of ethicists has been to ignore the relevance of physical touch to moral agency, metaphors expressing the social and moral value of touch pervade our language, suggesting that experiential wisdom holds the connection between touch and moral value close. In *Touching: The Human Significance of the Skin*, Ashley Montagu explains that tact was derived from the Latin word meaning touch, *tactus*, and that these two words were used interchangeably until the middle of the nineteenth century.[1] Tact is a delicate touch, and, as in timing the stroke of a drum with other players, tact possesses sensitivity in responding to one's circumstances. Very much like H. Richard Niebuhr's description of moral action as a "fitting response" within a web of ongoing relations extending over space and time, tact requires self-awareness, world awareness, and an ability to feel with those around you.[2] Thus, in our language, tactless people are "out of touch," "heavy handed," or have a "heavy touch." The "hard" to get along with are "touchy," "coarse," "slimy," or even "untouchable;" these people need to be "handled carefully," "treated with kid gloves," or "stroked." Others are a "soft touch," "smooth," or perhaps unworthy of one's attention if they are only "skin deep." Things and people "rub" us the wrong way as well as get "under our skin." And whether we are "thick skinned" or "thin skinned," some things make our "skin crawl." Reality itself seems "tangibly" or "palpably" this way or that. In *A Natural History of the Senses*, Diane Ackerman reminds us that crises are "touch and go," problems are "thorny," "ticklish," or "sticky," and when we say that something "touches" us, we mean that it stirs our inner life, that we are moved emotionally or care deeply.[3]

In all likelihood these metaphors are not misleading since tactility in early life experience contributes to our capacity for tact, both as fitting response and as caring. Touch is the first sense to develop in the fetus and the most mature sensory system for the first several months of our lives. Touch cells in our lips make it possible to nurse, and touch accounts for as much as 80 percent of infant communication. Along with food, touch is our first source of comfort as well as the primary signal of safety or danger. We house up to nine thousand independent nerves per square inch in the skin of our fingertips alone, making it difficult to imagine life apart from the body's tactile awareness. The ways we encounter the world through the sensations of the skin and stay informed of the movements and positions of our own bodies through their proprioceptory, sensory-laden musculature seems prerequisite to a sense of being. Occasional encounters with anesthesia, such as that used during dental work, offer some limited experience of the confusion that occurs when it becomes impossible to know where the body begins or ends as well as the danger in not knowing if one has cut, burned, bit, or otherwise harmed oneself. Indeed, as we will see in this chapter and the next, persons who cannot experience their own bodily feelings perceive the body as an external object rather than as self.

THE CENTRALITY OF TOUCH:
WITNESSES FROM THE WORLD OF AUTISM

To begin to understand how our sensory and emotional lives intertwine and how their interplay affects identity, perception, and agency, I turn to the insights of two women who were born with a condition that made touch physically painful and emotionally overwhelming. I consider them to be expert witnesses on the emotional and intersubjective disorders caused by sustained touch deprivation. Temple Grandin and Donna Williams suffer from Asperger syndrome (AS), a developmental disorder described as the less severe, "shadow," or high-functioning side of autism. In the last decade, researchers have begun to look at autism as a disease best understood on a continuum, placing the familiar image of autistics as severely retarded and incapable of language skills (Leo Kanner's studies) at one end of the spectrum and autistics linked to very high intelligence and linguistic proficiency (Hans Asperger's studies) on the other end.[4] The Asperger end of the continuum fades into learning disabilities such as Pervasive Developmental Disorders (PDD), Attention Deficit Disorders (ADD), dyslexia, and on into eccentric normality. One of the foremost investigators of Asperger syndrome, Uta Frith, suggests that, unlike Kanner patients, the most distinguishing feature of Asperger patients may be that they can learn by rote to "pass" in the world as eccentric and socially inept. Indeed, one study of persons known to be reclusive and eccentric yielded a very high percentage of people (76 percent) who actually met the criteria of Asperger syndrome.[5]

Asperger symptoms typically include sensory jumbling as well as uncomfortable sensory experience, such as hypersensitivity to light and noise. Asperger patients have difficulty touching other people or being touched by them; they experience overwhelming emotions relating to stress, anxiety, and fear—the fight-or-flight response—and they have extremely limited, if any, comprehension of social norms or social interactions. Like other autistics, Asperger patients are socially isolated, cut off from the intersubjective world by an inability to perceive the subjective life of others. They do not perceive people as creatures who think and feel. One boy with Asperger syndrome writes, "I really didn't know there were people until I was seven years old . . . I still have to remind myself that there are people."[6] It is often said of the sufferers of this syndrome that they treat people as furniture. One mother writes, "I seemed no more to him than a chair. He used my hand like a tool to pull open the refrigerator door for juice, as though the rest of me was just an unimportant accessory to the hand."[7]

Hans Asperger, working in the 1940s, felt that, given care, attention, and a kind of remedial pedagogy drawing together medical and educational practices such as rhythmic exercises, musical training, and dramatic events (*Heilspädagogik*), one could recover from this disease. Asperger also thought that those afflicted had special gifts to offer the world; he saw a special or unique kind of intelligence in them, "scarcely touched by tradition and culture—unconventional, unorthodox, strangely 'pure' and original, akin to the intelligence of true creativity."[8] While it has been suggested that Asperger intentionally overplayed the capacities of his patients and their ability to be useful in society, due to the real danger that the Nazi regime posed to misfits (and some today might accuse him of exoticism), I found, in reading the accounts of people with AS, that these people are intelligent, creative, and particularly insightful on the subject of sensory and emotional awareness.

The first published autobiography written by someone afflicted with Asperger syndrome was Temple Grandin's *Emergence: Labeled Autistic*. As early as the age of six months, Grandin resisted her mother's touch and clawed herself free from her mother's arms. She found the touch of skin on skin particularly repulsive. Unable to endure even brief contact such as a handshake or a pat on the shoulder, she also could not endure her own legs or arms touching each other. Grandin wore only certain fabrics and never wanted them washed. (Despite her mother's best attempts to hide the fact that she had washed her clothes, Grandin was never fooled.) She says that it still takes her three to four days to become accustomed to a new type of underwear, or to pants after wearing skirts, or to shorts after wearing pants. Diagnosed at the age of three with brain damage, Grandin was given every pedagogical advantage, to rescue her from withdrawal into a solipsistic world. Speech therapy, demand for eye contact, and highly structured body-mind activities like ball games helped Grandin become what she is today, a professor in the department of animal sciences at Colorado State University in Fort Collins.[9]

Grandin describes her autism as a disease affecting sensory processing, making her effectively "cut off by overreactions or inconsistent reactions from [her] five senses."[10] Her hypersensitivity to stimuli made normal contact all but impossible as a child, and her senses were so painful that at times they simply shut down. Grandin describes her ears at the age of two and three as "helpless microphones" transmitting everything indiscriminately and overwhelmingly, an experience mirrored in each of her senses.[11] She longed to be hugged as a child but found the prospect both pleasing and terrifying. She experimented with various textures and materials, such as silks, clay, and sandpaper, to integrate and extend her capacity to touch and be touched. Determined to make the tactile contact that her body denied her, Grandin wrapped herself in blankets, crawled under sofa cushions, wore poster boards sandwiched on her front and back, and had her sisters sit on her on top of pillows.

The social world was impenetrable to Grandin, perhaps because it is impossible to learn social interactions with intelligence alone. She remained without friends, finding the dynamics of human social relationships utterly incomprehensible—she decided that other children must be telepathic since they so easily understood each other. In the language and methods of science and technology Grandin eventually found ways to interpret and conceptualize experience, ways that were not plagued by references to emotions or social life. Not surprisingly, she and other autistics identify with the Star Trek characters Data and Spock, an android and a nonhuman species portrayed as operating on logic and reason alone. Like some autistics, Data and Spock stand outside human emotion and social interaction, perplexed and yet fascinated by it.[12]

In high school, in a paper on her hopes and dreams, Grandin wrote that she longed *"to build a device to teach me to feel for others and to teach people to be gentle and caring."*[13] At seventeen, Grandin was visiting her aunt's cattle ranch when she noticed the relaxed state of calves upon leaving the cattle chute, a device holding them tightly during branding and castration. She climbed into the cattle chute herself and discovered that its squeeze provided relief from overstressed nerves, relief that lasted for several hours. Grandin went home and fashioned a squeeze machine from a cattle chute and on a daily basis began using the machine to induce calm and to give her the tactile sensation of the hug that she could not receive from other people. The machine applies pressure to her sides, and that pressure is both substantial and comforting to her. Grandin believes that the tactile stimulation denied her as a child by her autism caused secondary neurological damage that led to the hypersensitivity she experienced as an adult. Therefore she regrets that she did not have the machine earlier in her life. Coming to use the machine at the age of eighteen, she reports that it "was more like aspirin instead of a cure. If I had used it as a child it may have helped prevent the problem by inducing changes in my central nervous system."[14]

Nevertheless, Grandin discovered that as her use of the squeeze machine continued, she required less and less pressure to initiate a comforting sensation. Eventually, and quite remarkably, through the continued use of the machine she gained two important types of connection: she learned to tolerate being touched by another person and she learned empathy, one of the most difficult feelings for autistics to master.[15] Grandin reflects, "When I was in the chute, I felt closer to people like Mother . . . and Aunt Ann. Although the squeeze chute was just a mechanical device, it broke through my barrier of tactile defensiveness, and I felt the love and concern of these people and was able to express my feelings about myself and others. It was as if an accordion folding door had been shoved back revealing my emotions."[16] She continues later: "*God, whatever that is, and chance formed the gene structure that made me and something happened in the process which disconnected the 'wire' in the brain that attracts a child to its mother and other humans offering affection. It was not until I was old enough and skilled enough to build the squeeze machine that the connection was repaired.*"[17]

After earning an undergraduate degree in psychology, Grandin went on to do graduate work on animal behavior and physiology, completing her Ph.D. dissertation on the effects of enriched and impoverished environments on pigs. Her interests in psychology and animal behavior are part of a search to understand herself and autism. Thus her autobiographical reflection, "My Experiences as an Autistic Child," includes section titles such as "Touch Deprivation in Lab Animals," "Chemistry of Touch," "Cholinesterase Inhibitors and Contact Comfort," and "Tactile Defense." Well versed in scientific research on tactility, she brings to that work her own experience as a student of touch and as a sufferer of AS. Grandin wants to understand how physical experience is tied to emotional development, and thus she explores connections of the sensory system to the emotional parts of the brain, such as the limbic system and the prefrontal cortex where emotional awareness resides. She speculates that the failure of emotional development in autistics may be related to their sensory deprivation and that this is also partially responsible for their inability to perceive other minds.

Grandin's knowledge of neurophysiology, animal behavior, and the physio-emotional dynamics of touch as well as her own experience of tactile deprivation make important contributions to an analysis of human eros. She has discovered that her tactile experiences with animals function very much like the squeeze machine in that touching animals leads her to feel calm and empathetic. She uses her talents in design and engineering and her capacity for empathy to design humane systems of animal management. Her second book, *Thinking in Pictures,* describes how she is able to use her sensory awareness to enter into the bodily experience of animals, particularly cattle, with whom she discovered close ties ever since entering the cattle chute. Witnessing to and respecting the necessity of touch as critical to the development of organisms, Grandin writes of AS, "Our bodies cry out for human contact but when contact is made, we withdraw in pain and confusion."[18]

Donna Williams finds it futile to explain to nonautistics that touch is painful. As a child, being hugged felt like a burning sensation; her head spun and she felt like fainting. In an effort to gain control over an existence in which touch was overwhelming, she constructed a world that was as dualistic as her own experience. In her world, even having her clothes next to someone else's in a closet was a threat because it was too much like being touched herself. For Williams, alienated from her own body as subject, things became symbolic expressions of her identity. If others touched her things in the world "out there," then those things, like her body, were disowned as "non-me."[19]

Unlike Grandin, Williams grew up having a category for practical touch; this allowed her to more easily endure being touched briefly when necessary for medical, safety, or instructional purposes. However, she explains that social or erotic touch was both sensually and emotionally beyond her. "It was one thing to deal with touch as a performance or dissociate from it all as an object of someone else's tactile infliction. It was altogether different when inner defenses had to stomach the awareness that touch was emotional, self-initiated, and personal. . . . It was damned hard to be touched when I had a feeling self intact."[20] On a walk one afternoon with a fellow she fancied, he held out his hand to support her climb. Williams says, "My heart sank. I became painfully aware of my inability to combine touch and feeling."[21] Whenever touch combined with emotion or intersubjective relations (as it did in this example) or with eye contact, she felt as if she were drowning or being eaten, submerged into the other. Eros was oceanic, like a tidal wave or death, overwhelming, and thus met with overload and shutdown. When confronted with connection, she entered the "Big Black Nothingness," where the bottom of her world fell out: "In my case, my mind knows that affection and kindness will not kill me, yet my emotional response defies this logic, telling me that good feelings and gentle and loving touch can kill me or at the very least cause me pain. When I try to ignore this message, I go into what would seem to be a state of shock, where what's coming in is either incomprehensible or has no significance. This state leads to my emotions committing suicide, leaving me without physical or emotional feeling and with a purely robotic mental response—if that."[22]

Donna Williams's first book, *Nobody Nowhere*, was translated into nine languages and was impossible to keep stocked in bookstores. Meant to act as a journal, to be tossed aside after helping Williams sort out her own experience, the text provided a much needed mirror for sufferers of this disease and a window for families and friends to understand a world unlike any they had known. Her second book, *Somebody Somewhere*, is a more confident, more philosophical text reflecting her emerging sense of body-self, captured in this chapter's opening quote, in which she affirms that her body is connected to the world and that her identity is to be found in that relatedness: "The outside of my body is attached to the rest, and it all belongs to me."[23]

Williams strikes me as less comfortable than Grandin with her autism in that she seems more frustrated with the absence of an emotional life and intersubjective world. Williams understands her life as waging two battles, the first to keep the world out, the second to join it, and she provides reflective meditations about sorting out fears in order to remain in touch with both self and world. As she puts it, "Meaning without inner experience was as empty as inner experience without meaning . . . I had no concept that a sense of 'self' and 'other' could exist at the same time."[24] More poet than scientist, Williams gives us rich descriptions of her struggle to escape from the isolated reality of the autistic to a relational sense of reality.

Many factors contribute to the differences between Grandin and Williams, supreme among them the fact that Williams grew up in an abusive family with an alcoholic mother who physically and mentally assaulted her. She had an older brother who teased her mercilessly and a father who, when he lived at home, was violent toward his wife but able to ignore everything else going on in the household. The abuse may have contributed complex developmental dynamics when combined with her autism. There is the further possibility of Fetal Alcohol Syndrome (FAS), known to create sensory and emotional problems that are quite similar to AS. Her autistic condition turned out to be exacerbated by and partially caused by multiple food allergies; this is true of autistics in 8 to 20 percent of cases.[25] Food, like sensory stimulation, trauma, and the effects of prenatal drug and alcohol use, alters the body's chemistry and brain development. Those chemical alterations can lead to hypo- or hypersensitivity, both of which Williams experienced, as well as to perceptual and emotional disorders.

Williams's sensory disorders are so profound that she is a victim of both inadequate exteroception and proprioception. We process sensations from the immediate external environment via a multitude of exteroceptors that can be divided into distance receptors (hearing, vision, smell) and contiguous receptors (touch and taste) located on sensory nerve terminals in the eyes, ears, nose, mouth, and skin. Body sense also arises from the inside by means of interoceptors from the viscera, which give us information about tension, temperature, and secretions, and by means of proprioceptors located on the sensory nerve terminals of muscles and tendons stimulated by movements of the body itself. The exteroception of Williams is mostly mono, meaning that she can feel either the phone in her hand or the cat on her lap but not both simultaneously. While we are rarely aware of and do not control them, proprioceptors keep us informed about our location in space: they let us know where our hands and feet are, for example, and help us maintain our balance. Oliver Sacks calls proprioception our sixth sense, derived from the Latin word *proprious*, to own itself.[26]

The first and most basic thing touch may provide for us is this sense of body ownership, the pervasive background feeling responsible for the sense of existing and the ability to construct "I am." Donna Williams never experienced that opportunity; instead her body blindness and sensory confusion left her body in pieces: "If I touched my leg I would feel it on my hand or on my leg but not both at the same time. My perception of a whole body was in bits. I was an arm or a leg or a nose. Sometimes one part would be very much there but the bit it was joined to felt as wooden as a table leg and just as dead. The only difference was the texture and the temperature."[27] Williams explains that she never knew where her body was and was surprised to discover, in conversation with a blind piano player, that he had a strong inner sense of body ownership even though he could not literally see his body in space. She found the location of her body in space by tapping it and then listening to the tapping or by means of a reflected image or by someone else's reactions to it. Unable to inhabit her body, she was "nobody nowhere," deprived of the feeling of Being.

Williams experiences her body more as a prison or a house of mirrors than as a means to know herself or to interact with the world. When she does feel something happening to her body, she says it is as if her body is an external object or even "a wall" between her inner mental world and the world outside her. Therefore she refers to herself as "you": "This was because 'you' logically captured my relationship to myself. One develops an 'I' in interaction with 'the world.'"[28] Because she perceives her body more as object than subject, Williams early in her life had to practice awareness of the necessity of eating and even, on occasion, breathing. Unable to differentiate cold from hunger or fear, she learned to generally ignore physical sensation entirely. Williams writes, "In twenty-seven years, I had touched my own hands many times. They were just lumps of flesh, blood and bones delineated by type, location, function, and image as something we call 'hands.' There was no emotional attachment to them, no personal belonging with them, no significance to the act of touching hands. It was merely a collision of two such objects in space."[29] Sensory integration work, such as rubbing her skin with brushes, trying to make connection to her torso, helped Williams acquire a sense of dwelling within her body for short periods of time. Her joy in discovering a body-self is obvious: "I had wondered what I wanted a body for. Now I knew. There was no greater feeling of self-security. This was the first security a baby knows long before it knows its mother. This was the first security in life, which had been missing. Connection with my body was the missing bridge across the impassable gorge that had stood between me and being in touch with feelings."[30]

Williams speculates that autism results when emotion does not function properly, and that this dysfunction in emotion leaves both body and mind unable to express themselves. Grandin would agree. Her analysis begins, however, with the autistic's lack of tactile stimulation as the ground of the original emotional disorder that separates mind and body. Grandin argues that touch deprivation creates abnormal biochemistry and an immature or damaged central nervous system. These biochemical imbalances go on to affect the capacity for both sensory stimulation and social relations, including the lack of an emotional life that includes compassion and empathy. Noticing similarities among the behaviors of autistic children, farm and lab animals raised in deprived environments, and traumatized and institutionalized infants, Grandin is convinced that, whatever the other etiologies of autism, lack of touch complicates or exacerbates an already-given organic dysfunction.[31] Thus we start this inquiry by examining the biochemical and behavioral consequences of touch deprivation. Once we understand the effects of touch deprivation on neurology, nervous systems, and behaviors, we can return to the lives of Williams and Grandin to reflect with them on how it is that sensory systems function either to cut us off from or to connect us to each other, the world, and ourselves.

TOUCH DEPRIVATION: ANIMALS, ORPHANS, AND AUTISTICS

As an anthropologist convinced that Western cultures had neglected the senses, Ashley Montagu wrote his book on touch to draw together the scientific literature then available on the relationship of touch to animal behavior and development. According to Montagu, researchers began to focus on the relationship between touch and physical health after Frederick S. Hamnett, an anatomist, published his (1922) paper on rats who survived the removal of thyroid and parathyroid glands because they were petted. In the process of studying gland removal, Hamnett discovered that

rats who were customarily "petted and gentled" were far more re-
silient than rats who had been given little tactile contact—and indeed they survived the operation.[32] Once scientists and social
scientists began to observe the biochemical and behavioral consequences of tactility, it became clear fairly quickly that touch affects
the development of all organ systems (gastrointestinal, respiratory,
genito-urinary), the somatosensory system, and the central nervous system.

Newborn animals, for example, must be licked to survive. If
neither licked nor provided alternative stimulation, lambs fail to
stand and subsequently die. Licking, particularly in the perineal region, teaches the newborn to defecate and urinate. Without tactile
stimulation in those areas, genito-urinary tracts fail to function.[33]
Intensified self-licking by the mother prior to delivery improves
her organ systems during labor, delivery, and parturition; but if deprived of self-licking, mothers fail to care for infants after delivery.
(Stimulation of the skin causes the pituitary to secrete prolactin
and thus is associated also with the possibility of nursing.) When a
newborn is taken away from its mother for several hours prior to
her licking it, some thread is broken, and a relationship is never
reestablished. Removing newborns also retards the physical recovery of the mother because her recovery is enhanced by the tactile
stimulation of nuzzling and nursing.[34] Montagu speculates that in
humans licking is replaced by labor, which provides the stimulation necessary to the development of organ systems. The contrac-
tions of the uterus stimulate sensory nerves in the skin and thereby
the peripheral and autonomic nervous systems as well as the principle organ systems.[35]

Just as Hamnett's experiment indicated, handling infants is
now known to produce faster learning and growth, greater emotional and psychological stability, the ability to withstand stress,
and greater capacities for physical and emotional healing. Handling calms, decreases fear, and increases weight and physical activity. While the skin's basic sensitivity seems given or innate, skin
sensitivity is heightened or lessened according to stimulation received. Rats who are stroked have highly developed nerve cells, in
the cortex, that process tactile sensations while those who are not
stroked display a decrease in the richness of these neural connections and in the size of those brain cells.[36] This means that

touch affects the capacity to be touched, to feel touch, and to enjoy touch. Organisms with little physical contact become hypersensitive to that contact and may grow up to find it uncomfortable. As Grandin puts it, the "sensorily deprived have an overly sensitive nervous system resulting in lowered thresholds to sensory stimuli."[37]

Studies on the weight gain that accompanies tactile stimulation show that it is due to biochemical alterations in metabolism rather than to the infant eating more. Experiments on infant rats reveal that contact with the mother, such as licking, inhibits the production of beta-endorphin, a chemical that slows metabolism and growth. Growth and activity are stunted when licking ceases, and this is apparently an evolutionary strategy to maintain the organism in the absence of a caregiver. When touch is reestablished, it signals the caregiver's return and reverses the process.[38]

Harry F. Harlow's well-known experiments on tactile deprivations of primates caused the primates irreparable brain damage. Convinced that one could use science to study love and intimacy, Harlow took infant monkeys away from their mothers and away from all other creature comforts such as a soft blanket or a stuffed toy to cuddle. He then periodically offered a choice between two substitute mothers, one constructed out of wire but equipped with a bottle to feed, the other a soft cloth mother the infant could cling to. Baby monkeys chose the contact comfort provided by a soft cloth surrogate over a wire surrogate that was rigged for nursing. In other words, tactile comfort was given priority over sustenance. Harlow concluded that the primary function of nursing is touching; food alone is never a substitute for the security provided by an embrace. When Harlow completely isolated infants and provided no surrogates, they became asocial and functionally autistic, retreating into a tiny, shaking fetal ball as if to find some small comfort in holding onto themselves. All of Harlow's monkeys were damaged in their sensory and social systems for their lifetimes, rendered incapable of communal and sexual relations. His work therefore underscores the importance of affection to the healthy development of every organism, though at the price of inflicting tremendous suffering. Studies since have shown that the need of piglets for contact comfort is so great that rather than moving to a heat lamp in the center of a pen where warmth but no direct tactile stimulation is provided, they will choose to lie against a solid surface like a wall until they die from exposure to the cold.[39]

Restricted environments also function as forms of touch deprivation. By preventing natural movement either through isolation or overcrowding, restricted environments inflict a form of trauma and stress, causing human and nonhuman animals to become hypersensitive to stimuli. Dogs isolated in cages remain hyperexcitable even six months after their return to a normal environment. Chickens on egg farms, when given no room to scratch the ground, stretch their wings, or move about, are driven to attack themselves and each other. Pigs chained to the ground to prevent their fighting in stalls too small for them gnaw on the bars of their cells because they crave tactile stimulation and motion. The stress induced by their isolation and restriction is so severe that it can lead to overwhelming anxiety, panic, and sudden death (Porcine Stress Syndrome). Veal calves kept in stalls with walls that prevent contact between them become hypersensitive to stimuli, but less so if they are raised in stalls with low walls that allow them to touch and groom each other.[40] Zoo animals are hypersensitive—they rock, pace, self-mutilate, and have difficulty with social and sexual relations. Human prison populations increasingly turn to forms of self-mutilation such as cutting, obsessive exercise, violence, and drugs to deal with the biological and psychological effects created by impoverished environments.

Montagu cites the first recorded experiment in human sensory deprivation by Frederick II (1124–1250), the Holy Roman Emperor, who wanted to see which language children spoke naturally and, thus, which language was more ancient—Greek, Hebrew, or Latin! Frederick forbade any contact, beyond feeding and minimal bathing, with a group of children. However, none of them ever spoke the primal language, for it was said that they died "without the petting."[41] Montagu claims that, as late as the 1920s, the death rate for infants less than one year of age in institutions throughout the United States was nearly 100 percent and that this had a lot to do with tactile neglect.

More recently, researchers have noted the damage tactile neglect has inflicted upon many children living in overcrowded, understaffed orphanages in Eastern Europe. In her essay "Attachment

Theory: The Ultimate Experiment," Margaret Talbot suggests that the types of maternal and sensory deprivations that Harlow inflicted on primates in the 1950s have now in effect been carried out on children institutionalized in Romania and the former Soviet Union. Since the collapse of communism in 1989, more than eighteen thousand of these children have been adopted in the United States, constituting what Michael Rutter, a child psychologist at the London Institute of Psychiatry, describes as the largest group of deprived infants ever available for study.[42] Some of these children seem perfectly fine, while 20 to 30 percent of them are severely disturbed, the differences due perhaps to the meeting of heredity and environment. Although the studies are just beginning, the parallels to what is seen in AS and in children affected by neonatal drug use are astounding. Indeed, Talbot points out that it is difficult to tell whether the institutionalized children were affected by neglect, Fetal Alcohol Syndrome, lead exposure, malnutrition, or any combination of these factors because the emotional and psychological damage is similar in all cases. One single mother who adopted a child living in a Russian orphanage until age two and a half said that so far he had been diagnosed with "attention-deficit disorder, schizophrenia, autism, Tourette's syndrome, [and] obsessive-compulsive disorder."[43] Her experience may indicate how central touch is to bodily and psychological development and may also witness to confusions in contemporary psychiatry about how to sort out these symptoms and diagnostics.

These orphaned children are described by their adoptive parents as overwhelmed by anxiety, hypersensitive to stimuli, oddly reckless, resistant to physical touch, and inclined to express emotions in undeveloped, artificial, or uncontrolled ways. There are babies in this group who at eighteen months are still not capable of making eye contact or holding their heads up, much less walking or talking. Psychologists suggest that they will need to be taught, just like autistics, to recognize emotions on the faces of others, in hopes of being able to someday feel emotions themselves. Feeling kinship with Anne Sullivan (the teacher of Helen Keller), Linda Crumpecher says of life with her adopted son, "There are times when I felt that what I was doing was trying to get his soul back. . . . This was a kid who at 5 didn't seem to have any cause-and-effect thinking, who didn't know that plants were alive but furniture wasn't."[44] Those who survive touch deprivation or abuse find themselves living in an estranged world, a world that is perhaps quite familiar to Donna Williams and Temple Grandin. Indeed, the lives of autistics are themselves experiments in tactile deprivation, since caress, an essential ingredient and basic need of all vertebrates, is denied to them, albeit by organic rather than cultural conditions.

Biochemical and Neurological Consequences

Once we recognize that the brain is neither determined genetically nor a tabula rasa (neither of which, taken alone, makes any sense from an evolutionary perspective), then it is incumbent upon us practically and morally to take seriously the fact that the brain's chemistry and circuitry remain very much open to experience and formed by it. A living organism rather than a mechanical switchboard, the brain is modified by experience; it does this slowly, and as it is modified it records the properties of its experience. The organic functioning of the central nervous system is not even completely developed to the brain stem at birth, and later structures such as the hippocampus continue development into puberty. Even then the brain remains quite flexible, open to restructuring by trauma as well as to healing and neural regeneration. Genetic paths are set along with autonomic systems; however, our sensory and emotional systems mature through late adolescence and are always in the process of redefinition by experience. The limbic system, which surrounds the brain stem, is physiologically mature only around puberty, and the frontal lobes of the cerebral cortex do not complete their growth until approximately age sixteen.

Because touch causes distinct biochemical changes in the central nervous system and is one of the first senses to become organically functional in many animals, touch affects neurological development. It is therefore quite possible that deficiencies in incoming tactile stimuli are partially responsible for the incomplete nature of brain structures affecting autism, such as the reduced size and function of the cerebellum. Grandin thinks that her sensory problems are associated with cerebellar abnormalities but that secondary forms of neurological damage were caused by withdrawal from touching.[45] Creating a biofeedback loop, touch deprivation produces a nervous system that is hypersensitive to touch and, therefore, animals that further withdraw from touch.

The process of lifelong brain shaping means that experience continues to "matter," that is, to literally materialize in biochemistry that affects brain structure and function. Experience affects cognitive and emotional processes by modulating neurotransmitters in the brain and hormones in the bloodstream. For example, the brains of rats raised in rich environments contain enhanced acetylcholine, which is known to facilitate transmissions of impulses across synapses, while rats raised in impoverished environments show reduced levels of acetylcholine. There are one to two dozen kinds of neurotransmitters in the brain, including acetylcholine and serotonin (5-hydroxytryptamine), the catecholamines adrenaline, noradrenaline, and dopamine (a modified kind of adrenaline), and endorphins (the brain's own internal or "endo" mimics of morphine). In *Enriching Heredity*, Marion Cleaves Diamond presents twenty-seven years of studies on the anatomy of mammalian forebrains, showing modifications in the cortical thickness and dimensions of nerve cells (distributions of spines, postsynaptic density, and number and length of dendrites) brought on by environmental conditions. She found that rats raised in environments in which they can move around freely with other rats and toys not only find their way through mazes more quickly than rats raised in restricted environments, but also have brains that are actually thicker and heavier, like well-used muscles. Diamond focused her research on the neocortex, the seat of higher functions of cognition as well as one of the most recent phylogenetic structures in evolution and the last to develop embryologically. She found that even in the womb the neocortex showed measurable biological changes in relationship to environment. (Diamond notes that this was not lost on the Chinese, who developed the concept of "intrauterine education" in literature that goes back two thousand years.)[46]

Impoverished environments hinder the development of neural pathways able to regulate chemicals that flood the central nervous system in response to stress. For example, rats raised in rich environments produce more serotonin, a neurotransmitter known to help control aggressive behavior and to increase the body's ability to suppress production of catecholamines such as adrenaline (associated with short-term emergency responses) and cortical steroids such as cortisol (produced during long-term trauma). This means that animals raised under conditions of stress end up more sensitive to stimuli but less able to cope with the short- and long-term effects of those stimuli. The retreat to violence as a response to stress is particularly seen in males, who are affected not only by the adrenal hormones but by testicular testosterone. Testosterone does not itself affect the amygdala, the part of the brain which sends messages about threat, but it heightens and quickens aggression once the message of threat has been sent. Larger rats bite the smaller rats, and the larger rats have lower blood pressure than the rats that are bitten.[47]

In *Emotional Intelligence*, Daniel Goleman analyzes the effects of touch on the brain development of humans as well as the effects of emotions on intelligence. Concerned about the emotional immaturity and ineptitude he sees in our society, Goleman shows how stress and trauma combine to leave our sensory and emotional lives too aroused to be either useful or comfortable to us, much as they are for Grandin and Williams. His thesis is echoed by Elaine Scarry's inquiry into torture, *The Body in Pain*, which found—like Grandin's experience in the squeeze machine—that only when the body is calm can connections with others and the world be maintained. Goleman explains that several areas of the brain known to affect emotional development are also known to be developed by touch, that is, by being physically comforted. These are the same areas of the brain that make it possible for the animal to comfort itself and keep distress to a minimum. One area includes the amygdala and cingulate gyrus, perched just above the brain stem, near the bottom of the limbic ring. These are neural structures of the limbic system and include the hypothalamus, hippocampus, olfactory bulb, and parts of the thalamus and cerebral cortex. The limbic system regulates motivational and emotional behaviors; it interacts with the hypothalamus in regulating anxiety, fear, and aggression as well as appetite, thirst, and sexual activity.

The hypothalamus and amygdala interpret the emotional significance of events and send messages (through the pons and the medulla) to the spinal cord. The amygdala acts as a kind of sentinel, scanning the world for signs of danger, and the more neglect or trauma the organism experiences, the more vigilant the sentinel. The amygdala also receives messages about fear from the vagus nerve, which regulates the heartbeat and much else. (For example, this nerve is sometimes cut to ameliorate peptic ulcers.) The vagus nerve is part of a pathway that shapes itself throughout childhood, sending signals to the amygdala and to adrenal glands, promoting secretion of catecholamines such as adrenaline, noradrenaline, and dopamine. Comforted children are able to suppress the trigger of the vagus nerve while emotionally and physically neglected or abused children are not.

A second area of the brain developed by comforting touch is located in the prefrontal cortex just behind the forehead. The prefrontal cortex—once the target of prefrontal lobotomies and the only part of the brain to receive information from all sensory systems—helps to regulate memory, emotional life, and reactions to stress. Emotional awareness resides in the prefrontal cortex, and it is part of the brain known to be central to human practical reason, social life, and decision making. Between ten and eighteen months of age, "the orbitofrontal area of the prefrontal cortex is rapidly forming the connections with the limbic brain that will make it a key on/off switch for distress."[48] If a child has been comforted when distressed, these pathways will be strengthened. Neglected and abused children (in that order) are primed to fight or flee while they are also less able biologically to cope with distress.

Temple Grandin says that she lived in a perpetual state of hypervigilance until she found relief in medication. She also knows that most people do not get to this state unless they experience severe trauma such as isolation, child abuse, or war.[49] Dennis Charney, a psychiatrist and director of clinical neuroscience at the National Center for Post-Traumatic Stress Disorder, claims that victims of trauma may never be the same biologically and that the specific cause does not matter: "All uncontrollable stress can have the same biological impact." The brain chemistry of Vietnam veterans reveals 40 percent fewer catecholamine-blocking receptors than is normal. With catecholamine secretion poorly controlled, one's system remains anxious, fearful, and hypervigilant. High amounts of the stress hormone cortisol can lead to uncontrollable flashbacks triggered by the slightest sensory provocation—a sound, taste, or smell. The brain's opioid system also becomes hyperactive and secretes endorphins, the brain's own morphines, to block feelings of pain as well as pleasure.[50]

Goleman reports that children with impaired frontal cortical functioning are impulsive, anxious, and disruptive; they are at high risk for academic failure, criminal behavior, and alcoholism.[51] Unable to settle down, they have trouble with abstract cognition and the processing of information and therefore cannot learn higher-level cognitive skills. Replete with anxiety, they are also anesthetized to pain and unable to empathize with the feelings of others. In places like Rwanda, Cambodia, South Africa, and Bosnia, as well as any home in which there is domestic violence, one would expect many generations of healing to be necessary. Under the right conditions, these bodily responses are appropriate survival adaptations, but under inappropriate conditions the combination of anxiety, anesthetization to pain, and the failure to feel empathy can be deadly. Healing proves difficult as trauma creates a "reactive brain" that is incapable of empathy and highly punitive, tied to the immediate present, immature with regard to problem-solving skills, and given to panic and impulsive behavior. Each loss builds on the other.

The experience of the lived body for children exposed prenatally to drug or alcohol addiction is so similar to autism that Danni Odom-Winn and Dianna Dunagan, the authors of *"Crack Kids*" in School,* advise parents of any child meeting the description of Pervasive Developmental Disorder (PDD) or Attention Deficit Disorder (ADD) to read all the literature they can find on Asperger syndrome.[52] Crack cocaine causes blood vessels to constrict, altering neurotransmitters that carry information from one nerve cell to the next. Effects include delayed language development, indecipherable and heightened sensory experience, an inability to generalize or empathize, mood swings, and behavioral problems. Researchers think that prenatal drug use affects the acetylcholine pathways necessary for normal brain cell firings and that this goes on to affect emotional stability. Emotions, once unlocked in PDD children, are described as "basic, extreme, instantaneous and prolonged."[53]

Hypersensitivity and Ritualized Behaviors

The experience of having to find an address in an unfamiliar city—say, Los Angeles—in traffic, with the radio is blaring, might lead any of us to feel nervous, to experience a quickened heart rate, perhaps even a sweating and shortness of breath. Perceiving the music

as highly irritating, the traffic as chaotic, and the experience of being lost as threatening, I know that I might turn the radio off (not
merely down) and try to find a place to pull over. For autistics and
other people with damaged nervous systems (as well as lab, farm,
and zoo animals), who have no way to turn off the chaos that con-
fronts them, increases in environmental stimulation can result in
self-destructive and ritualized behaviors.[54] If one cannot attend to
stimuli selectively and make sense of it, overload and shutdown responses to overload are inevitable. Any disruption in Grandin's
routine caused panic attacks and overwhelming fight-or-flight responses. She acknowledges once biting her teacher in the leg—her
tantrums came on quickly, like epileptic seizures, and had to run
their course.[55] Williams describes a similar experience, "Everything
was too colorful, too invasive, too constantly changing. I could
switch off emotion and self, it would be tolerable; a film of someone else's life with my body cast in the leading role. I could hold
on to self and emotion and awareness and overload under the
weight of everything coming into a mind with no sieve."[56]

Williams speculates that her distorted emotional life causes
many of her perceptual and developmental problems since her
awareness itself was "a puppet, the strings of which were set firmly
in the hands of emotional stress."[57] She thinks that her estrange-
ment from emotion forces her to function on a more sensory level
than other people and, thus, to miss the larger, more coherent picture most of us take for granted as the core of subjective life. However, when Williams registers complaints about the overwhelming
nature of stimuli and about an inability to maintain awareness
in shifting consciousness from one moment to the next, her
experience tells her that this is as much a failure of her emotional
connectedness as it is a sensory abnormality. Indeed, the interde-
pendence of the sensory and emotional systems is so complete
that, like an exercise in karma, as each system affects the other so it
affects itself.

Self-Stimulation. For the hypersensitive it is not, of course, simply a
matter of escaping all sensory stimulation. Humans and animals
deprived of sensory experience crave it just as profoundly as those
who are overwhelmed by it seek release. Individuals prevented
from having sensations push levers repeatedly to obtain light or

sound stimuli. A rat deprived of sense experience will work just as hard to get that stimulation as a rat that works for stimulation with an electrode implanted in its pleasure center. And if the deprived nervous system cannot get any outside stimulation, some form of self-stimulation will occur, including experiencing visions and hallucinations.[58] One key to achieving some kind of coherency, meaning, and freedom in action is to find the right balance in sensory experience so as to maintain both self-awareness and world awareness. For example, in search of sensory stimulation without overload, Williams climbed into a cupboard where the encroachment of the world was not a problem: "Here the bombardment of bright light and harsh colors, of movement and blah-blah, of unpredictable noise and the uncontrollable touch of others were all gone. Here was a world of guarantees, where things were controlled for long enough that I could calm down and have a thought or become aware of a feeling. I reached out to touch the fabric in front of me. I ran my hand over the silky surface of the patent leather shoes at my feet. I picked them up and ran them across my cheek. Here, there was no final straw to send me from overload into the endless void of shutdown."[59]

Retreat is one possibility for the hypersensitive, equivalent to our example of turning off the radio and pulling the car over. Ritualized behaviors such as rocking or tapping provide another possibility. Grandin proposes that "stereotypies"—repeated, ritualized behaviors and fixations—are adaptive responses of disturbed biological systems seeking homeostasis.[60] In other words, these behaviors mediate between the body's chemistry and environmental conditions in a search for tolerable, optimal stimulation. The self-stimulation of ritualized behavior works to screen out external stimuli by controlling the input of the environment. The ritual acts, in short, as a form of tactile defense allowing the brain to process, select, and give priorities to incoming information. The higher the arousal, the greater the fixation needed to calm the inner chaos and panic created by overwhelming sensory stimuli. Hence, pigs in enclosed environments have lower stress hormone levels when given a chain to pull than when they have no chain to pull.[61]

Under stress, all of us fall into ritualized behaviors that create appropriate or comforting chemistries, such as tapping or nail biting, as well as more sophisticated rituals, such as working out at the gym or consuming fatty foods. Bipolar people, for example, often self-medicate by using food, drugs, or alcohol to relieve overwhelming mood swings. In general, like caged animals and children with Fetal Alcohol Syndrome or Pervasive Developmental Disorders, autistic children tend to rely on the phylogenically older tactile and vestibular motion systems for self-stimulation. Educators working with PDD children report better results in calming and connecting with these children when using physical exercises based on touch and motion rather than hearing and vision. Visual and auditory exercises do produce calm, but educators find that children tend to withdraw more into worlds of their own using these stimuli rather than touch or motion.[62]

Grandin says that her nervous system gave her two choices, the same choices we have when we experience trauma or stress. She could either retreat to an inner world that acted, like Williams's cupboard, to minimize stimuli or overstimulate herself.[63] To maximize stimulation, as a child Grandin very much enjoyed the Round Up, a carnival ride in which the body is spun around in a circle, held in place by centrifugal force. The circular motion provided intense somatosensory input that calmed her nerves, as did "intense activities such as galloping on a horse, or strenuous physical labor."[64] Similarly, Williams gave herself "whizzies"—her name for spinning around in place with arms outstretched, like the dance of the whirling dervish—to produce calm. Vestibular stimulation, like the back-and-forth action of a swing, is known to initiate speech in autistic children and helps them as well as PDD children to focus.[65] Harlow's experiments found that monkeys raised on stationary surrogates developed more stereotypical rocking behaviors and social problems than monkeys raised on moving surrogates.

Motion, therefore, appears to be an important key to finding the homeostatic balance of stimulation that allows us to stay attached to self and world rather than shut down to them. Montagu describes rocking as erotic or autoerotic behavior—a form of self-caressing which renders a sense of wholeness or well being. He laments pedagogical practices in the United States in the 1880s that abolished the cradle, which simulates sensory inputs of the mother's own motion while the child is in the womb, replacing it with the stationary, "prison-like" crib. The cradle was pronounced a means to spoil babies by Luther Emmett Holt, whose guide, *The Care and Feeling of Children*, written in 1887, influenced child rearing for more than fifty years. Montagu reports that Holt was described as "austere and unapproachable . . . a highly efficient, perfectly coordinated human machine."[66]

Infants raised in institutions self-stimulate by rocking. Rocking cools and warms, it stimulates the skin and thus the internal organs, and it provides a feeling of attachment since the world appears to move with you. Donna Williams credits rocking with providing her a sense of security and release from built-up tension and anxiety. She thinks that both rocking and spinning may provide a feeling of containment, the feeling of being and dwelling comfortably in one's body, a feeling that infants normally acquire by being held. (This may also be why autistics are drawn to swimming pools in an effort to reproduce the feeling of being held by floating in water.) Rocking is observed in grief and mourning as well as in forms of meditation and prayer. Like the wringing of hands or the manipulation of rosary beads, rocking releases frustration and eliminates distractions. Similar to meditative breathing, rocking produces the kind of serenity and focus one sees in the faces of the Hasids as they rock while reciting the Torah in front of the Wailing Wall.

Ritual responses to external overload can take many forms, including linguistic repetition and visual fixation on an object. The mantra "Who's on first?" which Dustin Hoffman's character uses in the film *Rain Man,* provides a good example. The repetition of language blocks out chaos and focuses attention, much as it does in chanting and formal meditation. Grandin and Williams also give examples of using vision as a meditative way to shut out the chaos of the world. Gazing at the sand on the beach, Grandin recalls "studying the sand intently as if I was a scientist looking at a specimen under the microscope. I remember minutely observing how the sand flowed, or how long a jar lid would spin when propelled at different speeds."[67] Likening herself to a yogi, Williams says: "[F]rom the earliest I can remember I found my only dependable security was in losing all awareness of the things usually considered real. In doing this, I was able to lose all sense of self. Yet this is a strategy said to be the highest stage of meditation, indulged in to achieve inner peace and tranquillity. Why should it not be interpreted as such for autistic people?"[68]

It is possible that both ritual behaviors and meditative exercises are tied in our evolutionary history to neurological structures linking perception and cognition to feeling states that create adaptive somatic conditions. The autonomic nervous system works in connection with the limbic brain to construct the value-laden and emotional nature of experience. Composed of the sympathetic and parasympathetic systems, the autonomic nervous system controls fight-or-flight responses. Stress-related disorders, whether aggressive or depressive in nature, have their origin in the continual activation of the fight-or-flight response. The efforts of Grandin and Williams to stop these responses by means of meditative retreat or physical stimulation are in accord with what we now know about how meditation and ritualized motions affect the autonomic nervous system. Rituals like dancing or rocking tie into the autonomic nervous system by working up through the brain stem and limbic structures to the neocortex, producing the feelings of calm, alertness, and belonging. Meditation produces the same relaxation, beginning in the evolutionarily more recent cerebral hemispheres, referred to as the neocortex, and working its way down through the evolutionarily more ancient limbic brain into the autonomic nervous system. Slow, ritualized behaviors such as chanting or T'ai Chi enter into the quiescent (parasympathetic) system and create a sense of peace. But one can also enter into the arousal (sympathetic) system and produce the same effect by means of rapid motions such as dancing, twirling, or long-distance running, all of which serve to integrate the mind-body. While researchers used to think the sympathetic and the parasympathetic system were antagonistic, the most recent view is that either system, when driven to its extreme, causes a spillover effect in which both systems are fully engaged, producing experience described as rarefied states of consciousness.[69]

Ritualized motions such as drumming, dancing, and aerobic exercise have proven useful in treating anxiety attacks, obsessive behavior, ADD, post-traumatic stress disorder (PTSD), and chronic substance abuse, conditions associated with the inability of the brain to produce neurotransmitters necessary for self-soothing. Prozac and other drugs that increase serotonin in the brain also help put the arousal and quiescent systems into balance. Recent studies on aerobic exercise show that it encourages the secretion of adrenal hormones when we really need them and inhibits the production of those hormones when we are stressed. Additionally, when a stressful event is over, a well-exercised body eliminates adrenal hormones more quickly, reducing the likelihood of a disproportionate response to the next of life's chaotic intrusions. When performed in nonobsessive or nonaddictive ways, exercise also produces flexible mental adaptation, affecting the brain in much the same way that Prozac provides neurological plasticity to the depressed.[70]

While autistic and hyperactive children find motion a helpful therapy, they may do so for opposite reasons. Autistic children self-stimulate because they have a hypersensitive nervous system, that is, a nervous system with a wide-open volume control attuned to all sensory inputs. Self-stimulation is a technique used to filter out painful, external stimuli and find peace. However, hyperactive children often have nervous systems that are underaroused because they are undersensitive; their excessive activity is a means of providing stimuli to a system in need of it. Thus, the ritualized activity of autistics is designed to lower incoming stimuli, while the activities of hyperactive children are used to enhance stimuli. Both attempts can lead, if successful, to a homeostasis of body chemistry and environment as well as to experiences of embodied selfhood. The search for balance between the inner and outer worlds explains the seemingly counterintuitive therapy that prescribes amphetamines (or uppers) for the hyperactive. The amphetamines provide a needed stimulus to focus the nervous system, allowing the child to attend to the task at hand.[71]

Both Grandin and Williams take seriously the fact that forms of self-stimulation can function as a means of escape from intimacy and self-world relations. Like many of us, Williams found it easier to live in her own world, where life was like a movie that only occasionally came off the screen to affect her. Given her autism and life in an abusive household, remaining aware and responsive was a "joyless achievement." It demanded too much energy and felt "like a battle" rather than like belonging. Eventually, Williams says, "[I learned] to lose myself in anything I desired—the patterns on the wallpaper or the carpet, the sound of something over and over again, like the hollow thud I'd get from tapping my chin. Even people became no problem. . . . I could look through them until I wasn't there, and then later, I learned to lose myself *in them.*"[72] For Grandin, too, the world would easily cease to exist as she watched the Technicolor movies in her head or became absorbed in a spinning penny or the patterns in the wood of her desk. She lost herself and the world in daydreams as early as age two and a half. Yet her governess and her family did everything they could to keep her connected. She remembers her speech teacher gently grabbing her chin to force eye contact. As if given direction by Asperger himself, Grandin's teacher broke up her fixed stare and her body's immobility. Besides forcing her to make eye contact, the teacher insisted on activities that engaged Grandin in body-mind integration, such as jumping rope, skating, sledding, playing ball, or painting.[73]

Because stereotypies or ritualized behaviors have such a calming effect on the central nervous system, Grandin believes that the endorphins (or mimic morphines) produced by them may create a self-induced high in autistics, with the ritual etching itself into the circuitry of the brain in ways that make the behavior pleasant and self-enforcing.[74] (Stereotypies have been artificially induced experimentally by the injection of both amphetamines and endorphins into the brain.) Concerned that rocking can become as addictive as any drug, Grandin implies that stereotypies may be a menace, their sense of well-being a bit too seductive.[75] Both women are clear about the seductive nature of withdrawal from the world, the ease of finding comforting spaces and places in which one can enter a safe but solipsistic universe. But in the end, neither is fooled nor satisfied by that universe.

Self-Abuse. Williams and Grandin also take seriously the fact that painful rituals can be just as addictive as pleasurable ones. The desire to feel something rather than nothing, or something rather than an undifferentiated everything, causes some autistic, crack, FAS, and PDD children to go beyond self-stimulation to self-mutilation. Numbness is the flip side of the coin for the hypersensitive, and both hyperactive and autistic children have been shown to prefer stimuli that most of us would find painful to comforting touch or to no stimulation at all. Seemingly impervious to pain, these children can and do hurt themselves. Grandin remembers, as a child, "I sort of liked stimulation that was painful."[76] She warns caregivers not to misunderstand the nature of pain and pleasure in the autistic sensory system and end up rewarding a child when punishment is intended. Grandin gives an example of caregivers imposing physical restraints on a child after a self-injury. This could serve to reward rather than inhibit self-injury if the restraint is interpreted as a pleasant experience.[77] Grandin is talking explicitly about the sensory systems of autistics, but many people, the most famous being the Marquis de Sade, first realize their attraction to being whipped or spanked by suffering it as punishment at the hands of authorities such as teachers or priests.

When nothing else worked to help Williams escape her numbness, she hurt herself. Self-abuse assured her that she did in fact exist. Seeking a way out of her "mental prison," she hit, slapped, bit herself, and pulled her own hair, providing the contact needed to force her out of her own isolation. One of Williams's first memories of sharing any kind of experience with another human being was sharing painful physical sensation. She and a friend would amuse themselves by drinking water to the point of bursting, then choke themselves until they turned blue. They pushed in their eyes to create colors and screamed until their throats became raw. To produce some sense of intersubjective contact, painful stimulation proves to be better than no stimulation at all—neglected children fare worse than those who have been traumatized. Since the flip side of the coin of hypersensitivity is numbness, some autistics and PDD children do not appear to experience pain as painful. For example, when an eleven-year-old sunk his teeth into Williams's arm, she says, "There was a funny sensation to which I didn't know how to respond." She told herself to remember that people say "ouch" if bitten and that she must say "ouch" next time.[78]

Besides autistics and hyperactive children, young girls and women in our culture who feel imprisoned by their own bodies or psychologically and emotionally overwhelmed are increasingly given to self-mutilation. Mary Pipher's *Reviving Ophelia* brought to the attention of the public the fact that self-injury appears to produce physiological and emotional soothing. Self-injury is a cheap, fast, and easy way to use the body to produce a powerful sense of peace and calm; it is referred to as the new bulimia. An estimated two million people in the United States, most of them female, report the use of self-injury. Paula Watson, who began to self-mutilate at the age of seven, says, "Everything is spinning faster and faster and all these emotions are pouring out and they're going everywhere and you can't control them, you can't make them stop. And cutting makes them stop."[79]

Perhaps because people who abuse themselves find that cutting relieves tension, allows sleep, and provides a sense of being in control, the compulsions surrounding self-injuries are very strong. One woman says that she can't bring herself to watch a television commercial in which a finger is shown running along the cut edge of a can. While the point of the commercial is selling a can opener that leaves no sharp edge, watching the finger on the edge of the can makes her want to run her own finger along a very sharp edge because it feels so good. (Even telling this to a reporter made the woman want to cut herself.) The prevailing medical opinion is that cutting releases endorphins in the brain, just as Grandin suspects that rocking does. Grandin points out that there has been some success treating self-injury with naltrexone (Trexone), a chemical normally used on heroin addicts to block the brain's own opiates. Taking this drug prevents endorphins from being released during self-injury, allowing people who abuse themselves to begin to overcome their addiction.[80]

Even though she was numb to many forms of pain, Williams recognized that her mother's violence against her was violence, not caring. She remarks that what her mother did to her was much more severe than anything she ever did to herself, indeed, that her mother's physical abuse put her own efforts to shame: "I had always accepted my mother's violence toward me. Somehow it did not seem to matter too much. After all, it was only my body. Perhaps in some perverse way these extremes were the only physical sensations I could feel *without* being hurt. Gentleness, kindness, and affection terrified me, or at the very least, made me very uncomfortable."[81] With violence, Williams says, she always knew where she stood. She was regularly punched, kicked, rammed against the wall, locked out of the house, and referred to as "It." Her mother told her repeatedly, "You were my doll, and I was allowed to smash it."[82] In a particularly terrifying incident, Williams recalls the horror of nearly drowning on her own vomit while her mother forced a dishcloth into her mouth and whipped a cord across her face. There were threats of being institutionalized or sent to the same "heaven" her mother sent cats to—by breaking their necks in front of her eyes. Williams reflects, "It is hard to say whether the violence of my family made me the way I was."[83]

Ironically, Williams believes that her freedom was born in her mother's abuse because the abuse led her to the personality dissociations that she feels made it possible for her to avoid institutionalization. By the time she was two, Williams had "Willie," who felt no pain and was always in control and so was able to guide, defend, and hide Donna. Soon after that she came to have "Carol," the "dancing doll" to whom her mother was able to show affection. Wearing the personas or masks of Willie and Carol gave Donna the chance to retreat into the place of silent witness, to watch, wait, and see what would become of life and whether it would ever be worth coming back into her body and the world.

DONNA WILLIAMS: ON MASKS, MIRRORS, AND FINDING HER SELF

Early in her life, Williams found a sense of belonging in things, animals, and her own reflection in the mirror. Alienated from her body, her emotions, and other humans, she projected feelings into things and lived through or even in them. People with autism are known to be collectors of things and, like Williams, seem sometimes unaware that things would need a nervous system to think and to feel. Substituting things for persons, Williams composed a makeshift intersubjective world. "For me, the people I liked *were* their things, and those things (or things like them) were my protection from the things I didn't like—other people."[84]

Following this logic, Williams only ate food that symbolized the things she liked. For example, she liked rabbits, and since they ate lettuce, she ate lettuce. Jelly was similar to the colored glass she found to be so beautiful, and so she ate jelly. Living a fetish-like and animistic sort of existence, perhaps not unlike the worlds of many imaginative children, she saw things move more in accord with their readiness to do so than with any person's decision to move them. She told her shoes where to go so they could take her and talked to the carpet and to chairs. Williams gave things subjective life in order to be able to sense her own being and belonging, explaining, "[T]hings never thought or felt anything complex but they gave me a sense of being in company."[85]

Seeking proof, however literal, of the erotic nature of reality denied her, Williams longed to cut her doll open to search for the feelings inside it. Her therapist eventually gave her a universal rule, or a rule without exceptions (like the Kantian imperative) to follow—the only kind of rule autistics can understand—things need a nervous system to have intentionality or feeling. Having been repeatedly abandoned by people, Williams poignantly recalls how it felt to be also abandoned by things: "[This] new perception of objects as dead things without knowledge, without feeling, without volition nagged at me. I felt my aloneness with an intensity I had always been protected from. . . . Everything around me had no awareness I existed. I was no longer in company. Leaves didn't really dance and pictures didn't really jump off hooks on the wall and furniture didn't really stand around me. Damn 'the world.' It was an empty and ugly place."[86]

Besides connections to objects, Williams also connected with animals and eventually was able to use her relationships with animals to help her relate better to other people and to herself. Williams brought home stray cats from all over the neighborhood. A litter of kittens she found in a Dumpster became her symbol of the rainbow, a kitten for each color and for every aspect of the feeling world that eluded her. To Williams they were not only cats but symbols of her inner life and the need to care for it.[87] She placed a cat food tin next to her bed: "a symbol that I could commit myself to feed and care for the kittens that represented myself."[88] The cat food tin was her way of showing that she meant the commitment to herself to exist in the real world, not just in her mental universe. Since she cared for kittens and identified herself with them, she could also learn to care for herself in the world.

To assure her survival in the new "world of object corpses," Williams decided she must have some exceptions to the "logic of objects" given to her by her therapist. Exceptions to the dead world would include two toys she called Travel Dog and Moggin. By its mere physical presence beside her, the stuffed animal Travel Dog helped Williams accept the presence of her own body and her capacity to be with another. Similarly, in an attempt to recover her capacity for sensory touch, Williams constructed a puppet named

Moggin, a furry black cat she could wear on her hand. Moggin could be touched in ways that her own flesh could not, taking her still closer to actual physical encounter: "He could put his cat's paws around my neck and hug me, as I could neither ask nor tolerate to be hugged. Moggin was my bridge to touch and closeness as Travel Dog had been my bridge to maintaining self in company."[89]

Beyond the world of things, animals, Travel Dog, and Moggin, Williams had a feeling relation, one could even say an intersubjective relation, with her own reflection in the mirror. The mirror became another vehicle through which she gradually learned how to communicate with the world outside of herself. Her mirror reflection was the best friend Williams ever had in childhood, and for much of her life it was the only way she had to feel anything. Carol, Donna's mirror reflection, was named after a little girl who for a brief period of time befriended Williams but then abandoned her. In Donna's quest to experience relatedness, Carol came to live in the mirror. Donna reasoned that it was necessary for Carol to look like her in order to hide from others. Williams says that for four years she tried to walk into the mirror where her friend Carol lived. Finally, desperate to communicate and unable to find Carol either behind or within the mirror, Donna took on Carol's persona. Since she looked like Carol in the mirror, she would be Carol in the world.

Although she took on Carol's persona when she was with others, Donna's only true friend was in her mirror until a newly found, flesh-and-blood friend questioned the quality of the intimacy available in a mirror reflection. Although this observation initially angered her, Williams finally came to realize the emptiness of the world she had, in despair, created: "I came to realize that although the mirror had begun as an excellent strategy for breaking withdrawal, learning how to be social, fighting isolation, building language, and having body awareness, I had become addicted to its security. I had taken things too far. I would not truly learn ongoing closeness, touch, inner body awareness, and true sharing until I gave up the addiction. . . . Closeness, awareness, and self: these were the weapons against the addiction of the mirror world, for in the mirror world there were none of these things."[90]

Under all of this fleshless existence, some lingering desire for erotic connection drove her back into her body and the world.

Carol and Willie could act out the play but could neither help Donna feel nor express her feelings. Williams writes of Carol, "I had created an ego detached from the self, [a self] which was still shackled by crippled emotions."[91] Williams now came to recognize that Willie was an internalized version of her mother (Williams/Willie) and that her dependence on him caused a further retreat from both herself and others. As she puts it, "I was living as completely as I could within my own mind, and what I did express I expressed in a very symbolic and disturbing manner. I decided to murder a part of myself."[92] More often than we would like to admit, we use the unfeeling self to murder the feeling self, but Williams did the reverse—she murdered Willie, most appropriately, in ritual fashion. Donna dressed a small boy doll in jeans, colored his eyes green, wrapped his head in a cloth belonging to her grandmother, painted a small cardboard box black for a coffin, and buried him in the fish pond. His epitaph recorded that he must perish so that Donna could walk a stronger path. Looking back, Williams writes, "This incident was an expression of my desire to overcome the conflicts within that had made my world of nothingness so necessary. The conflict was caused, and always had been, by the necessity to give up control and interact with others. The more I tried, the worse became the conflict. The more I kept to myself, or kept others at a distance, the clearer things became."[93]

Her conflicts within were caused by the need to give up control and interact with others; yet the more she tried to interact, the worse the internal conflicts became. These are the torments experienced by the self in isolation. The more distanced, the more in control the self becomes, but the more the inner lives of everyone, including oneself, disappear. Such well-lighted and controlled worlds come with significant price tags, because in those mindworlds one finds only animated corpses. In such a world one can only live on the surface of the skin.

Williams's experience bears witness to the fact that whatever form solipsism takes, it is ultimately self-destructive. As she observes, the sanctuary one finds can easily become a prison: "I was sick to death of my attention wandering onto the reflection of every element of light and color, the tracing of every patterned shape, and the vibration of noise as it bounced off the walls. I used to love it. It has always come to rescue me and take me away from an incomprehensible world, where, once having given up fighting for meaning, my senses would stop torturing me as they climbed down from overload to an entertaining, secure, and hypnotic level of hyper. This was the beautiful side of autism. This was the sanctuary of the prison."[94] Once she began to climb out of the "self-made mind-house," the "world under glass" in which she found herself "suffocating," she also realized that Carol and Willie were nothing but masks created for acceptance in a world that was unacceptable. Her alternative personas then became "pathetic reminders of just how expensive cheap acceptance had been in 'the world.'"[95]

Without the distance her masks provided, Williams once again had to confront her sensory and emotional problems directly. Back in her body, she found herself wearing dark glasses indoors and putting cotton in her ears just to stay calm and focused. Williams's emotional difficulties stemmed in part from her failure to be aware of them as they happened—she had been letting her emotions pile up like laundry until the pile threatened to consume her.[96] Because she never felt angry when she was angry, Williams never became cognizant of the feeling that is anger, or any other feeling. The recognition that her emotions came all at once allowed her to confront the Big Black Nothingness that had always taken her down when she was touched emotionally: "I heard the roaring sound of silence in my ears and lost all sense of self-awareness as I stayed with the deathlike fear emotion gave me. I had found myself in a state of shock through allowing myself to keep a grip on feeling. Yet I had survived. . . . Donna was beginning to win the battle. . . . This time, however, she was not fighting to mirror someone else. She was fighting to come out to someone who was *her* mirror."[97]

Armed with pencils and paper, Williams knocked on the door of a family whom she had befriended and asked them to draw emotions for her. If she could learn to associate facial expressions with the emotions they represented, then perhaps she could learn to recognize emotions in others and in herself. Perhaps through facial expression she would gain an entry into the inner lives of others. After her friends drew faces representing emotions such as anger, happiness, and sorrow, Williams learned that she had been misinterpreting most human behavior. She had been mistaking two-thirds of people's behavior for anger when their expressions could have meant tired, busy, or excited. Learning this, she says, really did make her angry![98]

Beyond all of these incremental steps to touch and be touched, it was finally dealing with her food disorders that helped Williams to bear contact with the world and with her own emotional life. Food disorders, like sensory deprivation, trauma, and prenatal drug use, dramatically alter the body's chemistry and brain development. Williams is allergic to all meat except beef, all dairy products, soy products, potatoes, tomatoes, and corn. She is also hypoglycemic in the extreme. Williams believes that food intolerance can lead to forms of brain damage, echoing in food chemistry the same interplay that Grandin sees between touch and the brain, but she knows it is equally true that damaged brains can manifest themselves in food intolerances.[99] Sticking to a diet that eliminates these intolerances reduces her anxiety, which in turn helps Williams to accept her body as her own.

Controlling her diet, along with giving up her masks and mirrors, has made it possible for Donna Williams to finish a degree in education and to discover her capacities for caring in her work with autistic children. Williams married an autistic man and is making progress accepting change, identifying her feelings, and comprehending social relations. A victim of autism, child abuse, and chemical imbalances created by food allergies, Donna Williams nevertheless has come to acknowledge that life takes on an ontological weight in feeling that is not possible in cognition or narcissistic reflection alone. Against great odds, Williams is developing a life that integrates body, self, and erotic engagement with others.

TEMPLE GRANDIN'S SQUEEZE MACHINE
AND THE COW'S-EYE VIEW

While Williams's account of her autism stresses the difficulty of holding on to the self and having emotions at the same time, Grandin's story seems more about how difficult it is to have a life that includes emotional connection without the comfort and calm of physical touch. She tells us that the squeeze machine taught her to be gentle and that she learned to comfort others only after she had experienced the feeling of being physically comforted. In an

interview with Terry Gross on the National Public Radio program
Fresh Air (February 20, 1998), Gross asked Grandin if she understood love. She replied that she has never understood romantic
love and its trappings, and that she doesn't engage in sexual relationships because she finds them way too confusing, but that she
does understand love as care.

Grandin was able to feel the caring love of her mother and her
aunt initially through experiencing the comfort of the squeeze machine. The pressure of the machine's touch calmed her down and
made it possible for her to feel cared for and to care for others. At
the time she wrote, "I realize that unless I can accept the squeeze
machine I will never be able to bestow love on another human being."[100] Embrace by the machine so altered Grandin's state of being
that their Siamese cat, who had always run away from her, perceived the change and allowed himself to be stroked in the new,
softer manner made possible by the machine's embrace. "It enabled me to learn to be gentle, to have empathy, to know that gentleness is not synonymous with weakness. I was learning how to
feel."[101]

Grandin says that sometimes the boundaries of her body disappear into the strong tactile contact the squeeze machine provides, and she feels that she is floating, like her experience of the
Round Up. She thinks that both the Round Up and her squeeze
machine could help children with developmental disorders. Proto-
types of her machine are now being used to provide therapy for
autistic and hyperactive children, and models of her design have
been on display at MIT. Enthusiastic also about a touch therapy for
babies with developmental disorders, Grandin remains hopeful
that, like the gradual training of a wild animal by stroking, the tactile defenses of infants may be slowly broken down by touch therapy, thereby minimizing later physical and behavioral problems.
She is also enthusiastic about the Internet, which she thinks may
enhance an autistic child's capacity for sociality by freeing them
from the chaos associated with face-to-face relations, eye contact,
and other forms of body language found to be indecipherable. At
the same time, she recognizes that the Internet should not be used
to escape all interactions with flesh-and-blood others.

Perhaps not surprising in a society that habitually confuses
eros with pornography, the psychologists at Grandin's high school

tried to convince her mother to take the squeeze machine away from her. Because sexuality is the only relevant form of tactility in a neo-Freudian universe, the counselors feared the machine might be some kind of bizarre sexual substitute. (Similarly, Odom-Winn and Dunagan note in their discussion of crack kids that when you say self-stimulation, most educators think only of masturbation.)[102] The counselors, missing the point about emotional intimacy entirely, initiated the first serious conflict between Grandin and her mother by attempting, ironically, to eliminate the one thing that allowed Grandin to be able to feel emotionally close to her mother. Besides conjuring up signs of sexual deviance in their minds, the machine appears to have also blurred the comfortable boundaries they had constructed between animals and humans. Grandin says they implied that she thought she was a cow and called her use of the machine "sick." Her memory of the conversation is that the psychologist said, "Well, Temple, I haven't decided whether this contraption of yours is a prototype of the womb or a casket," to which she responded, "Neither." The counselor then said, "*We* do not have an identity problem here, do *we*? I mean, *we* don't think we're a cow or something, do *we*?"[103]

Grandin's relationship with animals, especially cattle, is a close one; she admits to and rightly prides herself on having the cow's-eye view ever since she first entered the cattle chute. Of course, she knows that she isn't a cow, but she does think that cattle have sensory and emotional experiences much like hers. Animals have a limbic structure very similar to that of humans, and Grandin takes the dominant emotion of cows to be the same as hers—fear. Cows pull away from touch the way she pulls away, and they are frightened by light and unfamiliar noises the way that she is. She uses her ability to feel what cows feel to design farm, transport, and slaughter equipment that lessens the pain inflicted on these animals. She claims that she has "a sensory empathy for the cattle. When they remain calm I feel calm, and when something goes wrong that causes pain, I also feel their pain."[104] Many people experience these same dynamics with their pets; the physical and emotional contact people have with their pets has been shown in many studies to promote physical and psychological health as well as quicker recovery from trauma or injury.

Grandin experiences with cattle a sensory and emotional immediacy that she finds impossible to experience with human children and with primates, both of whom are capable of complex social relations that Grandin readily admits to understanding only intellectually. Cattle do not confuse her with complex social dynamics. They respond to her tenderness; her touch calms them, and in touching them, she becomes calm and gentle herself, the way she does in the squeeze machine. She describes the way she extends her sentience into an animal to feel what it might feel: "I place myself inside its body and imagine what it experiences. It is the ultimate virtual reality system, but I also draw on the empathetic feelings of gentleness and kindness I have developed so that my simulation is more than a robotic computer model."[105]

Grandin acknowledges the irony of knowing that the same cattle chute which has helped her feel connections with others also holds cattle while painful acts like branding and castration are performed. Her name is synonymous with a circling or curved chute used to calm cattle on their way to these operations and to slaughter. She says, "It is a sobering experience to be a caring person, yet to design a device to kill large numbers of animals."[106] Yet she maintains that slaughter can be humane when done correctly, and so she actively seeks and finds ways to lessen the pain and anxiety of these animals—fully one-third of the cattle in the United States are now killed in machinery designed by Grandin. She considers her work in the slaughterhouse to be a form of "hospice care" because the cattle are made as comfortable as possible as they approach death:

> I am successful in designing livestock systems because I can imagine myself as an animal, with an animal's body shape and senses. I am able to visualize myself as an animal going through one of my systems. This "video" is complete with touch, sound, visual and olfactory sensations. I can play this "video" from two perspectives. The perspective is either me watching the animal, or me inside the animal's head looking out through its eyes. Many systems used in meat plants are designed poorly because the engineers never thought about what the equipment would feel like when it contacted the animal's body. I can imagine how the animal will feel, and set my own emotions aside. I can imagine realistically what the animal would feel because I do not allow my own emotions to cloud the picture. . . . Most people who love animals have such a negative emotional reaction to being in a slaughter

plant that their emotions interfere with really empathizing with
the cattle.[107]

In a culture insistent upon eating meat and taking very little
moral responsibility for it, Grandin finds herself doing some of the
moral work no one else wants to do by designing equipment to
provide a more peaceful and painless death. She has also worked to
get the industry to pay attention to abuses associated with over-
loading cattle in transport, calving on slippery flooring, and
"downer cattle" who are dragged from trucks or picked up by fork
lifts and to the impossibility of treating animals humanely when
under pressure to kill too many animals too quickly. One cannot
kill one thousand hogs an hour and do it humanely, she believes.
Grandin finds that the record of such abuses in the United States is
tied to the emphasis on profit. Whether or not one wants to question the morality of killing animals to eat in the first place, the fact
is that violence against animals occurs on a massive scale, with
minimal awareness of the pain inflicted on them, the effects on
workers, or the consequences for the planet.[108]

Grandin speculates that her autism protects her from emotional breakdown in what amounts to a very painful situation. Her
equanimity serves to promote caring acts that would be impossible
for other people, including those who eat meat but could not stand
to enter a slaughterhouse, much less perform the kill. In other
words, she is able to improve the conditions of these animals because she continues to feel empathy for them while being in the
kill area, assisting and performing the kill. She knows this is unusual because, having seen her colleagues at work, she has deduced
that numbness and desensitization are natural responses of humans to brutality.[109]

Grandin says that she learned the art of caring while operating
the "stunning pen" at Beefland. Beefland is the largest slaughterhouse in the Southwest (likened by her in grandeur and immensity
to the Vatican). When operated correctly, a "captive bolt stunner"
drives a retractable bolt deep into the brain, killing animals in-
stantly, she thinks, with less pain than branding: "Gradually I realized that to be an expert in the stunning pen was really the art of
caring. Paradoxically, I was learning to care at the slaughterhouse."[110] Her ability to maintain empathy during the activity of

slaughter is, she imagines, similar in intent and performance to religious acts of sacrifice. Religious sacrifice is about taking life in a serious and moral way, without the emotional deadening typical of the sadist and the mechanist. Grandin bows her head before approaching the slaughterhouse as a matter of respect and describes the experience of killing painlessly as Zen-like: an act of awareness, connection, and clarity in which one becomes the act. Quoting the Torah's restrictions against causing pain to animals, Grandin has worked hard to eliminate the hoist-and-shackle methods of kosher slaughterhouses, which even she cannot enter without suffering nightmares for days afterward.[111]

Grandin finds the most common management psychology in slaughterhouses to be "simply denial of the reality of killing." As if they had taken on the persona of Willie, managers distance themselves from what is actually happening at their workplace by using words like "dispatching," "processing," or "euthanasia," much as we too use distancing euphemisms when we order "ham," "pork," or "beef" for dinner. In factory farming the movement is increasingly toward ceasing to speak of an animal at all, referring instead to a "food-producing unit," a "protein harvester," or an "egg-producing machine." Managers and engineers avoid the kill area because it really upsets them, Grandin observes, and discipline is lax where managers refuse to spend time overseeing the handling and the killing. As would be predicted, this often means that the only people in the kill area are the sadists who enjoy and find pleasure in the maiming and killing. There are also the mechanical people, as Grandin calls them, who approach their work as something to be done without feeling, engaging in slaughter "as if [they were] stapling boxes moving along a conveyer belt."[112]

Most of the mechanical people kill the animals "efficiently and painlessly," she reports, and there are a few people who take the kill chute—the lowest-paying job at the plant—explicitly to prevent the sadistic people from doing it. Grandin notes that women are entering this previously male-dominated profession with the explicit intention of preventing pain to the animals. Her concern is that persons with healthy emotional lives cannot do this work without becoming increasingly desensitized or without devaluing the animal to justify the cruelties inflicted. Once the rationalizations kick in, then anything becomes possible. She reports seeing workers shoot out the eyes of animals prior to the slaughter or pick a live hog up by driving a steel hook through its shoulder. One slaughterhouse worker told her that as a child he was forced to kill a pet calf so he would never love one again. Grandin has a good sense of the role our relationships with animals play in our psychological lives, and she believes that if we can't respect animals, we can't respect ourselves.[113]

Grandin suspects that people who exhibit sadistic behaviors with animals cannot transcend that behavior to be compassionate in other areas of life. She is also disturbed to find at over half the auction markets she attends instances of young children being allowed to abuse animals without adult interference. She points to studies showing that children who enjoy abusing animals are much more likely to engage in sadistic behavior when they become adults. Cutting animals into pieces or lighting them on fire, along with a childhood that includes sexual abuse, rigid discipline, social isolation, bedwetting, and corporal punishment, are standard in the biographies of sadists and serial killers. Grandin mentions Albert DeSalvo and Edmund Kemper, serial killers who tortured cats when they were young.[114] Kemper cooked and ate parts of his victims as did serial killer Albert Fish, who claimed to be in a state of sexual excitement during the entire nine days it took him to eat Grace Budd, a nine-year-old girl whom he had abducted, raped, and murdered.[115] Fish wrote to Budd's parents that he particularly enjoyed their daughter's sweet buttocks, which he roasted in the oven. In more instances than one might imagine, serial killers consume their victims and are caught by blocked drains and strange odors that reveal their horrifying deeds. Fish's biography included childhood sexual abuse, rigid discipline, corporal punishment (including floggings that gave him erections), bedwetting, arson, and cruelty to animals. Fish claimed to be in love with pain—his own and that of others. Traced by police through the letter he sent to Budd's parents, Fish was caught and sentenced to death by electrocution, a sentence to which he responded by saying it would be "the supreme thrill" of his life.[116]

I think Grandin would agree with Marti Kheel, who has argued that "learning to respond to nature in caring ways is not an abstract exercise in reasoning. It is, above all, a form of psychic and emotional health."[117] Children who abuse animals learn to suppress their own capacities for feeling and denigrate others just as they become desensitized by watching hours of gratuitous television violence. Sadists are persistent in their complaints about being numb, and it may be this alienation from feeling that propels them to use the pain of others to feel vital and therefore real. Because workers tend to cope with the act of slaughter either by becoming numb or by coming to find pleasure in it, Grandin concludes that no one should be made to kill animals as a full-time job. Instead, we need to view forms of empathetic breakdown in workers in slaughterhouses (and wherever else we find them) as we would the illness of canaries in a mine, as signals of disease induced by toxic conditions. Grandin argues that such jobs should be rotated and that societies need to seriously address "the paradox . . . that it is difficult to care about animals but be involved in killing them."[118] Meat eaters need to consider not only the pain of the animal (and the impact on the planet of eating this high on the food chain), but also the emotional consequences of their actions on the people who do the handling, transporting, and killing.

In spite of Grandin comparing herself to the emotionless Spock and Data, it seems clear to me that Grandin's construction of the squeeze machine and her work with animals testify to the crucial role that touch plays in developing our capacity for emotional connection and compassion. In this, my own reading of Grandin's life and work is in opposition to that of Francesca Happé, who thinks Grandin "ignores or discounts the importance of our affective and emotional life."[119] Happé judges Grandin incapable of emotion not because she is able to work at the slaughterhouse with equanimity, but because, to Happé, her lack of emotion helps explain "Temple's merging of human and animal data."[120] Happé finds it "interesting . . . that [Grandin] has succeeded in a field which requires some 'empathy' for farm animals—since this is an area in which we are all left guessing and using scientific facts to infer 'feelings.'"[121] Empathy and feeling are here in quotations to imply that neither Grandin nor animals are able to feel the way the rest of us do. In other words, because Happé cannot credit animals with feeling or empathy, and Grandin seems to relate so well to them, it follows that Grandin is also without these sensibilities.

To make her case, Happé tells us that Grandin, in an attempt to feel what cattle feel, swam through a dip vat at the Red River

Feedyard in Stanfield, Arizona, a facility which Grandin herself had designed. Grandin wanted to know how traumatic the experience was chemically and otherwise, and to discover what she needed to know, she stood in line with about three thousand head of cattle. Like them, she became more and more nervous as her turn came, until, finally, she was dipped just like they were. (Ironically, the dip, replete with an organophosphate pesticide, had the side effect of calming her nerves for almost three years.) To Happé, Grandin's action "suggests perhaps a lack of ability to empathize, since she felt it necessary to put herself through the same experience in order to feel the same feelings. When we empathize with another person we generally mean that we *feel with* them, despite the fact that we are not actually *suffering with* them."[122]

Even though we who are not autistic can more easily feel what it is like to walk in the shoes of another human being than in the hooves of a cow, being willing to experience what others experience can suggest an enhanced rather than a diminished capacity for empathy. As an ethicist, I would argue that fasting brings us closer to all of those who are hungry since feeling hunger has an emotional and moral urgency to it that the idea of hunger does not. The idea that both Grandin and animals have the ability to feel, and feel with each other, does not occur to Happé because her dualistic position, like that of the psychologists at Grandin's high school, makes her suspicious of the boundaries Grandin is blurring. In her words, "[Grandin] does not seem to see the divide, which, rightly or wrongly, most people feel the need to construct between animals and humans. This is evident in her creation of the squeeze machine."[123]

In my view, Happé represents, however subtly, the kind of perspective that has long discounted the role of body and feeling, indeed, the role of touch and eros, in our moral lives. Moreover, as the work of Darwin and others has shown us, many of the lines we have drawn between humans and animals are purely arbitrary. A moral code that takes into account our common evolutionary heritage would respect what we share with animals by making central our capacities to feel pain and our abilities to engage in social relations. Yes, happily, Grandin does blur the distinctions between mind and body, humans and animals, sensations and emotions, because she experiences these distinctions as artificial constructions. She is quite aware that the nonautistic, or so-called feeling, world is reluctant to attribute feeling to farm animals or lab animals, and she recognizes further that to do so might require us to alter our behavior. As an undergraduate, Grandin went to the trouble of arranging a meeting with B. F. Skinner to speak to him about her conviction that animal behavior can never be fully understood through the behaviorist model of stimulus-response. Behaviorism, like Cartesian philosophy, views animals (and to some extent humans) as automatons. Grandin points out that during the reign of the behaviorist perspective, animals in labs, on farms, and in slaughterhouses were treated particularly cruelly—and, we might add, so were many children raised with a behaviorist model. She also sees disturbing parallels between the ways animals are mistreated and the ways people with physical and mental disabilities are mistreated. Perhaps, in the end, it is the holders of the dualistic perspective—the Cartesians, the Skinners, the Happés, and Grandin's high school counselors—who are most in need of the squeeze machine.

The first lesson in erotic morality that we can learn from the stories of Temple Grandin and Donna Williams is the importance of touch and emotion in connecting self to world. As I suggested earlier, because of their autism these women have learned to be aware of the boundaries and attachments, the barriers and openings, the prisons and sanctuaries that surround the self in its relation to others. That awareness made it possible for them to devise strategies to defeat their defenses and fears and learn to be touched in ways that allow them to be physically and emotionally at home in the world. For both women this is an ongoing process, as it is for all of us who struggle to maintain erotic relations. When I asked Grandin if she still uses the squeeze machine, she said that she no longer needs it to calm her nervous system (there are plenty of therapeutic drugs now on the market to do that) but that she continues to use the machine explicitly to help her experience empathy, that is, to feel closer to others.[124]

Williams and Grandin teach us that to reach out is to reach within. Many of their lessons are about being aware of and comfortable in our bodies; without feeling calm and comforted ourselves, we can never calm or comfort others. We need to be aware of our emotions and experience them in context, but we can't feel them at all if we live in sensory confusion. The external chaos that often surrounds us creates internal chaos, and internal chaos eliminates subjective awareness. We need, therefore, to find tolerable levels of sensory stimulation. As both women discovered, this means finding sanctuaries and rituals that do not become addictive or self-enclosed.

Grandin and Williams also remind us that the smallest acts affect our ability to feel connected to the world around us. Chemically and morally, what we consume can act to alienate us from others by altering our nervous systems and by drawing artificial lines between ourselves and the sources of our consumption. Grandin and Williams teach us that animals are important avenues to erotic morality. The sensitivity of animals to touch can quickly remind us that we too are embodied and share with them capacities for pain and pleasure. In our love of animals, we can learn to care for, respect, and love ourselves, for we too are part of nature. Williams and Grandin teach us, finally, how easy it is to respond to brutality by becoming anesthetized or desensitized. Whether one is the abused child, the slaughterhouse worker, or simply someone living a life of continual stress, the tendency is to identify with someone other than the person experiencing the pain. It is easier to put on the mask, become an automaton, or live in a mirror world, even when these identities lead us to false perceptions and unfeeling actions.

Given these lessons, it is no surprise to find that neither Williams nor Grandin seem very impressed by the so-called feeling world's capacity to feel. Grandin remarks that she is not sure which is more of a hindrance while working at the slaughterhouse, that she is autistic or that she is female. She is always given the grossest tour and has returned to her car more than once to find it covered in bull testicles or other body parts. Williams, too, is quick to realize how alienated our society is from feeling: "Look around you. Most people force themselves to do things against their natural emotional reactions. We live in a schizoid society." Neither of them need to be reminded that in Stanley Milgram's famous experiment it was "normal" people who administered the high-voltage shocks to other people simply because the experimenters instructed them to do so.[125]

In the next chapter we will examine how Western philosophy has traditionally failed to recognize the role of the emotions in moral life, in contrast to more recent research, in neurology and psychology, that affirms the importance of emotions for practical reason and agency. There we will turn to the work of Louis Sass and Antonio Damasio, among others, to show how dualistic philosophy, by divorcing the mind from the body and the emotions, more nearly describes diseases that afflict humanity than prescriptions for morality.

2

DISEMBODIED TOUCH
Body as Object

One sticks one's finger into the soil to tell by
the smell in which land one is: I stick my finger into existence—it smells of nothing.
Where am I? Who am I? How came I here?
What is this thing called the world?

—Sören Kierkegaard, *Repetition*

K ierkegaard describes the retreat of philosophy from the world and
thus from the embodied self as a form of sensual diminishment that
leaves us erotically adrift and lost in the midst of existence. Ludwig
Wittgenstein referred to this retreat as "the philosopher's disease,"
the burden of perpetual doubt and enclosed self-reflection borne by
those who privilege mentality over engagement in the processes of
living. The reflections of Donna Williams and Temple Grandin have
begun to show us how emotional life is interwoven with sensory
awareness and cognition. We can extend their insights by paying
attention to the ties between cognition and emotion emerging
from contemporary research in neurology and clinical psychology.
As the examples in this chapter will show, divorcing mind from
body creates a dissociated ego that, by eliminating erotic life, destroys the connections necessary for practical and responsible
agency.

Human cognition finds its evolutionary ground in our sen-
sory-emotional life, and our emotions remain the first and still primary means by which we give material expression to our being in
the world. As psychiatrist Peter Whybrow argues in *A Mood Apart*,
any attempt to disregard emotional awareness is to lose a tool essential to adaptive behavior. Ignoring emotion is "equivalent to

the ancient mariner throwing away his sextant, or the airline pilot ignoring his navigational devices."[1] Emotions put us and keep us on course. They also help us understand each other by acting as physiognomic expressions of temperament and inner states of being through which we enter the lives of others. The continued use of disembodied models of cognition, such as those used by theorists interested in artificial intelligence, leads everyone astray, particularly in popular culture, by conceptualizing the person as a mechanism. Their blatant disregard of the flesh reminds me of the films that I watched as a child in which the mad scientist saved the brain of his friend—and thus his friend—by suspending it in a vat of liquid. Attaching mechanical devices to the brain was magically all that was needed to bring the friend to awareness, to speech, and to feelings of dread, regret, and longing sans the body.

On the basis of neurological research and studies in evolutionary biology, Antonio Damasio has argued that the life of the mind originates neither in the brain in its entirety nor in the traditionally more privileged "thinking" or "higher" brain, the neocortex. Instead, cognition emerges in the totality that is the lived body, an organism in continual, reciprocal interaction with the world. There are therefore no strict boundaries between mind and body or between mind-body and world situatedness. Mentality is an event that includes the world horizon, and whatever it is that we refer to as "mind" must remain rooted to the body-world if we are to maintain intersubjective awareness and contact with reality or being. *Descartes' Error: Emotion, Reason, and the Human Brain* is Damasio's exploration of how our cognitive and emotional lives intertwine. He finds Cartesian dualism to be more typical of persons suffering injuries to the prefrontal cortices than the basis for normal human praxis. A neurologist by training, Damasio argues that sensations and emotions are expressions of our being in the world; they are the means by which the world is interpreted and becomes embodied in our flesh. The materialization of the world in the flesh is absolutely necessary for practical and moral life, because apart from that biochemical "mattering" there is no way for us to realize what "matters" as relevant or valuable in moment-by-moment living.[2]

Similarly, Louis Sass, has proposed parallels between dualistic modern philosophy and mental illness in *Madness and Modernism* and *The Paradoxes of Delusion*. Sass is a clinical psychologist who finds the emphasis in modern philosophy on detachment from the body to be dangerously solipsistic. Indeed, this is one of the great ironies of the Cartesian quest for certainty, as Kierkegaard's lament implies: the more distant mind from body, the more delusional we become and less able to find our way back home into existence. Once we recognize the importance of the senses and emotions in cognition, then the Cartesian certainty, "I think, therefore I am," appears similar in its solipsism to forms of psychosis. Descartes's description of the mind mysteriously residing in a barely corporeal, mechanistic, emotionless body or shell is closer, phenomenologically, to the experience of those who suffer mental disorders on the continuum of schizophrenia than to ordinary human awareness.

Sass considers Jean-Paul Sartre's *Nausea* to be the culminating modern example of "the crumbling of normal sensory and emotional reality."[3] One might recall that for Sartre's main character, Roquentin, the world frequently has no presence or being: "Nothing seemed true; I felt surrounded by cardboard scenery which could quickly be removed." Yet when confronted with particular things, such as the root of a chestnut tree or a pebble, Roquentin finds the experience completely overwhelming. His response to the pebble is this: "Objects should not *touch* because they are not alive. You use them, put them back in place, you live among them: they are useful, nothing more. But they touch me; it is unbearable. I am afraid of being in contact with them as though they are living beasts."[4]

DUALISM AND DEONTOLOGY

My working hypothesis is that deontological ethics, that is, the ethics of obedience to law and duty, is the only kind of ethic possible in an ontology which severs mind from body and culture from nature. A direct consequence of moral theory's flight from the body may be the formalization of moral discourse around absolute rules, rights, and duties. These are the legalistic, mathematical, and abstract values that emerge in the life of the disembodied subject who looks at the world from a distance to weigh and pass judgment. The values of intimacy, relatedness, responsibility, caring, and compassion are erotic values arising from sensory feeling and emotional connectedness. While one may want to argue that moral agency demands both types of values, erotic values have been dismissed in traditional moral theory at least partially because they muddy up the water: they create ambiguous and fluid boundaries by acknowledging the reality of change and interconnectedness. The flesh-and-blood presence of eros in the world cannot be reduced to the formalized abstractions of law or mathematics.

Representatives of fuzzy mathematics and chaos science or complexity theory have made similar arguments about the limitations of disembodied reason. These theorists wish to hold onto the ambiguous, fluid nature of the world of everyday life. Yes, in theory, a billiard ball will run the course plotted for it by Newtonian mechanics and remain predictable in perpetuity, but not in the real world where balls are never perfectly weighted nor tables ever perfectly leveled. What happens as one turns from the objects of classical physics, such as rolling balls, pendulums, and planets, to messy daily realities, such as weather, air turbulence, wildlife populations, the heart pumping blood, and water coming out of a faucet, is that one must face contingencies and interconnectedness.[5]

I read psychologist Carol Gilligan as making a similar argument. Gilligan's *In a Different Voice* describes the gestalt shift that occurred in her thinking about morality when she realized that Lawrence Kohlberg, her mentor, had set up artificial abstractions to measure moral development. The Heinz dilemma, for example, was one of Kohlberg's standard moral problems. It asks whether a husband, Heinz, should steal a drug which he cannot afford to buy for his dying (unnamed) wife. Yes, responds Jake, an eleven-year-old who sees this exercise as "sort of like a math problem with humans." On Kohlberg's scale of moral development, Jake is given high marks for his ability to recognize the appropriate hierarchy—life is worth more than property. Eleven-year-old Amy, however, stays closer to the body—in space, time, and community—and in so doing she opens Gilligan's eyes to the abstract nature of Kohlberg's question and fails Kohlberg's test by resisting the abstraction. Amy's voice is a different voice because, like chaos theory, fuzzy mathematics, and embodied life, her voice restores the messy variables: Does Heinz know how to administer the drug? Will his wife need the drug more than once, or perhaps even for the rest of her life? How will Heinz take care of his wife if he is in jail? Has Heinz spoken to the druggist in an attempt to explain the problem? Amy sees the issue in terms of embodied, ongoing relatedness rather than as a conceptual dilemma with properly weighted principles.[6] One can see how holding onto the body complicates the situation, but it has the distinct moral (and epistemological) advantage of holding onto the world, that is, to the realities which confront us in life rather than in thought alone.

Western ideas about reason and logic, having abandoned concrete bodies, are founded more on mathematical abstractions than on lived experience. By contrast, Jain philosophy, which first arose in India in an ascetic sect that respected the reality and diversity of the world by rejecting the idealist tendency in Hinduism to see each separate being as unreal when compared to their unity in Brahman, takes embodiment seriously. The Jains are perhaps best known for their pious practices of nonviolence toward all forms of life—sweeping as they walk and wearing masks so as not to disrupt even the world of bacteria and insects. Their radical sense of being in touch with all kinds of bodies helps account for the fact that Jain logic reflects a less rigid attitude toward truth statements than, for example, Aristotle's laws of logic, according to which, following the law of the excluded middle, every statement is either true or not true. Jains, however, describe seven categories by which statements can be judged as true, each of which reflects a kind of humility that acknowledges the incomplete and uncertain nature of knowledge. For example, one of their truth claims is "maybe it is and it is not and is also indeterminate."[7] Philosopher Sara Ruddick has made a similar argument about the thought structures of caregivers. Because in caring for infants one meets the embodied, unpredictable, full, and complete presence of another, the epistemology of caregivers is attentive to ambiguity and flux. Ruddick writes, "On my view, the attentive love of mothering requires concrete cognition, tolerance for ambivalence and ambiguity, receptiveness to change and recognition of the limits of control."[8]

It has been repeatedly said of autistics that their morality is Kantian or deontological in nature, that is to say, that autistics have strict law-abiding attitudes and can only understand rules without exceptions. I am speculating that they must do so precisely because they are alienated from their own emotional lives and thus the interior lives of others. Acting from abstract and absolute rules rather than subjective connection, Barry, who has

Asperger syndrome, says, "I am never going to kill anyone since I would hate to die in the electric chair or get life imprisonment."[9] Perfectly suited for behaviorist justice systems, autistics see the correspondence between behavior and punishment as one-to-one, or as an easy problem in mathematics. The context of the act, the life of the other person involved, and all other social and emotional connections are irrelevant to such a cost-benefit analysis—just as in the moral game theory, the Prisoner's Dilemma, the point is to choose a course of action based on logic alone.

People with autism appear to turn to universal rules because they are distanced from their own subjective lives and the lives of others. Autistics generally cannot pretend, conceal, or lie, and they describe indiscretions in detail without shame or embarrassment. Because they are largely unaware that others have subjective lives, they cannot hurt others intentionally. At the same time, they are rigidly legalistic when searching for guidelines for behavior. Unfortunately, since they fail to understand that others have a subjective life, they also fail to understand that others can break the law, and so they can be easy prey for those who would take advantage of their indiscriminate trust. Both Grandin and Williams give heartbreaking accounts, as do the relatives of less-functional autistics, about the way they are mistreated by those of us who, allegedly, can feel. Donna Williams tells a horrendous story about being invited to a party only to discover that "she *was* the party." After being raped and beaten, she wandered around for two hours trying to make sense of what had happened. Williams then returned to the house where she had been raped to apologize for her mistake, whatever it was.[10] Grandin readily admits that when she is away from the moral issues that she authentically understands through her own erotic sensibilities—her love for her family and her work eliminating the pain of livestock—she is forced to make decisions by reference to a "vast data bank" and the process of elimination.[11] She likens herself to an android in this instance because she realizes that it is impossible to learn social intimacies or capture subjective experiences with the processes of abstract cognition alone. Her own experience with animals and with the squeeze machine supplies firsthand evidence for this.

Perhaps just as Temple Grandin found a comforting world in scientific abstraction—a conceptual life unencumbered by emotions, feelings, irony, or social intimacies—so some of the most important intellectuals of Western philosophy, including Plato, Descartes, and Kant, found security in descriptions of truth that excluded erotic sensibility.[12] In *Emotion and Embodiment,* Glen Mazis describes Plato as a keen observer of the emotions. Plato recognized that by tying us to the sensually perceived world and to our own bodies the emotions undermine the autonomy of the knower. According to Mazis, Plato correctly saw that *"each* emotional apprehension is a way of *becoming more enmeshed in each perceptual object and more integrated with the body."*[13] But it is precisely this enmeshing that led Plato to reject rather than affirm the emotions as part of the project of coming to wisdom. The emotions, in Plato's view, cannot convey truth because by forcing body and world upon us, they question self-sufficiency, control, and fixity. Plato writes that "each pleasure and pain seems to have a nail, and nails the soul to the body and pins it on and makes it bodily, and so it thinks the same things are true which the body says are true."[14] Referring to such feelings as "bewitchings" that overcome us, Plato sought to ascend from the delusional earthly cave that he equated with the world of the flesh by means of the transcendence provided by reason, just as his student Euclid attempted to eliminate the ambiguities of existence by subjecting life to the principles of geometry.

Kantian Bodies and the Panopticon

In *Cognition and Eros,* Robin May Schott argues that the divorce between cognition and feeling in Kant's philosophy can be attributed to his need to repress eros. Schott points out that every time Kant speaks of feeling in his major philosophical work, *The Critique of Pure Reason,* he is careful to say that it leads neither to knowledge nor to any information about the external world.[15] Like autistics, Kant appears to have ordered all aspects of his life according to rigid schedules so as to eliminate any change or spontaneity. He never had a lasting intimate relationship and is said to have lost the opportunity for marriage by thinking about it for too long. Not surprisingly, Kant also found sexuality to be problematic and viewed it as purely genital activity divorced from any emotion. Because he so distrusted eros, he understood sexual relations as inevitably turning one's partner into an object, violating his moral principle to treat all persons as subjects.[16]

Of all the senses, Kant said he favored vision because "it is far-thest removed from the sense of touch."[17] Schott notes that Kant uses the word "Anschauung" to describe sense perception, or em-pirical sensation. The more commonly used word is "Empfind-ung," which can mean either physical sensation or emotional feeling, whereas "Anschauung" means to look at or view (and "Schau" means an exhibit). Conditions appropriate to knowledge and moral action therefore require the ideal Kantian subject to be a spectator viewing an exhibit. In his daily habits Kant became such a spectator himself, viewing his body from a distance. As Andrew Cutrofello suggests in *Discipline and Critique,* Kant may have trained for this identity while submitting to his abusive father's punishments, learning as a child the trait of the masochist to cre-ate a program replacing "instinctive forces with transmitted forces."[18]

Every philosophy student has heard stories about the walks Kant took each afternoon, so regular and punctual that his neigh-bors set their clocks by them. What is less well known is that on these walks Kant was applying a kind of calculus to his flesh, divid-ing motions into discrete, indivisible, and controlled moments. As Cutrofello describes it: "The event of stepping is being reduced to a series of measured instants. The parts of his foot will be restrained to step as one—not heel first, then the ball of the foot, then the toes—but all at once as a unified, law-governed stepping ma-chine."[19] Whereas one might expect a mind-body dualist to ignore his body, according to Cutrofello, Kant, to the contrary, was ob-sessed with it: "From the moment he woke up (at 4:55 A.M. every day) until the instant when he fell asleep at night, no detail of his daily routine was too insignificant to escape disciplinary control."[20] He not only tried to control his walking but his breathing and swallowing. In short, Kant appears to have lived in ways that mechanized life by reducing it to habitual and discrete moments devoid of erotic connection. Unlike Grandin, who built a machine to allow her body to feel, Kant seems to have made his body into a machine to avoid feeling.

The central modern symbol of the gaze that imposes objectify-ing distance between viewer and viewed is Jeremy Bentham's ar-chitectural design known as the Panopticon, a structure first built in 1871. Adopted by Michel Foucault as the organizing metaphor for *Discipline and Punish*, the Panopticon, an early version of Orwell's Big Brother, is a building constructed to allow maximum and continual surveillance of populations in prisons, asylums, schools, and factories, or of subjects of any experiment. In the Panopticon a central tower opens onto visible cells placed in a circle around the tower. Observations radiate from the central tower to cells arranged in multiple levels, with each cell backlighted to provide maximum visibility. By radically separating the observer and the observed, the Panopticon leaves the powerless ones exposed, or exhibited, and places the power in the relentless gaze that, for whatever reason, studies them. If this is successful, the subjugated, who know they are being observed but cannot see their observers (due to the elaborate design by Bentham), will eventually subject themselves to continuous monitoring by internalizing the gaze of the external authority. This is how discipline replaces punishment, argues Foucault, as the dominant force of the modern era. The discipline is complete when the subjugated objectify themselves even when the observation tower is vacated.

Jeremy Bentham clearly knew the power of the gaze. A philosopher, jurist, and economist, he had his own body preserved through a primitive form of taxidermy—and in that state still continues to oversee meetings in London at University College, which he founded. Taxidermy was one of the original forms of exhibiting bodies and grew up, not coincidentally, with both the fixed-gaze world of photography and the fixed-motion world of workers on factory lines of the industrial revolution.[21] Since of all the moral philosophers of his time Bentham was the most adamant in his support of the rights of animals, one could perhaps regard turning his own body into taxidermy as an act of identification with animals who were being subjected to the same process in the growing spectacle of culture's triumph over body/nature. A strict vegetarian, he argued that it was neither reason nor speech which gave one moral rights, but feeling. To Bentham, the capacity to feel pain and pleasure was the ground upon which all moral issues should be addressed. Yet insofar as he also viewed pain and pleasure as qualities that could be calculated mathematically—and in his design of the Panopticon to keep watch over subjected populations—he anticipates behaviorist experiments in engineering morality.[22]

In *Discipline and Critique,* a work that plays Kant's *Critique of*

Pure Reason against Foucault's *Discipline and Punish,* Cutrofello argues that Foucault could have used Kant's life to exemplify modernity's choice of discipline as the foremost model of power. The rationale behind Kant's attempts to control everything related to his bodily life was to achieve a virtuous character. In service of a bodily discipline that leads to virtue, Kant had one cup of tea daily and trained himself not to desire another, just as he trained his body to awaken without desiring even a moment more of sleep. It is this discipline, referred to as the moral law within, that Kant said raised his worth to the status of "a life independent of all animality and even of the whole world of sense."[23] It is also this intense control which has led philosophers and psychologists such as Theodor Adorno and Jacques Lacan to associate Kant's discipline with that of the Marquis de Sade. Whether in the name of virtue (Kant) or of vice (Sade), in punishing and disciplining the body the forms of action are identical; both men present "a ruthless and thorough-going attention to detail in their regimented attempts to manipulate bodies."[24] Both find a kind of pleasure and, indeed, freedom in absolute obedience.

We will return to this comparison in the next two chapters, which consider sadism and asceticism, respectively, but it is important to note here the ways that Kant's moral theory suffers from the requirement of the individual to divorce himself from sensual existence. I say "himself" because for Kant this moral requirement is impossible for women, who are "by nature" identified with the senses rather than reason. Similarly, Kant believed that whereas the white race is capable of progress and education, other races can only be "trained." Because his skin was so thick, Kant suggested, the training of an African slave should include physical punishment that was most effective when using "a split bamboo cane instead of a whip."[25]

But beyond the identification of women and native peoples with the kind of eros he feared, Kant's moral theory poses untenable limitations on the moral subject to act solely from duty or obedience to the moral law. Severed from the conditions of his embodiment, the virtuous man is described as insensible and indifferent to the needs of others. So pure is this obedience to the law, according to Kant, that morality is proven to be the highest form of duty when it actually offends our inclinations or feelings.[26] This may help to explain why Adolf Eichmann asserted that his actions on behalf of the SS were moral as defined by Kant's philosophy.

DESCARTES' ERROR: GAGE AND ELLIOT

In *Descartes' Error,* Antonio Damasio argues that feelings and emotions are absolutely necessary to practical reason, that is, to the way we negotiate the social, political, economic, and moral worlds of everyday life. A neurologist by training, Damasio began to reflect on Descartes's error—the dissociation of reason from the body—when he came across patients with frontal lobe injuries who fit Western philosophy's criterion of rationality to a tee. They were intelligent and unemotional, with good language skills and an excellent ability to form abstractions. These patients, however, also shared two symptoms in common: they could neither experience feelings nor act rationally in the world. "Flawed [practical] reason and impaired feelings stood out together as the consequences of a specific brain lesion, and this correlation suggested to [Damasio] that feeling was an integral component of the machinery of reason."[27] Damage to part of the prefrontal cortices (the most anterior part of the frontal lobe) appears to have disconnected the patients' capacity for abstract and logical thought from bodily sensations relating to emotional states. While their abstract thoughts remained intact, their emotional lives had vanished, along with the ability to hold a job, maintain a relationship, act in ways advantageous to them as individuals, and engage in appropriate social behavior.

Damasio hypothesized that these patients could no longer make their way in the world because the dysfunction of their feeling and emotional lives made decision-making impossible. If so, the Cartesian-Kantian assertion that decisions are best made by reason divorced from emotion and body would be seriously questioned, indeed, in error, as the title of his book asserts. After all, by dualistic accounts, these patients are precisely what philosophy had ordered—abstract thought freed from emotional baggage. Even better, these patients appeared to feel no pain or pleasure and were not able to identify with anyone else's. Plato might say that they had no "nails" to hold thought down. For Damasio, however, this portrayal of the "cool head" also perfectly describes the sociopath: someone who is very intelligent but acts without feelings for others.[28]

To clarify the role feelings play in rational behavior, Damasio begins his work by telling the story of Phineas P. Gage, a foreman working in New England on the construction of the Rutland and Burlington Railroad. In the summer of 1848, a distracted Gage pounded an iron rod into explosive powder without first checking to see if his assistant had covered the powder with sand, which would have directed the explosion into the rock. His assistant had not, and the resulting explosion caused the tamping rod to enter Gage's left cheek, pierce the base of his skull, pass through the front of his brain, and exit at high speed through the top of his head. "The rod . . . landed more than a hundred feet away, covered in blood and brains."[29] Gage not only lived, but got up, spoke to his men, and rode in an ox cart to the hotel of Joseph Adams. Getting out of the cart with some assistance, he waited for Edward Williams on the porch of the hotel for over an hour, chatting with Adams. Apart from the loss of vision in his left eye, Gage was said to be "cured" in less than two months. However, his likes, dislikes, manners, and competencies changed completely. Harlow, the doctor of record during Gage's recovery, wrote that the "equilibrium or balance, so to speak, between his intellectual faculty and animal propensities" had gone.[30]

Though prior to the accident he was an excellent and well-liked foreman with a keen sense of personal responsibility, Gage became grossly profane and cared little for his workers. People who knew him said that "Gage was no longer Gage."[31] Like autistics, he developed a habit of collecting things, showed no respect for conventions, and made decisions not in his best interest. Also like many autistics, personal relationships were lost to him. He drifted, unable to hold a job, follow through on a project, or anticipate the future. Eventually, he became a circus attraction, carrying the tamping iron with him and showing his wounds. Available documents suggest to Damasio that Gage developed epileptic seizures and died of a major convulsion in May of 1861. No autopsy was performed at the time, but Hanna Damasio, also a neurologist and wife of Antonio Damasio, used Gage's skull and neuroimaging technology to reconstruct his brain in three dimensions and found damage to the prefrontal cortices on both hemispheres. These are areas of the brain central to emotional awareness, social life, and decision making.

Antonio Damasio became interested in Gage when he was asked to see a patient named Elliot, who had frontal lobe damage caused by the removal of a tumor. Elliot had also undergone a complete change of personality. He was no longer capable of holding a job; yet he was intelligent, skilled, and healthy. Having lost all of his savings, he drifted, and he divorced and remarried repeatedly. He showed no emotions nor cared about others, and he was now arrogant and cruel when he had once been modest and polite. Elliot came to Damasio to see if, having lost everything and being unable to work, he qualified for disability payments. In time it became clear that Elliot's abstract reasoning systems were not damaged but that his emotional life was gone, as he himself recognized. He told Damasio that his ability to feel had changed since the removal of the tumor, and that topics which once evoked strong responses no longer created any reaction in him, positive or negative. "Elliot was able to recount the tragedy of his life with a detachment that was out of step with the magnitude of the events. He was always controlled, always describing scenes as a dispassionate, uninvolved spectator. Nowhere was there a sense of his own suffering, even though he was the protagonist . . . the magnitude of his distance was unusual."[32]

Damasio goes on to describe another patient who had frontal lobe damage since birth and had never developed normal social behaviors or been able to hold a job. Like many victims of Asperger syndrome, he was frustrated by change, manifested stereotyped behaviors, and possessed intense knowledge of esoteric subjects. Like others with injuries to the frontal lobes, he had difficulty experiencing pain or pleasure and seemed to be without a theory of mind, that is, without a sense of his own interior life or that of others. After witnessing repeated deficiencies in decision making and emotional sensitivity in patients with these injuries, Damasio became convinced that even though they could conceptualize and articulate a value system, their values were not felt and so were not acted upon. The values literally did not matter.

To test his hypothesis that reduced emotional capacities may fundamentally and adversely affect one's ability to engage in practical reason and action, Damasio first had to show that the emotional lives of patients with frontal lobe damage were missing. To do so he used a skin conductance test to measure responses of the nervous system to emotional images. Measurable changes occur in the skin when one is touched emotionally (which is why autistics fail these tests as well). When one is subjected to sexually explicit or horrifying images, the autonomic nervous system increases secretion of fluid in the skin's sweat glands. While changes in heart rate and skin temperature could also be measured, Damasio turned to the skin conductance test because it is reliable and easily performed, with no discomfort to the patient. The secretion of fluid into the skin may not be visible to the naked eye, but it can be detected because it blocks a low-voltage electrical current.

The skin conductance test reminds us of a very important, if obvious, point: emotions are physical. One reason that distorted or limited body awareness leads to a distorted or limited emotional life is because emotions manifest themselves in the body. While not all feelings are emotions (for example, feeling hot or cold, wet or dry), we tend to call emotions feelings because, normally, we do feel them. As William James argued, there is no disembodied "mindstuff" out of which emotions can be constituted apart from their bodily manifestation. Emotions physically alter our state of being, constituting a response to our being in the world moment by moment. While patients like Elliot were able to generate skin conductance responses in relation to being surprised or even taking a deep breath, Damasio found that they did not respond to stimuli that were emotionally complex and/or tied to someone else's experience. Damasio refers to this condition as "'acquired' sociopathy."[33] Graphic scenes of violence and people in pain as well as sexually explicit images were flashed before the subjects and drew unequivocal results: no patient with frontal lobe damage generated any skin conductance response. Damasio's patients could describe what happened in the films, but they felt nothing. Their senses apparently had become like a video camera, recording the world but in no way engaged by it. Indeed, one patient said he knew that what he was seeing was horrible, but that he could not feel the horror: "*his flesh no longer responded to these themes as it once had.*"[34]

Here Mazis's philosophical analysis is helpful. Like perceptions, he says, emotions take in the world around us; however, as suggested by its Latin root, e-motions move us to act in relation to that which moves us. The motion is both the movement of the person into the world and the movement of the world into the person. For Mazis, the material and the emotional intertwine so completely that "'mattering' in the sense of e-motional investment is also 'mattering' in the sense of apprehending, feeling, the expression of the physiognomy of the physical."[35] What is missing in the lives of Damasio's patients is precisely this "mattering" by which the body gives meaning to and communicates its relationship with the world. Playing on the motion in e-motion, Mazis argues for a circling of the flesh, an embeddedness in the world by which we move into our own being as the being of the world moves into us. This is a process of simultaneous entering, or "touch-touching," of self and world, inner life to inner life. Mazis uses Merleau-Ponty's term, the "flesh of the world," to describe the erotic interminglings presented as one breaks through to the inner life from the surface of the skin. This seems to be what happened to Temple Grandin in the squeeze machine: the comforting touch she experienced allowed her empathetic emotions to materialize, so that she could learn what it felt like to love and be loved.[36]

Somatic Markers and Cost-Benefit Analyses

Having confirmed the loss of emotional life in patients with frontal lobe damage, Damasio went on to study the role that feeling and emotions play within practical reason, the world of everyday life and work. To test the ability of his patients to make sound decisions based on lived experience, Damasio used a card game that required them to gamble. The rules were consistent but participants were not told the rules beforehand, assuring that players had to apply their experience of the game to the game, just as we must apply our experience of life to life. What these patients did while playing the game resembled what they did in everyday life— they lost over and over again by taking unrealistic risks. They persisted in all ways to make the least advantageous choices, going after big payments with more abundant and larger penalties rather than smaller payments with fewer and smaller penalties. Persons without frontal lobe damage also pursued the larger returns a few times, but when they lost, they eventually learned from their experience and took the more prudent path involving surer, smaller returns. Elliot and other emotionally impaired patients failed to learn from their losses, but like gambling addicts, their losses didn't seem to count. Because they failed to feel the pain of loss, they did not anticipate or fear losing. To be moved one way or another, something distinctive in the quality of relatedness needs to bear either positive or negative significance. Without that manifestation, all options appear neutral or equally possible.[37]

Damasio found, in essence, that patients with this kind of brain damage have an almost impossible task before them as they face the challenges of everyday life by trying to apply a new cost-benefit analysis to each of the choices life presents. Even though Elliot could do mathematics perfectly well, he failed at practical decisions because they demand judgments concerning a wide variety of concrete and therefore complex and ambiguous possibilities, all of which must somehow be brought to awareness and weighed as one comes to a decision. Elliot found himself very much in the situation Grandin faces when filing through her "data bank" in order to anticipate how the mysterious other might respond to her action. For someone standing outside looking in, such an analysis can theoretically last forever since every decision includes a maze of variables with exponentially multiplied future scenarios. Grandin says she gets through social situations by scanning her memories about similar situations and then making the most logical determination available to her given that information. She is forced to imagine people's intentions and motivations by drawing upon stored memories that act as a reservoir of typical responses. Not too surprisingly, she says that in business dealings it works fairly well; the rules of behavior are fairly clear and she's become adept at anticipating responses. But it is much more difficult in daily, personal life to read the inner lives of others by formal abstractions, much less to pick an appropriate response from a data bank of possibilities.

Damasio's patients were lost because they were deprived of a basic mode of communication with the world: our situatedness, or the internal recognition of what is happening to us as reflected in our bodily being and in the bodies of others. He concludes that we use our feelings and emotions much more than traditional philosophy ever realized to help sort through the maze of possibilities presented by the practicalities of our existence. We don't simply decide "in our heads" whether to buy a house or enter into a relationship, or even what to eat for dinner; we narrow choices by feeling what to do. Indeed, practical reason appears impossible if one does it by cost-benefit analysis alone, without the use of what Damasio calls "somatic markers." Somatic markers are described as body states tied to images and events derived from our past. Somatic markers are remembered significances which link the experiences of our lives with the feeling states those experiences produced, either pleasant or unpleasant. As a way to register our present situatedness, somatic markers offer alarms and beacons to guide our decision-making lives. By applying lessons from the past to the present in a continual monitoring of the body as it conceptualizes and perceives, somatic markers help us narrow choices and predict outcomes.

Damasio maintains that there are two levels to the encoding of our embodied, emotional lives in the brain. The first level depends upon the limbic system circuitry, particularly the amygdala and the anterior cingulate. Responses from this system are innate in the sense that we are born ready to respond to sensory stimuli with both pain and pleasure and what he calls primary emotions such as fear. The limbic system of Elliot and patients like him is intact, which accounts for why Elliot responded with fear when someone surprised him during the skin conductance test. But what Elliot and those with frontal lobe damage cannot do is form systematic connections between primary emotions and situations, that is, they cannot create secondary emotions, of which somatic markers are a special instance. Elliot, in other words, could not extend his feeling of fear given in the moment of fear to a situation in which he might do well to feel fearful. To do so, the neural network must expand beyond the limbic system to the prefrontal and somatosensory cortices which, in Elliot's case, were damaged. It is this neural extension, linking feeling with past experience, present world awareness, and future possibilities, that Damasio associates with secondary emotions. The feelings and images generated from these secondary neurological linkages are what he calls somatic markers.[38]

Even with highly functional somatic markers, one can still reason about choices and go on to apply some kind of cost-benefit analysis to the options available, but having feelings about choices eliminates many incompatible possibilities and puts the remaining choices more clearly in focus. Damasio explains that somatic markers don't deliberate for us but that our decision making is enhanced by their existence and thwarted by their absence because these "emotions and feelings *have been connected, by learning, to predicted future outcomes of certain scenarios.*"[39] Somatic markers act as emotional appraisals and thus imply in their very existence the sense of world engagement that we have described as "mattering." Feelings bring with them subjective and moral content, the sense that we are in the world rather than an external observer, regarding the world through a pane of glass. By making present our connectedness with the world and our fellow beings, feeling states help us find our way.

When neural networks are properly established, the body's regulatory systems act in conjunction with cognition, so that when we see an image of horror, we not only understand it but respond to it and feel it in our flesh. Without the feeling capacities of the body, assessments about what may be a good or bad response become more or less indiscriminate. (Thus the autistic's need for rules without exceptions.) Contemplating the relation of emotion to reason in evolutionary terms, Damasio argues that it just makes sense that the systems responsible for biological regulation (sensory feelings, emotions, drives, and instincts) would remain in intimate contact with the systems responsible for reasoning and decision making, since both are concerned with survival. The dualistic paradigm wherein the supposedly primitive brain is identified with biology, whereas the newly enlarged neocortex of the so-called civilized brain is identified with reason, is a caricature of the far more complex truth in which body, brain, and environment interact with each other. "Emotion, feeling, and biological regulation all play a role in human reason."[40]

Prior to, during, and after the development of the neocortical structures in evolution, Damasio says that the role of feeling has been to "mind the body." Sensory and emotional feelings work to extend conscious awareness by providing ongoing information about the body-mind's situatedness in the world. Feelings are cognitive structures that are distinctive only in the sense that they specifically place the body in the context of the world by *"representing the outside world in terms of the modifications it causes in the body proper."* Mentality had to be first about the body, Damasio argues, and then it could go on to be about other things, real or imagined.[41] Cognition depends upon our biochemical lives capturing the interactions with the environment to stay linked to practical agency and reality. In evolution the cerebral cortex incorporated the already existing network of feelings to represent our situatedness in the world; and once the cortical structures became capable of abstract thought, sensations and emotions continued to provide a cognitive awareness linking the worlds of inner and outer. In evolutionary terms, emotional intelligence comes first. Neocortical structures refine the human ability to categorize feelings by means of somatic markers, offering the blessing and the curse that is our ability to have feelings about our feelings.[42]

For the human body to prepare the ground for consciousness such that it can acquire functional strategies or fitting responses to situations, both the connection of the limbic system to the neocortex and sensitivities to pleasure and pain are essential. Damasio speculates that it is our past history and present experiences of pain and pleasure that trigger the body-mind states we use to form somatic markers. Pain, in particular, puts us on notice; indeed, people born with "congenital absence of pain do not acquire normal behavior strategies."[43] This would help explain why Gage and Elliot, both indifferent to pain and pleasure, could no longer negotiate the world practically and meaningfully. These same patterns repeat themselves in persons who have been overwhelmed by trauma. In Damasio's words, "We came to life with a preorganized mechanism to give us the experiences of pain and of pleasure. Culture and individual history may change the threshold at which it begins to be triggered, or its intensity, or provide us with a means to dampen it. But the essential device is a given."[44]

In this embodiment of experience, the human being is neither tabula rasa nor fully genetically determined. Experience shapes neurological areas where the limbic structures interact with the neocortex, or, more precisely, where the amygdala intersects with the prefrontal cortices, to establish the connections we use to negotiate our way through the world. This means that the neurological and biochemical structures associated with somatic markers are very much open to unique, personally acquired representations. We are all born with sensitivities to pain and pleasure and with basic fight-or-flight responses, but these secondary linkages emerge from our particular experiences in unique ways to guide our decisions. While we are not tablets open to each and every engraving, on the level of practical agency, I read Damasio as proposing that our neurological contingency is radical: "The entire prefrontal region seems dedicated to categorizing contingencies in the perspective of personal relevance."[45]

No essentialist, Damasio understands the self as created moment to moment. We are guided by somatic representations from the past to help us encounter the present and anticipate the future, but the living material of the self is reconstructed continuously. Furthermore, the same somatic markers necessary for practical reason can, when nonadaptive, also impair it. The embodiment of experience allowing us to make decisions in our practical lives by an intuitive rationality based on feeling can leave us just as dysfunctional as Elliot if the somatic states induced paralyze us or are experienced out of context—as often happens in post-traumatic stress disorders. After the experience of trauma, the brain cannot easily erase the life-saving responses of fight or flight when external threats are reduced. Thus, for example, a car backfiring today can take the body back in time and space to Vietnam, 1969. Damasio concludes, "The buildup of somatic markers requires that both brain and culture be normal. When *either* brain or culture is defective, at the outset, somatic markers are unlikely to be adaptive."[46] As examples of "sick cultures" that produce nonadaptive somatic markers, Damasio mentions Germany under the Nazis, Cambodia under Pol Pot, China during the Cultural Revolution, and the Soviet Union in the 1930s and 1940s, as well as "sizable sectors of Western society."[47] Damasio does not specify what he means by these "sizable sectors," but I want to extend his analysis by further considering the consequences for our culture of rejecting the body and eros as sources of moral wisdom.

THE PHILOSOPHER'S DISEASE

Maxine Sheets-Johnstone calls Descartes's philosophy a "cultural disease." She writes, "Cartesianism tells us that we are schizoid creatures, one-half of which is little more than a mechanical rig for getting us about in the world."[48] Her analysis in *The Roots of Think-*

ing, like the work of Damasio, describes cognition as intimately tied in evolution to the physiognomic nature of bodies, that is, to the material and emotional manifestations of inner and intersubjective life. Historically, the Cartesian philosophy of the body as a machine or shell separate from subjective life and spirit is often cited as the beginning of Western culture's retreat from the flesh. However, Sheets-Johnstone suggests that Descartes's body is still the only body our culture really knows. She sees body as extended substance not only as an esoteric idea discussed in university philosophy seminars, but as an image portrayed daily in tabloids, television programs, popular magazines, and advertisements.[49]

Sass also argues that the material and psychological conditions of the modern era are the legacy of Cartesian dualism.[50] He is struck by the fact that many elements of experience occurring in schizoid personalities and schizophrenics appear to describe Cartesian and Kantian metaphysics from the inside out. As a clinical psychologist, Sass is careful to say that he is not diagnosing the leading proponents of dualistic philosophy as schizophrenic. However, because he takes body-mind interaction seriously, he is interested in the state of mind of anyone who is intent on rejecting the sensual world as a source of truth, preferring the paradigm of mechanism to organism. Dualistic philosophy gives so much ontological weight to the thinking subject and so little to material-biological being that its vision of rationality invites critique as utterly self-enclosed.[51] Eugen Bleuler, the Swiss psychiatrist who coined the term schizophrenic, used it to refer to the splitting (schism) of psychic or mental functions (phrenos), or more precisely, to the splitting of cognition and emotion, a split that is central to modern philosophy.[52] Sass understands schizophrenia as existing on one end of a continuum that also includes schizoid personality traits, so it does not seem too much of a stretch for him to imagine that proponents of dualism manifest some of the characteristics of schizoid personalities.

Schizophrenic Bodies

It is particularly ironic that mental illnesses such as schizophrenia have been viewed in our ancient and modern history as well as in popular culture as being ruled by Dionysian, irrepressible drives, sensual abundance, bodily abandon, and spontaneity. Sass quotes a character from Tennessee Williams's play *Suddenly Last Summer*:

"*Dementia praecox*—it reminds me of a night-blooming tropical flower."[53] In the dualistic model the diagnosis of insanity is conceptualized as involving "a shift from human to animal, from culture to nature, from thought to emotion, from maturity to the infantile and the archaic."[54] Madness is linked in the dualistic tradition to the beast in us and to the unfettered desire that compels those who are released from the restraints of virtue provided by the light of reason.

Sass's thesis is that mental illness is actually quite the opposite of this characterization. Diseases like schizophrenia are better described as alienation from emotional life and bodily sensation combined with heightened mental activity or overvigilant conscious awareness than as heightened emotional life and increased sensuality combined with a lowering of mental activity. What dies in the schizophrenic is "not the rational so much as the appetitive soul, not the mental so much as the physical and emotional aspects of one's being; this results in detachment from the natural rhythms of the body and entrapment in a sort of morbid wakefulness or hyperawareness."[55] Rather than thought processes being overwhelmed by bodily libido, it is more likely in schizophrenia that the body is overwhelmed by its thought processes. The illness is therefore too much mentality, not less; too little connection of self with the body, not more.

Schizophrenia is like the philosopher's disease insofar as it involves relentless, obsessive self-reflection. According to Sass, it is this excessive self-awareness, not alienation from reason, which leads to delusion, disorganization, and fragmentation. The disorganization and fragmentation of experience is evident in the following statement by a patient named Henry: "There seems to be something that offers, to my recollection of being an infant, to seeing confused colors, and acknowledging that the world consists of tools, and that everything that we glance at has some utilization, some use, purpose. It means something. We could also consider that to be paranoiac. But I'm not so sure. It's a fact that, I'm not so sure what I mean by a fact . . . I'm trying to say something beyond a dichotomy between recognizing objects in the world and recognizing my own distortions, what I rather mean is my own hypothesized objects."[56] Schizophrenics describe themselves as "feeling dead yet hyperalert—a sort of corpse with insomnia."[57] Their awareness of awareness with no grounding in a lived body means that their mental lives slide from perspective to perspective, reason becoming like a house of mirrors where anything and everything is equally possible but questionable. Henry is clearly plagued by questions of a metaphysical nature, about whether and how meaning, self, and the world exist.

In *Betrayal of the Body*, Alexander Lowen traces how the schizophrenic's withdrawal of the self from the world is seen in the withdrawal of the self from the body, as evidenced by the body's lack of vitality and responsiveness. Vacant or masklike stares, blank eyes, and unvarying and inappropriate smiles replace physiognomic engagement. Sufferers from a variety of schizoid disorders share tendencies to be emotionally flat or constricted, as evidenced by a monotone way of speaking. Incapable of pleasure, or anhedonic, the body functions by rote, more like a mechanism than an organism. Such a person eats because it is 12:00, not because he or she feels hungry.[58] Like autistics, people with schizoid disorders not only find it difficult to express their own emotions, but also find it difficult to read emotions in the faces of others and to maintain interpersonal relations.

People with full-blown schizophrenia have trouble accurately identifying sensations and perceptions and giving meaning to them. At the most extreme end of the continuum, they experience terrifying perceptions and confusing jumbles of ideas, stimuli, and sensory messages. The dissociation through which the movement of one's own arm is not felt as one's own can lead to the terrifying sense of being manipulated externally, as if one were a puppet on a string. Their own mental images can also be experienced as coming from a source outside the self. In *The Autobiography of a Schizophrenic Girl*, Renée begins her recovery with the chapter entitled "I Learn to Know My Body." Prior to that time, Renée, who had experienced trauma in her early life and long periods of catatonia, would speak as if outside her own body, saying something like "the arm is sick" instead of "my arm hurts."[59]

All persons with schizoid disorders experience some form of alienation from the body and, with it, disruptions in a coherent sense of self and a meaningful world. Some schizophrenics withdraw into fantasy or into the rare, rigid posturing that comes with catatonia, that is, complete unresponsiveness to the world. The muscle rigidity can become so severe that blood flow to the surface of the body is restricted, causing the patient's skin to appear blue or even transparent. In the worst cases, the skin actually becomes cold, just as when patients begin to recover feeling, the skin grows warm, soft, and "in the pink."[60] In *Welcome to My Country,* Loren Slater describes the skin of her catatonic patients as nonabsorbent: "not a sponge, as all good skin should be, absorbing the world, reading within its pores the curves and textures that shape the stories of our lives."[61] Much of this deadening of the body seems to compensate for the fear of overwhelming sensory and emotional feeling, as it did for Donna Williams. Referring to a patient who had been molested repeatedly as a child by his father, Slater likens catatonia to the immobility response of rabbits: "the last adaptive mechanism in a series of stages animals go through when they sense their demise. . . . This comforts me and also strangely saddens me. I know there are limits to the horrors of the world. I also know our bodies sometimes leave us before we have left them."[62]

When Renée's illness began, she first lost the feeling of practical things, so that everyday activities like singing, drawing, and calisthenics terrified her. Then everything in the world proceeded to get less and less real; the house became a pasteboard cutout, her sisters and brothers robots. Well aware of their own detachment, patients say that they perceive the world but do not feel its reality. Intelligence remains, but perception becomes more like a video camera than a means of engagement. Typically patients say they experience the world as if through a pane of glass, and to break through that glass, they sometimes burn, cut, or otherwise harm themselves. Images of death and machines frequent their accounts:

> I am only an automaton, a machine; it is not I who senses, speaks, eats, suffers, sleeps; I exist no longer; I do not exist, I am dead; I feel I am absolutely nothing.

> I can't feel or relate. I used to feel emotions like physical pain and I couldn't stand it. So I blocked off. I can't empathize with people. . . . I can't work because there is nothing in me. Perhaps my nervous tissue has been destroyed. . . . I used to think everyone else was an automaton. Then I saw them relating to one another and I realized I was the automaton.

> I felt as though I were in a bottle. I could feel that everything was outside and couldn't touch me.
>
> *I had to die to keep from dying:* I know that sounds crazy but one time a boy hurt my feelings very much and I wanted to jump in front of a subway. Instead I went a little catatonic so I wouldn't feel anything.[63]

Agency obviously becomes highly problematic when inner life is cut off from the world. Value judgments appear to exist but to not really matter because, with sensory and emotional life askew, they are not given adequate bodily expression. Sass gives examples of a patient calmly eating food she believes with complete certainty to be laced with poison and another washing dishes without complaint while completely convinced that she is the Queen of England.[64] A second problem born from the death of eros is the confusion of self and world. Having no self and living in a universe in which there is nothing but self become equally possible, even compatible, perspectives in disembodied mentality. The patient who says he is omnipotent also says that he does not exist.[65] "All the clocks of the world feel my pulse," says one patient. "When my eyes are bright blue, the sky gets blue," says another.[66] Renée's localization of feelings in things progressively accompanied her own loss of subjective awareness. Along with the vacillation between all self and no self, the world seems either too much alive or totally dead, as it was for Roquentin in Sartre's *Nausea.*

Cartesian Bodies and the Influencing Machine

Little has been written about the way Descartes related to his body, but it has been said that he did much of his thinking lying in bed, motionless and with a fixed stare.[67] Wittgenstein, who has been described as having autistic and schizoid personality characteristics, defined the philosopher's disease as dependent upon this immutable stare, the frozen inactivity by which one is forced into an experience of experience rather than an experience of the world— possibly a description of the consciousness with which he himself was afflicted. To Wittgenstein this disease is the burden of perpetual doubt borne by those for whom distance becomes so magnified that one finds no foundation upon which to stand. Consider, says Sass, Michael Polanyi's analogy of a blind man walking with a cane. Such a man can use a cane to maneuver his way down a path perfectly well and can remain very much in touch with the world unless he becomes too aware of the sensation of the cane resting against his hand. When heightened awareness of the cane touching his hand replaces awareness of the cane's contact with the world, the lived connection between self and world is broken and he is stopped short. Once contact with the world is lost, then heightened attention to the stream of sensory experience makes one's situation even worse by taking the life and coherency out of it.[68] No longer in touch, the self turns back in upon itself and the inquiry into reality begins. Where is the path? Is the cane still touching the path? Is the cane still touching the world? Is there a world for the cane to touch? Like Descartes's own meditations, everything about the world can quickly become questionable, and as the existence of the world becomes questionable, one is increasingly plagued by internal doubts about reality, agency, and selfhood. Perhaps the cane in one's hand is itself an illusion manipulated by someone or something else. Perhaps this is not a cane. Perhaps this is not my hand.

The disease of solipsism can never be cured by thought, Wittgenstein argued; it can only be cured by movement and by action, even if only through the motions of our eyes, which act to embody us in the world by making self-world engagements evident. The fixed stare only continues to drive one inward so that eventually the break with the world leads to a break with one's own lived body, causing one to doubt the reality of everything, including self and world. Of course, after having doubted the existence of the entire material universe, "the sky, the air, the earth, colours, figures, sounds, and all external things," as well as his own body, "hands, eyes, flesh [and] blood," Descartes found that he could not doubt doubt.[69] Since doubt was an act of the mind that he could not doubt without incurring a logical contradiction, he concluded that mind was indubitably real, and also the deductions of the mind—God, mathematics, and the extended substance of the entire physical universe devoid of subjective life. The world remains, but bodies are alien, and one's inner life is severed from the outside. The entire material world is described by Descartes as nothing but "extended substance," and animals as nothing but automatons—self-moving mechanisms—without feeling. Like Plato, Descartes recognized the way emotions take material reality in the flesh, but he saw them as impediments to reason, referring to them as "animal spirits," his own name for their ability to bewitch us.[70] Mentality alone is deemed subjective, and mentality—attributed only to humans—is encased within extended substance, that is, a material world devoid of subjectivity. This creates a very awkward situation for human beings, since the body is only an object or container that houses an isolated mental subject. Consciousness is mysteriously held in an object that it has nothing to do with, a situation that Gilbert Ryle referred to as "a ghost in a machine."[71]

Schizophrenics experience the world much as Descartes appears to have done in his philosophical reflections, including the perception that bodies are alien or mechanistic and the tendency to engage in metaphysical doubt. However, to the schizophrenic there is no point at which doubt stops. The schizophrenic's question to Descartes might be, Why stop there, at the mind? If you are going to doubt, then doubt! Isn't it possible that someone or something else may be projecting ideas and images into your mind? Perhaps one's entire body is an object through which some outer entity is working, as was the case for Natalija A., who found herself completely under the influence of a machine. A former philosophy student, Natalija suddenly began to live as disembodied Cogito, completely divorced from her own body. She believed she was being influenced by an electrical machine made in Berlin, which acted, she speculated, by telepathy. Natalija was so intimately connected to the machine that when it was struck, she felt the blow.[72]

The influencing machine is a classic delusion in schizophrenia and a perfect symbol for the feeling that one's perceptions and actions are fundamentally bewitched. The influencing machine is described by schizophrenics as producing cinematography in the brain, motor phenomena in the body, and sensations that are ineffable.[73] Anything that might have been viewed as intentional or purposive when the self was embodied is seen as imposed in this totally mental universe. Rather than say, "I speak," one would say, "It talks out of me."[74] For Natalija, the influencing machine replaced her lived body and world with mental images and sensations projected from without—utterly the opposite of Grandin's squeeze machine, which extends her body into the intersubjective world and renders sensory and emotional connections her own.

Blaise Pascal posed the same question to Descartes about the mind's supposed indubitability. Why stop doubting with evidence of the mind alone? Pascal, a mathematician, founder of modern probability theory, and inventor of the adding machine (the direct ancestor of our computers), was convinced that the kind of certainty Descartes wished to obtain by reflection could only lead in the end to a skepticism so total that one would be left with nothing to know or to believe in. Perhaps due to his knowledge of the limitations of mathematics, Pascal argued that a philosophy of first principles that ignored feeling would be meaningless, indeed impossible, because it would be hopelessly narcissistic. What we believe in, he said, must come to us by connection with something outside ourselves. Pascal tried to tie feeling to reasoning in his well-known statement, "The heart has its reasons that reason knows not."[75] He rejected the God of Descartes for the same reason that he rejected the quest for certainty: God cannot be the first principle of anything by thought alone; instead, one must have a feeling of the reality of God to be assured of the reality of God. In other words, God must have subjective presence to have validity. This feeling of the presence of God took place in a spiritual encounter that Pascal never doubted. His famous "wager" that the benefits of believing in God, even if we are wrong about it, outweigh the costs of not believing at all was aimed only at those who had missed this kind of spiritual experience.

Within a century of Pascal, the sacramental world—a world in which one experienced the subjective presence of God—was well on its way to being replaced by the paradigm of mechanism and utility. The sacredness of the world was on neither the capitalist nor the scientific agenda, giving rise to the metaphysic of object-corpses. Deism viewed God as a creator entirely removed from his creation, a kind of influencing machine or all-powerful deus ex machina who affected the world but remained himself unaffected. To the delight of the vivisectionists, centuries before Skinner, animals too were posited to be automata. Apparently, animals were sufficiently different from us to feel no pain, pleasure, or emotion, but they were sufficiently like us to act as subjects in every kind of experimentation in medicine and science. On the horizon lay social sciences like Skinner's behaviorism, which would go on to see human beings reduced to stimulus-response mechanisms as well, with behaviors understood as the products of external forces acting upon them. In a phrase reminiscent of Natalija A.'s influencing machine, Nobel prize–winning geneticist Herman J. Muller writes, "Man is a giant robot created by DNA to make more DNA." Or consider the more elaborate fantasy of Timothy Leary: "We are all neurogenetic robots programmed to leave the earth and destined by our genes to shed this skeletal husk of the human body."[76]

CULTURAL INFLUENCES: BODY AS OBJECT

In *Technology as Symptom and Dream,* Robert Romanyshyn gives a historical account of our retreat from eros by suggesting that the triumph of a viewer-based, linear aesthetic adopted since the fifteenth century helped make possible our detachment from feeling. From then on we have looked at the world from a distance, as if through a window or a lens. The glass between us and the world divorces the inside from the outside and accentuates the distance between the observer and that which is observed while also increasing the distance between private and public life. Such a cultural aesthetic reduces sensory experience to the eye, robbing the viewer of the rest of the sensual body—smell, taste, touch, and hearing. Romanyshyn further likens this aesthetic to Hannah Arendt's description of modern alienation as the "twofold flight from the earth into the universe and from the world into the self."[77] To Romanyshyn the fixed gaze of a linear aesthetic suggests "a vision incapable of empathetic e-motion, a vision incapable of being moved by what it sees."[78] Like Damasio's patients, one knows but does not feel; one sees but the flesh does not respond.

Romanyshyn finds the objectifying gaze of modernity not only in the Cartesian body (1628), but also in the industrial worker (1700–1848), the robot (1928), and the astronaut (1945). He calls each of these disembodied creatures "skeletons in the closet" of the corpse, the "most visible image of the abandoned body [and] what the human body becomes in our increasing distance from it."[79] Just as the subject is alienated from the object and the mind from the body, so the industrial workers are alienated from the products of their labor and become themselves objects or commodities. The workers' bodies become more mechanisms than organisms on an assembly line that divides their bodies into discrete motions engineered to be ever more efficient—much as Kant did to his body while taking his evening walk. The workers' mechanization is incomplete only in comparison to a robot, Romanyshyn's third symbol of the rejection of the lived body, because a robot is able to go through the same motions of production as the human workers, but without the burden of embodiment, such as the need for food or sleep or health care.

Robin Schott turns to Marx's analysis of commodity fetishism to understand how capitalism works to diminish our capacity for subjectivity and intersubjectivity. Commodities act as substitutes for displaced erotic needs partly by allowing us to seek identity and gratification in them rather than in flesh-and-blood others. However, it is not just that eros is reduced to the desire to consume things—things appear to take on a life of their own, as Marx argued, while the life of workers and the reality of the material earth retreat or disappear.[80] This confusion of subject and object is all the more complicated by the fact that bodies themselves are increasingly regarded as standardized and exchanged commodities. Gail Faurshou writes of postmodernity that it is "no longer an age in which bodies produce commodities, but where commodities produce bodies: bodies for aerobics, bodies for sports cars, bodies for vacations, bodies for Pepsi, for Coke, and of course, bodies for fashion—total bodies, a total look."[81]

Finally, according to Romanyshyn, in the twentieth century the astronaut became the ultimate symbol of transcending the body, with the flesh encased in a suit that acts as an impenetrable barrier between the senses and the outside world. Like a child without a functioning immune system who lives in a bubble, the astronaut floats in solitary splendor miles out of touch with all that matters in human existence. While few of us are astronauts, the windows through which we observe the world are increasingly divorced from the conditions of embodiment. Movie, computer, and television screens are clearly technologies that lend themselves to the fixed gaze of a spectator who substitutes virtual bodies for corporeal bodies. Susan Buck-Morss, in "The Cinema Screen as Prosthesis of Perception," argues that the screen has become just that, a prosthesis of sense, the surface of which "functions as an artificial organ of cognition."[82] She is concerned that the screen as prosthesis doesn't merely duplicate what we perceive but alters it in ways that make violent and pornographic acts toward others more acceptable.

Allen Feldman provides excellent examples of just that phenomenon in his essay "From Desert Storm to Rodney King." Feldman describes how the Iraqis often disappeared in film footage of the Gulf War shown to Americans, creating an experience more like a video game than a military operation. He also explores how the manipulation of film by the defense team working for the police who beat Rodney King was able to make King's pain disappear and the violence seem rational. The stop-action, frame-by-frame analysis divided experience into discrete, robotic moments, eliminating the subjective body and leaving the jury with the impression that King was the agent in charge. Rodney King, the jury reported later, was in control of the situation and was "asking for it." Feldman likens the way King's body was treated—breaking apart whole motions into more robotic or frame-by-frame displays—to the industrial worker, and he finds the defense's manipulation of the video along with its "discourse on reasonable violence [to be] the indirect heir of labor-efficiency performance analysis."[83]

Romanyshyn's analysis therefore leads us into the concerns of the next chapter by reminding us that, by definition, dualism violates reality by cutting everything into two. The result is that in such a system our representations of progress, sanity, or moral virtue will always be half-truths. Each half-truth creates a corresponding half-truth, both of which are caricatures of any reality that is taken whole. In this case, the Western intellectual tradition's half-truths about embodiment leave behind shadows of feeling: the repressed desires and sublimated sensuality of the self projected onto marginalized, scapegoated others. More than just an error, dualism becomes a danger to society when purity systems use the repression of eros to define the borders between male and female, culture and nature, and mind and body; and once one has turned the body into an object, it is a small step to see the body as the Other, a threatening container of one's own denied desires.

SADISTIC AND PORNOGRAPHIC TOUCH
Body as Other

> For isn't it eros we rediscover in the child's world? The beauty of the child's body. The child's closeness to the natural world. The child's heart. Her love. Touch never divided from meaning. Her trust. Her ignorance of culture. The knowledge she has of her own body. That she eats when she is hungry. Sleeps when she is tired. Believes what she sees. That no part of her body has been forbidden to her. No part of this body is shamed, numbed, or denied. That anger, fear, love, and desire pass freely through this body. And for her, meaning is never separate from feeling.
> —Susan Griffin, *Pornography and Silence*

Palpable expressions of our being in the world, feelings are forceful presentations of our situatedness and therefore important guides for morality. The erotic self, I want to argue, is a given part of our evolutionary heritage, a part shared with other animal life on this planet. The function of the limbic system and, later, the cortical structures in evolution was to express and interpret one's state of being in material forms that unify mind and body. Many of these feelings are clearly visible to others. The biochemical "matterings" that Descartes ridiculed as animal spirits are products of millions of years of evolutionary history; they allow us to know our own feelings and intentions as well as to read those of others. While Descartes denigrated the animal spirits as impediments to reason, I am here using the term to mean the somatic markers which help us develop the emotional intelligence necessary to become more than observers and allow the world to become more than an exhibit.

We who are not autistic can more easily come to know what it is to meet another endowed with subjective life and to experience the feeling of loving and being loved. When we touch "the flesh of the world," we are thrown into intersubjective space where our inner lives meet and transform each other. To wage war on the animal spirits—to shame, numb, or deny the body—threatens not only the development of our inner lives but also the ability to comprehend and respond to what is going on around us. To paraphrase Maurice Merleau-Ponty, it is only the extent to which I experience my flesh as my own that I can perceive the world "as flesh of my flesh."[1]

In the last chapter we saw how a diminished capacity to feel hampers decision making, no matter how intact other cognitive functions might be. The alienation of Damasio's patients from their feelings and the feelings of others was caused by brain abnormalities, but a similar kind of alienation can be induced by cultural practices that encourage us not to feel. Studies show that persons avoiding emotional arousal "experience a progressive decline and withdrawal, in which *any* stimulation (whether it is potentially pleasurable or aversive) provokes further detachment." One thereby becomes "less and less responsive to various stimuli that are necessary for involvement in the present."[2] Dissociation from the erotic self can happen as a result of war, accidents, malnutrition, child abuse, and other forms of violence or, as we will see in this chapter, as a result of pedagogical practices and ideologies bent on creating morally pure and obedient children. The effects of trauma include anesthetization to pain, a lack of empathy, and the inability to identify emotions that might serve as appropriate guides for action. When the body becomes Other, attacks on the subjectivity of the flesh can lead to conditions which approximate autism and other feeling disorders, including hypersensitive nervous systems, the inability to experience pain and pleasure, the adoption of extremely rigid and punitive value systems, and a fragmented sense of self.

The contingency in human neurological development is radical, and interaction with the environment determines the extent to which we can touch the world and be touched by it. We have already seen how our sensory and emotional lives affect our perceptions of the world and constructions of identity by attending to what Temple Grandin learned in the squeeze machine, namely, that compassion and empathy are predicated upon feeling comforted by and comfortable in our own bodies. Grandin's ability to find a way beyond neurological conditions preventing meaningful sensory and emotional life speaks to the significance that individual experience has on biological givenness. Her pedagogical exercises and use of the squeeze machine enabled her to transcend the organically produced sensory chaos that worked to make any emotion beyond fear or anxiety impossible. Such a story says volumes about what bodily movements, eye contact, and comforting touch can do.

The opposite and much sadder story is told more frequently, that is, when social factors interact with biological states to reduce one's capacity to feel. The story of Donna Williams testifies to the ways an abusive family can exaggerate an already problematic sensory system (or act to create one): "Home was the place where spastics and retards 'deserved to die'. . . Cigarettes seared flesh, and the belt buckle hit something again and again. 'Cry and I'll fucking kill you.'"[3] Why connect one's subjective life to such a body? Better to adopt a persona like Willie, who was impervious to pain and remembered these experiences only abstractly, without connection to the self who experienced the pain. Ultimately, if experience of the body is found to be too negative and sensations too painful, the ego splits or dissociates from the body and the body becomes Other. Abused children talk of "being gone" and of the relief found in leaving the tortured body behind. These same children frequently grow up to repeat sadomasochistic forms of touch in bulimic or alcoholic binges, self-injuries, or violence inflicted upon others. (Typically, we find males acting out their alienation from feeling in violence against others since they are taught to associate their own feelings with weakness, whereas we find females acting out their alienation from feeling in violence against themselves since they are taught to associate female bodies with feeling.) Melinda, who was sexually assaulted repeatedly by her father, her brother, and his friends, gang raped, and forced to kill animals, describes her dissociative disorder in this way: "I can remember learning how to float up to the ceiling and I could even float out the window, I was very talented. I learned to do that around age four. I remember searching inside myself since I had nowhere else to search, for how to do that. I remember doing that. I split . . . split off from myself. Too, I created parts of myself to handle these things. It's a survival mechanism, and it has nothing to do with your creativity and intelligence. It has to do with a survival instinct."[4]

Neonaticide provides a good example of how extreme the alienation of self from body can be. Some young women who are overwhelmed by and made to feel ashamed of their pregnancies (in a society bombarding them with the message that sexual attraction is everything) appear to be able to dissociate from their bodies in such a radical way that they do not "know," in spite of all evidence to the contrary, that they are pregnant. Unable to face the reality of their situation and already conditioned to take up the gaze that transforms their bodies into objects, some young women are able to continue the delusion up to the moment of birth. They then describe the experience in terms that are clearly dissociative: "I watched myself deliver the baby"; "I don't think I felt pain, but I must have felt pain because I remember hearing myself scream." The fetus is seen as a foreign entity, an alien that passes through them—hence they throw the "object" into trash bins, chutes, and Dumpsters because "it" has no reality to them as a living being.[5]

When wars on the animal spirits become understood as moral wars on decadence and pathology, then a society not only loses its capacity for feeling but also tends to scapegoat those who are associated with feeling. This can clearly be seen in Alice Miller's analysis of pedagogical practices in Germany prior to the rise of the Nazis.[6] In *For Your Own Good,* Miller offers an affirmative answer to Damasio's question about whether a culture can induce feeling disorders akin to those caused by brain damage. Miller is concerned that the suppression of feeling permeates so many areas of our lives that we hardly notice it anymore and that our capacity for emotional intelligence is being destroyed by cultural practices that fail to take our erotic lives seriously. Miller believes that sadists are, with few exceptions, made and not born, and she speculates that virtues such as courage, integrity, and the capacity to love may not be virtues at all, but "the consequences of a benign fate."[7] Miller argues that anyone can be raised to be a sociopath and that, if we are trained early enough and consistently to repress feelings, any of us can learn "to live in a dictatorship without minding it," even to identify with it enthusiastically as ordinary people did in Nazi Germany.[8]

To Miller the atrocities of history become much easier to comprehend when we begin to realize that the need to inflict pain is tied to the sensory and emotional numbness that accompanies traumatic stress disorders and to the compulsion to reenact the abuse as either the victim or victimizer. One can then stop looking for a magic bullet, such as a criminal gene, and begin to investigate how some societies become abusive by socializing people to be alienated from their own bodies and emotional lives. Alexander Lowen concludes his work similarly, fearing that we do great harm to children by causing them to be ashamed of their bodies and guilty about their feelings. Therein we create emotional illnesses that take the joy out of life and eliminate the immediacy of feeling, or what he calls "the animal aspect of our being."[9] Clearly a critic of deontological ethics, Miller writes, "Morality and performance of duty are artificial measures that become necessary when something essential is lacking. The more successfully a person was denied access to his or her feelings in childhood, the larger the arsenal of intellectual weapons and the supply of moral prostheses has to be, because morality and a sense of duty are not sources of strength or fruitful soil for genuine affection. *Blood does not flow in artificial limbs; they are for sale and can serve many masters.*"[10] Robert Jay Lifton believes that their dissociation from feeling helps to explain how Nazi doctors were able to block out the horror of what they were doing. He writes, "Fundamentally, dissociation serves as a psychological facilitator for deterrence, helping to reduce the kind of psychic stress that would be morally useful and appropriate. It is, in other words, a form of adaptation, by means of which people remain sane in the service of social madness."[11]

The issue is an important one for Western culture, not only because our lifestyles, technologies, and ideologies support the posture of detached spectator and consumer, but also because we bear the weight of a moral heritage that is bent on the mastery of eros. Moral puritans have portrayed the sensory and emotional aspects of our existence as degrading parts of our animal, instinctual, and evil nature, not only in dualistic philosophy but also in religion and psychology. When a society imagines erotic life to be part of the pathology to be conquered to achieve moral, physical, or spiritual health, it becomes harder to see that the real disease is the supposed cure. The purity systems constructed around the divorce between mind and body, culture and nature, and male and female portray the squeeze machines of nature as beastly and lascivious. The animal spirits that act to bind us to each other, inner life to inner life, are to be tamed by duty and discipline. Morality thereby becomes a purification exercise intent on escaping the flesh by extricating humanity from nature. Here we find the pervasive and insidious cultural equivalent of Donna Williams's autism: "I had to get this bastard thing off me. I gripped it and pulled at it and bit it. It was my body."[12]

Augustine's doctrine of original sin, the idea that from the moment we become flesh we are condemned to a life of sin, has engendered in Western society forms of discipline severe enough to be called child abuse. It is significant that Augustine experienced his own body as controlled by outside forces. Much like Natalija A., who attributed her sensations to the influencing machine, Augustine attributed his desires for food and sex to sensations coming from outside him. Susan Bordo likens Augustine's experience to that of the bulimic, who experiences feelings of hunger not as part of the self but as an "alien invader." Augustine remarked that he felt captive to "the law of sin that was in [his] member."[13] It is this kind of alienation, Bordo argues, that produces a self identified with control, because when the body is experienced as "ontologically distinct from the inner self," the body becomes "the enemy," the locus of *"all that threatens our attempts at control."*[14] The doctrine of original sin arose not coincidentally in an era in which Christianity was aligning itself with political power, rejecting its identification with the slave and peasant classes of its birth to facilitate its adoption as the state religion of the Roman Empire. As newly identified with the politics of control, this form of Christianity began to equate moral virtue with mastery of the body and, eventually, with mastery over anyone associated with the body, such as animals, women, indigenous peoples, homosexuals, and Jews. We might therefore say of Augustine and his followers what Andrew Cutrofello says of Kant: how different his ethics might have been had he been concerned with overcoming political forms of domination rather than overcoming nature.[15]

We will further consider the pornographic nature of the moral puritan's war on desire. In *Pornography and Silence: Culture's Revenge against Nature,* a book that Susan Griffin says was inspired by the work of Hanna Arendt and Susan Sontag, Griffin describes pornography by its striving for subjective disconnection from and complete mastery over bodies as objects of pleasure. In order to accomplish this, as Simone de Beauvoir once observed about the

pornography of the Marquis de Sade, distance is never abandoned.[16] In the work of Sade, sexuality becomes an extension of
the panoptic gaze that turns the body into an instrument of the
will. Jacques Lacan understands Sade's pornography as completing
rather than contradicting Kantian philosophy because it demands
the will over the flesh, control over feeling, distance over intimacy,
ritual over spontaneity, and the law over desire—in short, it demands that the body become Other. Pornography eclipses inner
life and turns bodies into pasteboard images that can be manipulated without fear of being encumbered by the subjective presence
necessary for actual erotic encounter. Griffin writes of pornography, "Like a piece of furniture, she must be pictured from the side,
and particular parts of her body, those intended for use—her
breasts, her vulva, her ass—must be carefully examined. And yet at
each turn of the body, at each face or curvature exposed, we see
nothing. For there is no person there."[17]

EMBRACING THE ANIMAL SPIRITS:
EVOLUTION AND THE SQUEEZE MACHINES OF NATURE

Historically our culture has chosen to emphasize only the aggression and violence found in nature, but it is difficult to imagine the
evolution of social existence apart from a more cooperative emotional intelligence. Not only acts of aggression but also acts of
compassion are found in nonhuman nature as they are found in
human nature, and there is evidence that these two ends of the
emotional continuum are reciprocally linked in our biology, one
side or the other being privileged by experience. Felicity de Zulueta
writes, in *Pain and Violence,* that "the neural pathways for altruism
and aggression may be reciprocally related, so that aggression reflects a deficit in endogenous opiates, whereas their secretion reduces aggression by promoting social comfort and play."[18] If in
human and nonhuman animals altruism and empathy have not
been selected against, then clearly the ways we care for others and
know that we feel what they feel must have adaptive value. This
was Charles Darwin's position in *The Descent of Man* (1871) and
The Expressions of the Emotions in Man and Animal (1872).

While Darwin argues that moral feelings such as altruism
and empathy arise from social instincts rather than from the in-

stinct for self-preservation, he insists that the ability to come to the aid of others confers advantages for survival. In compassionate action self-preservation and social preservation are convergent. To make that case, Darwin provides numerous examples of empathetic behavior in animal societies and questions John Stuart Mill for thinking that morality depends upon learned behavior when the animal world shows so many examples of it. Darwin describes, for example, how social animals suffer when separated from their companions, how animals help each other with grooming, how mothers are tender with their infants, and how orphans, the elderly, and the infirm are cared for in many animal communities.[19] On the basis of such observations, Darwin argues that humans are not separate from nature. As James Rachels argues in *Created from Animals: The Moral Implications of Darwinism*, Darwin insists of nonhuman animals "that, in an important sense, their nervous systems, their behaviours, their cries, *are* our nervous systems, our behaviours, and our cries, with only a little modification."[20] Darwin's work demonstrates that, with regard to emotional life and intelligence, differences between humans and other animals are matters of degree rather than kind. Mental states are expressed though emotions so that physical and mental meanings intertwine. Moreover, on the basis of our common evolutionary heritage, Darwin suggests that any animal, "endowed with well-marked social instincts, would inevitably acquire a moral sense or conscience, as soon as its intellectual powers had become as well developed, or nearly as well developed, as in man."[21] In other words, animals with more advanced cognitive skills would be able to develop moral responsibility out of their social instincts by recognizing that their aid is likely to be reciprocated.

Although Darwin underestimated the extent to which animals participate in learned social behaviors that might be described as culture, his work does not perpetuate the dualism between culture and nature found in the works of many other major Western thinkers. Our common evolutionary heritage and the embodied nature of mentality affirm a continuum of all animal life rather than imply ontological distinctions between different kinds of beings. (For example, his studies on worms suggest that the ways worms create and move through their shaped burrows implies a kind of awareness that deserves to be called intelligence.)[22] By maintaining that differences in feeling and reason are matters of degree among animals, including humans, Darwin opened himself up to the charge of anthropomorphism. But anthropomorphism, defined as the fallacy of seeing human traits in nonhumans, is it-self a product of culture-nature dualism. A culture's understanding of what is and what is not anthropomorphic varies according to how human beings understand their place in nature. Indigenous peoples would never use the term since humans and animals are assumed to be in kinship relations and therefore expected to feel similar things. Thus American Indian writer Linda Hogan describes anthropomorphism as "one of those terms that can change com-passion and empathy into pathologies."[23] When the Russian biolo-gist Peter Kropotkin published *Mutual Aid* in 1902, a book that, like Darwin's work, emphasized mutual assistance as essential to evolu-tion and survival, Kropotkin was dismissed by American and Euro-pean scientists as a socialist and somewhat of a crackpot, according to Stephen J. Gould. Frans de Waal adds that Kropotkin witnessed the ways animals help each other even more clearly than Darwin because his observations were made in Siberia, where life is ex-tremely difficult and the survival of the group is far more impor-tant than the survival of the individual.[24]

Donna Haraway gives many examples of how Western science has been distorted by cultural prejudices denying animals feeling. In *Primate Visions,* Haraway discusses the work of Japanese prima-tologists, who never regarded the existence of intentions and emo-tions in animals as in any way suspect. She refers to their writing about primates as "ethnographic" because it takes seriously both the personalities of individual animals and their cultures. Con-cerned about ways the clinical, objectifying gaze distorts the find-ings of science, Haraway contrasts the Japanese scientists, who paid attention to "the complex physiognomy of personality," with Western primatologists, who, prior to the influence of female ob-servers such as Jane Goodall and Diane Fossey, distinguished an animal merely by its external markings—e.g., a white left shoul-der—as if there were no subject there.[25] The physiognomy that manifests emotions and intentions is the same physiognomy that scholars who do not fear anthropomorphism find essential to the evolution of life in society. Social existence requires that we are not autistic, that we are able to recognize and respond appropriately to the pleasures, pains, joys, and sorrows of others.

Mindreading: The Importance of Eye Contact and Facial Expression

Certainly, few infants of social animals would survive alone, and thus one would expect to find the capacity for empathy in any animal whose young depend upon a social network to nourish and protect them. Biologist Mary Clark argues that one reason feeling and thought are not found in distinct areas of the brain is because the cortical structures coevolved with the increased importance of social life.[26] Any strengthening of group ties that enhance the survival of mothers and infants would help to ensure the survival of the whole, just as any realistic assessment of the intentions of others would be invaluable to the creation of a secure society. Infants of highly social communities appear to be born with very strong capacities for empathy, and their emotional development is tied to the inner lives and feelings of those around them.

Virtually from birth, infants are upset when they hear another infant crying, perhaps because in the first months of life we appear to live within others as much as within anything we might call a self. Up to the age of one, one baby upon seeing another cry will wipe his or her own eyes or upon seeing another child fall will crawl off to be comforted. The ability to develop empathy appears to be most affected in primate societies by whether or not caregivers mirror the infant's own emotional and sensory feelings. Delight met with a hug and a smile reinforces an acceptance and awareness of the feeling of delight. In reflecting back like for like, the infant's feelings and the caregiver's response, neural pathways are established that promote emotional development.

The response in kind is an affirmation that has biological consequences, including the development of neural connections corresponding to a strong sense of selfhood, an accurate body image, and the ability to trust one's feelings. The mirroring process reassures infants' sense of being in touch with the dynamics of life, that is, of knowing themselves, their bodies, and their emotions as well as being able to intuit those of another like them. Since the brain appears to use the same pathways to generate an emotion as to respond to one, when joy is met with joy, infants are given both the emotional capacity to experience joy and the ability to respond to joy in the lives of others. This is not just imitation. It is touch-touching, the transformative process of relatedness that Mazis calls a "circling of the flesh" and that Felicity de Zulueta calls the "psychobiological state of synchrony."[27] We enter each other and come away transformed.

C. Nadia Seremetakis captures the transformative process through which eros arises when she describes watching a grandmother feed a child by molding bread crumbs with her own saliva and then transferring the food to the child's mouth. The grandmother gives nourishment an ontological and intersubjective ground that Seremetakis calls "the materialization of the person and the personification of matter."[28] Eating food from the mouth of her grandmother provides an opportunity for the child to realize her own material nature and the intersubjectivity of the flesh. While feeding the child, the grandmother points to the child's body and back to her own, linking their inner and outer realities: "By naming the child's gaze 'my eyes,' the grandma exchanges body parts and establishes vision as a social and sensory reciprocity. She calls the child 'my heart' for the emotions in this awakening are as sensual as the senses are emotive. This act of sharing and naming parts and senses constructs one heart for two bodies, as one food was baked with saliva for two mouths, as one soul is raised for two persons, as one pair of eyes is imprinted on two bodies."[29]

Two recently published texts begin where Darwin left off by arguing that the awareness that others have a subjectivity like ours, the so-called theory of mind, develops through our bodily relations to others, more specifically, through eye contact and facial expression. In *Mindblindness: An Essay on Autism and Theory of Mind,* Simon Baron-Cohen argues that brain development is tied in evolution to the need for social intelligence and that eye contact, in particular, is essential to the adaptations by which we come to discern cognition in the flesh. Besides the comforting caress of the squeeze machine and her time spent with animals, it was being forced to make eye contact as a child that Grandin credits most with helping her transcend her autistic prison. (Recall also that eye contact caused Donna Williams to shut down because the other person was simply made too present.) Eye contact seems to affirm that we have touched the inner life of another being.

Baron-Cohen combines the study of developmental psychology with evolutionary biology and cognitive neuroscience to argue that eye contact is a form of mindreading and a biological foundation of social intelligence and that eye contact makes possible appropriate responses to the behavior of others. Physiological changes occurring with eye contact are abundant. As if we have been physically touched, eye contact causes increased galvanic skin responses, increased electrical activity in the brain stem, and a rise in the heart rate.[30] In human infants eye contact usually produces a smile, as does the game of peek-a-boo.[31] Mary Clark argues that a possible explanation for enlarged breast development in women is to promote eye contact between the nursing mother and child. There is no biological necessity for enlarged female breasts simply for the purpose of lactation, and the thesis that eye contact is crucial for the development of social relations far outweighs the speculation (by male scientists) that breast enlargement occurred in evolution to enhance the sexual attractiveness of females.[32]

Baron-Cohen notes that the sclera of the human eye is very white when compared to the eyes of other primates, and because this allows the eyes to stand out more vividly, it could indicate the high level of communication necessary to human social life.[33] Adaptive advantages of knowing you are being watched go back in evolutionary history to the eyespots on butterflies and reef fish warning away potential predators. In addition, eye contact has great adaptive value because the experience of looking together at the same thing assumes that we are subjects together, and since we are subjects together, your eye movements can convey important information to me, possibly showing me a food source or a predator. Primates quickly learn to use these same social skills to trick and manipulate each other, clearly indicating perception of another like being. For example, a chimp might purposely look away from, rather than toward, a food source in the attempt to distract a companion and thereby keep the food for itself, just as, in a bid for attention, a chimp in the zoo might pretend its arm is stuck in the cage. Frans de Waal argues that even to be cruel, one must have some sense of what the other is feeling; sadistic behavior implies some form of understanding the feelings of others in order to determine what might hurt them.[34] Such examples show the reflexive recognition of intersubjective life on a level to which autistics remain mindblind. Although Grandin is able to recognize fear and anxiety in animals—for example, upon arriving at the slaughterhouse, she knows, by their wails, when the calves have been taken from their mothers—presumably, like cows, she does not have the ability to deceive others by feigned expressions of feeling or to understand when others are doing that to her.

Jonathan Cole, a neurologist and the author of *About Face,* argues that facial expression is the primary way we come to perceive that others have consciousness like we do. He finds a direct association between facial animation, the experience of emotions, and the ability to form social relationships. Cole's theory is supported by the fact that autistics who cannot read facial expressions are also socially isolated, as are people with Möbius syndrome, a disorder characterized by the inability to make facial expressions.[35] Research over the last two decades shows that our biochemistry actually changes when we smile or frown. Therefore, apart from professional poker players and sociopaths, faces provide important access to truths about the inner lives of others. We respond physiologically not only to the faces we make but also to the faces we see, so that looking at someone's angry, joyful, or fearful face actually quickens our pulse. Mental and physical illness interferes with our capacity both to make and to read faces and may help explain how children of depressed parents become detached in their relations with others. The face shuts down in depression (as it does with the masklike face of the schizophrenic), revealing the death of the inner life. Abused children have a great deal of trouble deciphering the meaning of faces, and even as adults they tend to read every expression as anger, just as Donna Williams did.

WAGING WAR ON THE ANIMAL SPIRITS:
THE INFLUENCING MACHINES OF CULTURE

Because our body-minds are affected not only by love but by brutality, the reverse of the process of mirroring is also true. The biological propensity for empathy can be eliminated fully for the lifetime of even the most social animal, and there is a well-documented relationship between the severity of childhood abuse and the tendency to victimize others. Daniel Goleman points out that children raised by parents who discipline them severely but otherwise take little interest in their lives or children who grow up with no discipline at all tend to respond to others in pain by attacking them. Young children need guidance to develop their capacities for empathy just as infants do in nonhuman primate societies. Without an appropriate balance of discipline and care, infants of social animals have sadistic impulses and lack what Goleman calls even "the most primitive sort of empathy, the instinct to stop aggression against someone who is hurt." Indeed, the sadistic impulse is to attack rather than defend the weak in order to distance oneself from any hint of weakness.[36]

Harry Harlow's study of rhesus monkey infants is a case in point about how empathy can become short-circuited. Harlow's decision to study the consequences of maternal rejection on primates was part of an attempt to understand what would happen to children if women went to work. It did not occur to Harlow to study the children of women who were working, and since he could not find examples of infant rejection in any naturally occurring primate community, he decided to create mechanical mother surrogates to reject rhesus infants.[37] Harlow and his colleague Stephen J. Suomi at the University of Wisconsin described their first creations in this way:

> The first of these monsters was a cloth monkey mother who, upon schedule or demand, would eject high-pressure compressed air. It would blow the animal's skin practically off its body. What did this baby monkey do? It simply clung tighter and tighter to the mother, because a frightened infant clings to its mother at all costs. We did not achieve any psychopathology.
>
> However, we did not give up. We built another surrogate monster mother that would rock so violently that the baby's head and teeth would rattle. All the baby did was cling tighter and tighter to the surrogate. The third monster we built had an embedded wire frame within its body which would spring forward and eject the infant from its ventral surface [i.e., its front]. The infant would subsequently pick itself off the floor, wait for the frame to return into the cloth body, and then again cling to the surrogate. Finally we built our porcupine mother. On command, this mother would eject sharp brass spikes over all of the ventral surfaces of its body. Although the infants were distressed by these pointed rebuffs, they simply waited until the spikes receded and then returned and clung to the mother.[38]

Some surrogate mothers had heads, some had heads that were on backwards, and some had no head at all. One surrogate mother pumped cold water through her body and was known as the "ice cold mother"—as opposed, of course, to the "hot mama." Donna Haraway remarks, "Like viruses and sadists, Harlow's repetitiveness was innovative and visionary."[39]

Infants interacting with these mechanical surrogates demonstrated behavioral problems but not the psychosis Harlow expected. Meanwhile, researchers in Harlow's lab had also been experimenting with the complete isolation of rhesus infants for up to eighteen months, placing them in a stainless steel chamber hours after birth. The animals emerged from the chamber functionally autistic and showing no affect other than fear. This gave scientists the idea of producing real, flesh-and-blood "monster mothers" by taking an infant that had been isolated in the "well of despair" and allowing her to conceive. The problem was that none of the socially isolated monkeys knew how to have reproductive sex (which certainly calls into question the uniqueness of human learned behavior).

Undaunted, Harlow applied for and was granted more than a million dollars by the National Institute of Mental Health to study "primate love" by developing a piece of lab equipment known in print, says Haraway, as the "rape rack."[40] The new monster mothers would be isolated in the well of despair and then raped. Haraway describes these surrogates as autistic, technologically raped rhesus monkeys who, when forcibly impregnated, became engineered parts of an "experimental apparatus" meant to produce psychopathology in their young. She claims that they were not considered animals but "natural-technical objects" or "wetware," a kind of hardware made out of flesh and blood.[41] Having finally produced the mothers Harlow had only previously imagined, he wrote, "Not even in our most devious dreams could we have designed a [mechanical] surrogate as evil as these real monkey mothers."[42] He reported, "They tended to show one of two syndromes. One pattern of the motherless mothers was to pay no attention to their infants. (Any normal monkey mother hearing one cry would have clasped the baby to its breast in no time flat.) The other mothers were brutal or lethal. One of their favorite tricks was to

crush the infant's skull with their teeth. But the really sickening behavior pattern was that of smashing the infant's face to the floor,
then rubbing it back and forth."[43]

Remarkably, Harlow never really did succeed in inducing permanent psychopathology in the rhesus infants cared for by monster mothers. Instead, the infants kept coming back until either
they were killed or the mothers began to heal themselves through
contact with the infants, coming to show more normal nurturing
patterns even after all the horror done to them.[44] Harlow's experiments reveal that what every infant needs is a fully dedicated caretaker and comforting touch, whether or not that caretaker is the
biological mother. (Thus Harlow claimed that his work liberated
women to enter the workplace.) As the research of Emmy Werner,
Ruth Smith, and others has since shown, children are quite re-
silient in dealing with trauma as long as they have a familiar caregiver who is emotionally and physically available.[45]

Monster Fathers

Alice Miller thinks that we will find the origin of the human sadist
in the "desperate fantasies of a child who is searching for a way out
of a hopeless situation."[46] These are very often children who are
taught to believe that duty, obedience, and the suppression of feelings are paths to the good and honorable life. That moral paradigm
has, in Miller's view, acted to support countless institutions that
work by producing submission through violence, including the
military and all totalitarian regimes. To make her case, Miller appeals to the pedagogical practices of nineteenth-century German
society, in particular, the work of Daniel Gottlieb Moritz Schreber,
a physician whose work was central to the development of child-
rearing principles in Germany prior to the rise of the Third Reich.
Schreber's eighteen books and numerous pamphlets on household
totalitarianism went through more than forty printings and were
popular when members of the Third Reich were infants. While
Schreber had counterparts then and now, the goal of producing
perfectly dutiful infants was especially relevant in his own time
and society, where the perfection of culture being achieved in the
industrial worker was supposed to be paralleled by the moral and
physical perfection of the child.

Schreber's pedagogy provides the opportunity to ask what

happens to moral agency and moral reasoning in a society when spontaneous interactions, emotional connections, and embodied wisdom are replaced by rigid bodily discipline, the concept of duty, and moral purity. Like Miller, psychologist Wilhelm Reich argued that rigid bodily habits and mechanical forms of motion function to cut the self off from inner and intersubjective life. Rigidly enforced discipline leaves no possibility for feeling comforted in the body or for what we have called mattering and entering. Reich viewed emotional anesthetization and muscular rigidity as functionally identical and thus understood the military as engaged in training that resembles Schreber's child-reading practices—both producing persons who, like Damasio's brain-damaged patients, were incapable of feeling and of making their own decisions. In *The Mass Psychology of Fascism,* Reich wrote, "German fascism was born from the biological rigidity and crippling of the former generation. Prussian militarism, with its machine-like discipline, its goose-step, its 'belly in, chest out!' is the extreme manifestation of this biological rigidity . . . social freedom and self-regulation are inconceivable in rigid, machine-like people."[47]

Schreber's practices began when the infant was five months old, with every detail of the child's life ruled by mechanical orderliness. The caregiver was to leave crying infants alone. If the infant continued to cry, Schreber recommended responding with "stern words" and "threatening gestures" prior to "mild corporal" punishment. One was never to pacify or give in to the child's desires. To break the child's natural bodily rhythms, feeding was done on a strict schedule rather than according to hunger or food preferences.[48] Schreber's writing specifies in detail what and when children up to age seven should eat and drink at each meal. Children did not eat with their parents but were made to sit completely still and watch their parents eat, even if the children themselves were hungry. (John B. Watson, the founder of behaviorism, advocated similar child-rearing techniques, including feeding children on schedule rather than on demand and warning parents not to show their children physical affection.) When Schreber's children wanted to run and play, he made them sit perfectly still. Anything that appeared to amuse the child was removed. Principles of child rearing included threatening to take away love for failed obedience, replacing self-confidence with submission and shame, and teaching the art of self-denial. Miller calls these the techniques of a "poisonous pedagogy" that was designed to conceal the abuse of the child in the child's love for the parent. The child learns to associate abuse with love, perpetuating patterns of abuse into the next generation.[49]

In an effort to understand Schreber's motivations, Morton Schatzman quotes B. F. Skinner: "We can achieve a sort of control under which the controlled, though they are following a code much more scrupulously than was the one under the older system, nevertheless feel free."[50] Schatzman reports, in his text *Soul Murder*, that the Schreber household contained, on the wall of the children's room, a punishment board that listed under each name every misdeed to be reckoned with at the end of the month. Infants were bathed only with cold water after three months of age. The entire family was made to swim in the lake early each morning, even if the ice had to be broken first.[51] Eyes were sprayed with cold water and eye movement exercises were performed daily. A great deal of attention was paid to keeping the bodies of the children straight at all times, including sitting with weight distributed absolutely evenly. Schreber invented an apparatus that attached to a desk or table and pushed up into the abdomen to correct the children's posture. The children were also made to wear corrective bracing. The *Schrebersche Geradhalter* (or Schreber's straight-holder) was an iron crossbar that pressed onto the shoulders and collar bones, correcting the posture of children as they worked at a table and also preventing them from crossing their legs. The *Kopfhalter* (or head holder) was invented by Schreber to keep the child's head from falling forward or to the side. It fastened to the child's hair on one end and to the child's underwear at the other, pulling the hair when the head was not straight.[52] The children were strapped into their beds on their backs at night, with their hands unable to touch their own bodies lest any self-soothing bring comfort or pleasure.

To prevent masturbation, children were threatened with genital amputation as well as amputation of their hands and cautery of the spine. The sexual organs and the perineum were washed daily with cold water, and "pollutions" were countered with enemas. As we find in some forms of religious asceticism, Schreber suggests having children view corpses to induce disgust with their own bodies and to deal with their sex drive. Any delight in the embodied self would, even momentarily, diminish the need and respect for external authority—and could lead to a fantasy life that could not be controlled by the father.[53]

Schreber was not alone in his obsession with repressing sexual pleasure. Common practices meant to eliminate masturbation in children during the nineteenth century were truly remarkable and were part of a sustained attack on pleasure, an attack that placed the genitals into the camp of Cartesian animal spirits. Masturbation was thought to damage minds and bodies, and therefore leading psychiatrists found it responsible for every possible disorder, including insanity, cancer, heart trouble, hysteria, and emaciation (anorexia). Masturbation was defined as a psychiatric disorder by 1828, and a French physician writing in 1855 likened its effects on civilization to plague and war.[54] Methods for the prevention of masturbation for men and boys included "enclosing the penis in bandages, infibulation (the placement of metal wires or rings through the prepuce in order to forestall its retraction behind the glans), section of the dorsal nerves of the penis in order to prevent sensations in and erections of the penis, blistering of the prepuce, and wearing spiked or toothed metal rings on the penis at night, which would bite into the penis if it became erect."[55] For women and girls, the methods included "ovariotomy (i.e., cutting into an ovary), clitoridectomy (i.e., removal of the clitoris), infibulation of the prepuce and labia majora, surgical separation of the preputial hood from the clitoris, blistering of the prepuce, vulva, and insides of the thighs, and, before going to sleep, putting the legs in splints, or tying them one to either side of the crib or bed."[56] In females masturbation was referred to as "moral leprosy," and clitoridectomy was suggested as a solution to the problem as late as 1894. Schatzman argues that during the latter part of the nineteenth century such practices were not atypical but closer to the institutional norm. He quotes Alex Comfort, a biologist and English author who refers to the sexual puritanism in this time period as "comic-book sadism": "By about 1880 the individual who might wish for unconscious reasons to tie, chain, or infibulate sexually active children or mental patients—the two most readily available captive audiences—to adorn them with grotesque appliances, encase them in plaster of paris, leather, or rubber, to beat, frighten, *or even castrate them,* to cauterise or denervate the genitalia, could find humane and respectable medical authority for doing so in good conscience."[57]

Schreber was a devoutly religious man and based his regimen of discipline on the Augustinian doctrine of original sin. He prescribed eliminating the weakness of desire by "suppressing everything" in the child. The child was born evil, but purification could be achieved by the death of spontaneous feeling along with any independent or creative spirit. In short, the child's will would be taken away, placing the child on the side of the strong rather than the weak. Schreber added to the doctrine of original sin the premise that his age was "morally soft" and "decaying" due to a lack of discipline at home and in school. Better child rearing would lead to a better society, indeed, in his view, to a better, stronger "race." Schreber viewed those who did not meet his moral ideals as "ill" and his program as health therapy. He recognized moral illness in the relaxed postures of others and in their decadent slumped shoulders. Thereby his attack on impure bodies for the health and advancement of the race forms a preamble to succeeding eugenic and behaviorist programs, including those of the Nazis, who, eighty years later, used both philosophies to begin their own cleansing. Passages in Hitler's *Mein Kampf* (1939) show a similar disdain for "weakness, cowardice, laziness, softness, and indolence" and the "moral and physical decadence" of his time.[58] Although Schreber claimed to be doing what is in accord with nature (by which I suspect he actually meant God), his pedagogy was centered on eliminating natural or spontaneous motions and emotions. Such an approach takes away the squeeze machines provided by nature and replaces them with the influencing machines provided by culture. It does not seem very far from the schizophrenic's influencing machine to this statement by Herman Goering: "It is not I who live, but the Führer who lives in me."[59]

The philosopher Johann Gottlieb Fichte described the Zeitgeist of Schreber's pedagogy in this way: "The new education must consist essentially in this, that it completely destroys freedom of will in the soil which it undertakes to cultivate."[60] Fichte embraced and extended Kant's philosophy by making duty the highest form of human self-realization, higher even than reason—even against the protests of Kant, who, to his credit, saw reason as a necessary part of the critique that must accompany duty, lest duty be followed blindly. Fichte interpreted Kant's deontology to mean that a person becomes moral by adopting his or her vocation in society without question. Doing one's work in pure obedience would fulfill one's divine vocation, which for Germans, Fichte believed, was to raise up the rest of civilization through the supreme conquering of the will. Adolf Eichmann later made a similar claim when at his trial in Jerusalem he admitted creating a version of Kant "for the household use of the little man." In the household version, the Kantian categorical imperative, which requires one to be willing to make one's moral principle into a universal law, became "Act in such a way that the Führer, if he knew your action, would approve it."[61]

Like the legacy of Aristotelian biology, in which the child is born from unformed female/nature/matter ready to be formed or "rebirthed" by male/culture/spirit, the "second birthing" of Schreber and Fichte is part of what Donna Haraway calls a "politics of reproduction" that serves the status quo by transforming erotic female nature into a more immaculate and rational cultural conception.[62] For Schreber and Fichte, creating the right environment to engineer an obedient and orderly society was everything. Pure culture would triumph over unformed and impure nature in their rational rebirthing. However, an equally possible vision created by the dualism of culture and nature is that of the eugenics movement, which claimed that biology was destiny and set about interpreting physiognomies as indicative of character and intelligence. Darwin's cousin Francis Galton coined the term "eugenics," or "good in birth," in 1883. However, Galton too would make a mockery of the subjectivity of the flesh as Darwin understood it by associating morality with breeding experiments and with measurements of bodies and body parts. Even though behaviorism and eugenics held diametrically opposed philosophical positions in their approaches to the process of cultural rebirthing, they became bedfellows in their social experiments because both rejected the importance of Darwin's social instincts as the basis for producing the good citizen.

PATHOLOGIZING EROS

Part of the assault on the animal spirits includes the reading of emotions and desires as illnesses; and, as Sander Gilman has argued, it is a short step from pathologizing eros to eradicating the bodies with which eros is identified. In Western culture women were typified by their animal and/or sexual nature in prevailing medical theory since the Greeks, whose biological science considered the womb to be an animal. Along with homosexuals, Jewish men were stigmatized as feminized males who cut their penises to resemble the clitoris and simulate menstruation. In medicine and natural history blacks of both sexes were identified with uncontrolled sexuality and exaggerated genitalia.[63] According to Gilman, Europeans of the nineteenth century thought that the lowest or most animal-like humans were the Hottentots. Blacks were described as having animalistic sexual appetites strong enough to compel black women to copulate with apes, and Hottentot females were prized attractions at European social events, where they were exhibited nude to display their protruding buttocks. Georges Cuvier, a French anatomist, did an autopsy on Saartje Baartman, a twenty-five-year-old female Hottentot who died after having been exhibited in Europe for five years. Her genitals were mounted for public display, and Cuvier said that they were overdeveloped sexually in ways similar to those of the orangutan and the chimp. Her genitals "proved" that she was lascivious; the "overdeveloped" clitoris and the plumpness of the labia majora were said to be indicative of her animal nature. The significations attached to Baartman's genitals were later extended to prostitutes and lesbians, who, in defying the sexual norms of society, were said to carry similar physical stigmata.[64]

According to Gilman and G. S. Rousseau, these projections of repressed feeling can also be found in cultural representations of witches, monsters, and female hysterics. The ethno-pornography begins with the Catholic Church's *Malleus Maleficarum*, a document on witchcraft; it is obsessed with female genitals and their connection with demonic forces. The witch, like the hysteric, was associated with animals, sexuality, and the devil, the religious equivalent of pathology in the Middle Ages. Her seizure and torture are told in as much clinical sexual detail by the *Malleus*'s authors, Dominican monks Heinrich Kramer and Joseph Sprenger, as the Marquis de Sade and other upper-class eighteenth-century French writers. The witch was said to cavort with the devil, kissing his navel, his penis, and his anus. Once captured, she was stripped, shaved, and pricked as they searched her breasts and genitals for the devil's mark, a numb patch of skin considered to be incontrovertible evidence of witchcraft. Methods of torture used against the witch reflect a preoccupation with sexuality, a preoccupation found also in the diagnosis and treatment of female hysteria. As the French physician Pierre Janet said of doctors devoted to the study of hysteria in fin de siècle Paris, by means of their own search for numbness, were they not like the priests of the Middle Ages?[65]

Soul Murder

Had he lived long enough to see it, Schreber may have been disappointed to discover that none of his children were able to stay sane in the service of social madness. Daniel Gottlieb Schreber had no problem inducing in his children the psychosis that Harlow tried to produce in infant monkeys. Even though Schreber's rebirthing was designed to eliminate the child's will, his elder son, Daniel Gustav, shot and killed himself at age thirty-eight, after having been diagnosed with a "progressive psychosis" and "melancholy." We know less about the three daughters, but one was labeled "hysterical," and a nephew said that another was "mentally no longer quite right." The second and only other son, Daniel Paul, was an eminent judge until he was institutionalized as paranoid and schizophrenic, once at the age of forty-two and again for the rest of his life at the age of fifty. Living in asylums from 1884 until his death in 1911, Daniel Paul became one of the most highly discussed patients suffering from of what was called schizophrenia in the nineteenth century.[66]

As Mary Shelley's Dr. Frankenstein came to realize too late, one's creation is rarely what is intended, particularly when designed with a rationalist agenda that disrespects biological processes. The monster, although plagued by sensory disorders and afflicted with a yellowish skin too tight and too thick to fit him, still seemed capable of more empathetic connection than his scientist father. The monster liked music, flowers, and children. His body, like our own evolutionary bodies, was a creation of many parts. Constructed out of bits and pieces from the cemetery, prison, and slaughterhouse, the monster felt connected to the whole in a way inaccessible to the father who singularly birthed him. Thus, Shelley portrays the monster as acting out of respect for his composite body by living his brief life as a vegetarian, since he did not want to eat someone to whom he was related so intimately.[67]

Schreber's second son, Daniel Paul, did not become famous, as one might imagine, for being the insane son of a preeminent pedagogue who had assured his followers that his practices would prevent rather than induce psychosis. For fifty years, no one saw the irony or recognized any similarities between Daniel Paul's mental world and the tortures of his childhood. The distinction between public and private life was profound, and the order of the day in the emerging field of psychoanalysis, much as it is today, was to seek organic rather than social causes. The disconnection presumed between mind and body worked also to hinder recognition of the role trauma played in mental disorders. Yet many of the men who commented on Daniel Paul's disease, including Freud, who was himself attempting to tie childhood experience to mental illness, knew both the father's work and the psychosis of the son in great detail and still failed to make any connection.

Daniel Paul became well known instead because he wrote one of the first accounts of schizophrenia by a sufferer of the disease, *Memoirs of My Nervous Illness*, a text that was read and commented on by all leading psychoanalysts of the day. Louis Sass suggests it was Daniel Paul's autobiography that Ludwig Wittgenstein had before him as he wrote about the philosopher's disease—the world of solipsism, which could never be cured by thought, but only by engaged living.[68] Even Eugen Bleuler, the Swiss psychiatrist who invented the term "schizophrenia" in 1911, partly with Daniel Paul in mind, saw him as uttering meaningless words. His vocabulary was considered an organic reaction to the disease rather than a story about the role his upbringing played in his dementia. Finally, in 1959, an American psychoanalyst, William Niederland, pointed out that there were some very striking similarities between Daniel Paul's visions and his father's pedagogical practices.[69]

"Soul murder" is Daniel Paul's own term for what happened to him as a result of the abuse he suffered. Continuing to live out that abuse, Daniel Paul felt "miracles of heat and cold" and thought that his eyes and eyelids were targets for miracles as little men pulled them "up or down as they pleased with fine filaments like cobwebs." There was the "coccyx miracle," which made sitting and lying down impossible, and the "compression of the chest miracle," which made breathing difficult. Completely alienated from the natural process of eating, Daniel Paul had no idea when he was and was not hungry. He claimed that he had no stomach, yet sometimes the "miracles" brought him one just before mealtime so that he could eat. "It is," says Schatzman, "as if the father taught his son a language of sensory stimuli by which to experience parts of his own body."[70] Ever obedient to his father, Daniel Paul attributed the abusive actions to God. He wrote that God does not know "how to treat a human being," that God's absurd ideas are *contrary to human nature,*" and that God's "actions have been practiced against me for years with the utmost cruelty and disregard as only a beast deals with its prey."[71]

In the end Daniel Paul cast his lot with the shadows, the selves upon whom feeling is projected by those who have repressed their own. He created a mental world and a new persona in which he could appear to himself to be obedient to the wishes of his father and still hold onto his feelings. In his mind he was transformed into a female. Having had a dream, prior to his breakdown, that it "must be rather pleasant to be a woman succumbing to intercourse," Daniel Paul eventually began to believe that his transformation into a woman was actually taking place. At first, he believed the transformation to be for purposes of sexual abuse by his therapist, but ultimately he came to envision the transformation as necessary for him to have a new and special relationship to God. His theology made the transfiguration pure—he would be "penetrated" by God and this would bring about the world's redemption.[72]

Freud developed his theory about the cause of paranoia in relation to this case, locating the origin of the son's paranoia in the defense of his psyche against homosexual love. (Schatzman believes that the father may have excited homosexual tendencies in the child by washing the genitals and perineum daily as well as by the use of enemas to punish "pollutions.") In any case, the elder Schreber is obsessed in his writings with penetration, and he actually spoke to his children about wanting them "to become *penetrated* by and to *wed* God."[73] This religious scenario may have given Daniel Paul's surrender self-respect, and it may also have allowed him to gain a sense of his own internal agency, that is, to understand this transformation as an act of will rather than just another humiliating, external action upon him.[74] It is certainly also possible to read Daniel Paul as a person whose soul has not actually been murdered after all, someone who, having endured all manner of desensitization by his father, was still trying to find a way to feel. Perhaps a trace of spontaneity survived and allowed him to seek his own sensuality in the only place his society allowed it—the symbol of the fallen female. His transformation is not only from man to woman, but from dutiful, upright, ascetic man to "voluptuous harlot," one of the two extremes that dualistic constructions of feeling allow.[75] The opposition, like all dualistic constructions, is a caricature; however, it helps to clarify how constructions of sanity and madness go straight to the heart of constructions of gender and to the limitations we place on males by disallowing them attributes associated with femininity.

Luce Irigaray suggests that Kant took on the role of the female in his daily rebirthings, even though he judged any confusion of sex roles to be immoral. Wrapped up tight each night in a sheet that provided a cocoon (or womb) in which to sleep, Kant emerged each morning at the original moment of his birth (4:55 A.M.), assisted by a "man's man," his servant (or midwife) Martin Lampe, a war hero in the Prussian military.[76] To Irigaray and to Cutrofello, what Kant was really trying to give birth to was the possibility of identifying with the values of his mother, Dorothea Regina, rather than the regimen of his abusive father. "'If only I had been a girl when I learned my mother's discipline,' he seems to say later, recognizing his failure but unable to do anything about it."[77]

Hysterical Females

It is not surprising that hysteria would emerge in the Schreber household as it did in many others during the nineteenth century. Physical restraints placed on affluent women in Victorian society were similar to those used in Schreber's pedagogy, as it was the intent to master the eros of women by destroying their pleasure, freedom, and will. The clothes of Victorian women alone composed a type of isolation chamber and caused sensory trauma similar to what animals raised in restricted environments experience. The imprisoned body, like the disciplined body, cannot express itself erotically. According to Barbara Ehrenreich and Deirdre English, corsets have been measured as exerting from twenty-one to eighty-eight pounds of pressure on internal organs, sometimes causing bent or fractured ribs. In extreme cases, corsets were tight enough to force the uterus out through the vagina. Women were caged in bustles and wasp-waists, and illness itself was seen as part of feminine beauty in the nineteenth century, much as the anorexic look is favored today.[78] A woman wearing a corset could barely sit or stoop and could not move her feet more than six inches at a time. She fought fainting spells, loss of energy, and oxygen depletion, thus neatly achieving the desired look while helping to support prejudices concerning her weak constitution.

Women suffering from hysteria complained of numbness combined with hypersensitivity to sensory stimuli. They showed signs of mechanical or jerking motions, muscle spasms, an awkward gait, paralysis, convulsions, swooning, amnesia, and a stare that doctors reported as seductive, even though the physiognomies of hysterics are described as mechanistic and immobile. Cures included clitoridectomy and electric shock therapy. Charlotte Perkins Gilman, who documented her hysteria in "The Yellow Wallpaper," found herself totally numb, a victim of physical and psychic pain turned inside out.[79] When Gilman explained to the preeminent American neurologist S. Weir Mitchell that her symptoms became worse at home and disappeared when she wrote, he prescribed never taking up the pen again as long as she lived. Expected to do no work, including the rearing of her own children, Gilman rejected his cure and went on to describe the affluent wife as "a tragic evolutionary anomaly, something like the dodo," a heavy, flightless bird with no real function but sex and reproduction.[80]

While a male like Daniel Paul might imagine becoming a voluptuous female in the effort to feel, females were caught in the double bind of being at once coerced into identification of the self with the body while also taught not to be truly at home there. Even today, women are never to appear too hungry or thirsty, too angry, or too athletic, and certainly not too sexual, just as men are not allowed softness, empathy, or caring. World champion bodybuilder Bev Francis complains that due to her musculature she has been called "a transsexual, a man, and a lesbian."[81] Sandra Bartkey points out that if the socialization of women is done "correctly," the female accepts that she is and is not her body. By virtue of being female she is reduced to the destiny of reproduction, but she is to live "perpetually at a distance from her physical self, fixed at this distance in a permanent posture of disapproval."[82] By taking up the male gaze that reduces her body into parts—breasts, legs, thighs, "a nice piece of ass"—she is dismembered, objectified, and offered eugenic replacements such as breast implants and other forms of cosmetic surgery. Lauren Slater remarks that as a recovering anorexic and therapist she found herself perfectly placed to treat misogynist males since she understood "the urge to whip and dominate, to discipline and even delete the female form. . . . Like any real man, for years I lived by my fist and not my flesh."[83]

With very few exceptions, the medical establishment failed to connect the cultural restrictions placed upon the minds and bodies of women to hysteria, as it had failed to connect the abuse of Daniel Paul with the mental universe he created. Instead, physicians continued to look for organic causes equating femaleness itself with hysteria. William Harvey, a zoologist and anatomist known for his discovery of the circulation of the blood, said that women were slaves to their biology, their lives determined by the "furor of the uterus" in a parallel drawn between "bitches in heat and hysterical women."[84] Yet, as Sander Gilman explains, hysteria acted as a code word for "difference," and the medical establishment of Europe eventually turned its gaze away from women and toward Jews as the next group of humans living on too many threatening borders. Hysteria in Jews was diagnosed as caused by bad blood, a weak constitution, the stresses of modern life, and deviance associated with excessive and incestuous sexual behavior. Francis Galton presented the Jewish physiognomy as capturing the pose of the hysteric, but the pose was said in this context to be "calculating" rather than "seductive." Hitler expanded the diagnosis of Jewish hysteria into sexual impropriety by associating the Jew with spreading syphilis and with running parlors of prostitution. He credited movements to emancipate women as products of "the Jewish mind," the Jewish male having "more than a touch of woman in him." S. Weir Mitchell helped support that prejudice by asserting that the skin of the hysteric around the genitals was very like the skin of the syphilitic Jew.[85]

Freud, as a Jew, had little problem seeing through the anti-Semitism in the association of the Jew with hysteria. Indeed, he and Pierre Janet had already come to think that trauma, not the animal womb, was actually the cause of hysteria, particularly trauma associated with sexual abuse. Janet called the effects of trauma "dissociation," and Freud initially argued that if the cause of hysteria was trauma, the disease could certainly extend beyond gender lines to males, a proposal for which he was greatly ridiculed. Freud recanted his statement about sexual abuse as the cause of hysteria after being attacked by his colleagues, who were offended by the social implications of his hypothesis. He had, he said, mistaken the sexual fantasies of these women for reality. His patients had not lived out sexual abuse but rather desired it.[86]

World War I proved trauma to be the true etiology of hysteria after soldiers in the tens of thousands were diagnosed as having a disease with no known organic cause but with symptoms similar to hysteria. These men were plagued by shaking, awkward jerking movements, numbness, paralysis, and staring. Many veterans with the symptoms of hysteria were shot as deserters and cowards, accused of being weak, effeminate, too emotional, or homosexual— the ghost of the animal womb still in play. Referred to as shell shock and then finally as post-traumatic stress disorder, the condition was not taken seriously as a medical problem until after the Vietnam War. Only after the women's movement did anyone recognize that post-traumatic stress disorder plagues more women, due to domestic violence, than men, due to war.[87]

PTSD was not a formal diagnosis in psychiatry until 1980. However, Abram Kardiner, who worked with Freud until 1923, when he left to study the effects of war, published *The Traumatic Neuroses of War* in 1941, defining the characteristics of PTSD for the remainder of the twentieth century. Kardiner realized from his clinical observations that trauma brings with it a general numbing of sensory and emotional feeling, a breakdown in trust, a failure to be guided by empathy, and a somatic condition in which sensory and emotional stimulations of any kind, positive or negative, lead to further detachment. In other words, all the ways we have access to inner lives are broken down: numbness replaces feeling, the stare replaces eye contact and facial expression, rigidified and mechanical bodily motions replace spontaneity. Trauma inhibits the development of inner life and increases reliance on external forces to regulate internal emotional states. The inability to name somatic states hinders appropriate response to the world and is tied in the research of Henry Krystal to "the development of psychoso-matic reactions and to aggression against self and others."[88]

Hitler and the Making of Dutiful Citizens

Adolf Hitler grew up in a home very much like Schreber's, a small totalitarian regime under the rule of a brutal father who did well in the civil service. The father demanded absolute obedience from his son and whistled for Adolf as if he were a dog. His infliction of vio-lence upon his son was described as "constant and unequivocal."[89] Taught early on to dissociate physical pain from emotion, Hitler learned to be silent when his father beat him. The pain Hitler had to escape included both the abuse by his father and the pain en-dured by his mother, Klara. Klara not only lived with a brutal and womanizing husband from whom she could protect neither herself nor her son, she also lost a three-year-old, a one-year-old, and an infant to diphtheria four months before she began to carry Adolf in her womb.

Miller thinks that Hitler, like other children who have no way to express their sorrow, learned to deny his pain, to associate feel-ing with weakness, and to identify with the strength of his father. Suppressing all signs of weakness in themselves, abused children lie in wait for an object of projection that will allow feeling to live again.[90] Freud describes this process as the paranoid projection by which "an internal perception is suppressed, and, instead, its con-tent, after undergoing a certain degree of distortion, enters con-sciousness in the form of external perception."[91] In the projection of feeling, one's subjective life is turned inside out and reified, thereby appearing to come from the outside, much like the sensa-tions and images produced by the influencing machine.

Hitler finally discovered an object of projection that allowed him to idealize his parents and to express the rage tied to the hu-miliations of his childhood. The scapegoat could provide psycho-logical distance from his childhood role as victim and let him torment the weak and fearful parts of himself which he now saw conveniently embodied in the world all around him: "Wherever I went, I began to see Jews."[92] To a whole society of people raised to suppress their feelings of pain, pleasure, anger, and empathy, Hitler offered the Jews as objects of projection. Of course, since the feel-ing self one wishes to destroy is actually within and therefore never really dies, the circle of projection grows larger and larger, as it did for Hitler, coming to include anyone considered weak or impure— homosexuals, gypsies, the mentally ill, and the disabled. Susan Griffin describes Heinrich Himmler's identity as composed of a similar obsession over those whom he was not: not a Jew, not a queer, not a female. "Everywhere he casts his eyes he will discover a certain word. Wherever his thoughts wander he brings them back to this word: *Jew. Jude. Jew.* With this word he is on firm ground again. In the sound of the word, a box is closed, a box with all the necessary documents, with all the papers in order."[93]

When children are raised so that "not a trace of vital spontaneity survives," Miller believes we get citizens like Adolf Eichmann and Rudolf Hess, dutiful people who do what others tell them for the sake of an ideology.[94] Divorced from the realities of suffering, their own and everyone else's, they stand outside of erotic life looking in. These are people who pride themselves on not having an inner life and who never progress beyond idealization of the parent. They are the sons and daughters that Schreber longed to produce. Disciplined not to act spontaneously or on the basis of his feelings, Eichmann had trouble making decisions. He joined the same groups as his friends and took jobs others suggested, ending up working for the SS more or less by default. Eichmann avoided choice at all costs because making decisions demands engagement with one's inner life as well as the outside world. He ate, for example, by routine rather than desire because he experienced no preferences outside of established habits. If his routine was disrupted, he obsessed but could not come to a decision. Divorced from feeling, dutiful citizens live by routines and rules as much as possible and fear change. But because they look to external authority for self-definition, they are glad to carry out someone else's orders. Their obedience to external authority allows them to relinquish personal responsibility and, in the name of those who punished them, go on to punish the weak. This is the "trick" Hannah Arendt ascribes to Himmler in *Eichmann in Jerusalem.* Arendt saw that the most serious problem that had to be solved for the SS to do its work was to overcome "the animal pity by which all normal men are affected in the presence of physical suffering. The trick used by Himmler . . . consisted in turning these instincts around, as it were, in directing them toward the self. So that instead of saying: What horrible things I did to people!, the murderers would be able to say: What horrible things I had to watch in the pursuance of my duties, how heavily the task weighed upon my shoulders."[95]

Eichmann showed no hint of emotion throughout his trial, during which witnesses described in horrifying detail the atrocities he had committed against them. Yet he blushed when he forgot to stand for the reading of the verdict, ashamed of having momentarily forgotten social decorum. These are the same dynamics revealed in Stanley Milgram's experiment designed to see how much pain a human being would inflict on another when given the command to do so by someone else. When the command was given by a "scientist" for them to apply electric shocks to a "learner," twenty-six out of forty subjects obeyed to the end. They gave the most potent shocks possible (thought to be 450 volts) even though the "learners" screamed and cried out for mercy or did not move at all, feigning coma or death. The same people that were completely submissive to authority were also completely dismissive to the person in pain—and it became clear in the experiment that these two attributes worked together. The extent to which one is submissive to a dominant authority is the extent to which one dismisses a subordinate's subjectivity. Eichmann blushed, given his respect for authority, but he remained untouched by the pain of others, because to the one who is cut off from empathy, expressions of pain only confirm that others are weak and therefore all the more deserving of punishment.[96]

When Milgram reenacted the experiment by requiring his subjects to act less directly to administer the shocks, the number of people willing to complete their jobs rose to thirty-seven out of forty subjects. (Conversely, when the subjects were required to act more directly, having to force the learner's hand onto a metal plate that carried the electric current, the number of willing subjects dropped to 30 percent.)[97] By the same token, Judith Halberstam suggests that the monster as we knew it—the monster as an aberration of nature so horrible it could not possibly be human—died in 1963 when Arendt published "Report on the Banality of Evil." Refusing to see Eichmann as a monster, Arendt instead "recognized the banality of a monstrosity that functions as a bureaucracy." In Arendt's words, "The trouble with Eichmann was precisely that so many were like him, and that the many were neither perverted nor sadistic, that they were, and still are, terribly and terrifyingly normal."[98]

THE MASTERY OF FEELING:
SADISTIC AND PORNOGRAPHIC TOUCH

The association of feeling with weakness has tremendous moral consequences for society because it produces the same dynamics that define sadistic and pornographic forms of touch. Susan Griffin writes, in *Pornography and Silence,* that "to touch, to move, to breathe" are activities of the flesh that carry within them the potential for erotic engagement with others, indeed, that it is "difficult to experience any sensation without emotion."[99] As Schreber and Kant also clearly realized, basic human activities such as breathing and walking, let alone eating and sex, can be sources not only of physical sensations but of emotional connections. But for anyone who fears those emotional connections, and particularly for the pornographer and the sadist, who need to strip sensation from intersubjective life to make pleasure possible, every possible source of erotic engagement must be broken. The problem of breaking off emotional connection is particularly acute with reference to sexuality, Griffin explains, because sex (like food) has the power to force the mind back into body and thereby into potential emotional connection. Therefore, the pornographer and the sadist preclude every source of erotic connection by the use rituals, discipline, and forms of brutality to gain mastery over the body and feeling, like Kant's daily regimen or the discipline Schreber imposed upon his children.

The Marquis de Sade, after whom sadism is named, said he first realized his sexual preference for pain when being whipped as a child at the hands of priests. His pornography therefore plays upon the hypocrisy of moralism as represented by the church, the institution from which he claimed to learn the art of sexual release through corporal punishment. The lesson for moral theory is that desire is the other side of the law: those who keep most strictly to the law may, like Sade, come to find pleasure there. Sade's pornography is filled with the religious imagery of crucifixes, altars, and chalices as well as nuns, priests, virgins, and whores. Righteousness is defiled and then vindicated, and each demands the other.[100]

When the virgin is raped, she is made to confess and is punished so that she can become the "dirty whore" who is further subdued and denigrated. It is this mutual satisfaction of law and desire that led Lacan to remark that "the Sadian fantasy situates itself better in the bearers of Christian ethics than elsewhere."[101]

Similar to Sade's use of religious imagery are genres of pornography that revolve around the theme of parental discipline. The pornography associated with parental discipline appeals to individuals who, like Sade, come to find pleasure in pain and humiliation. There is some evidence, for example, that Hitler could only come to sexual arousal through constructing scenes that reproduced his abusive childhood. It has been reported that he reached full sexual satisfaction while watching "a young woman as she squatted over his head and urinated or defecated on his face" and that he hired prostitutes to tie him up and kick him.[102] Hitler was also known to have spent time in his private rooms watching films shot by his own officers of men and women being tortured. Nazi and SS memorabilia—whips, boots, uniforms, insignia—are still commonly found in consensual and nonconsensual forms of sadomasochism and couldn't be clearer in their association of mastery with pleasure.

Sade's pornographic writings portray the feeling of pain as the height of sexual pleasure, but, as Griffin argues, the real point of sadism and pornography is the pleasure of being in control of the feeling self that is symbolized by the female body. Sade was not imprisoned, after all, for self-flagellation—which he could have excelled at in many monasteries—but rather for raping five young women whom he drugged, one of whom he skinned alive. As David Morris writes in The Culture of Pain, "The libertine taste for extracting pleasure from pain is not entirely, as Sade insists, a matter of anatomy and physiology. It also depends on a paradoxical deadening of the emotions in order that cruelty might be enjoyed to the utmost."[103] Indeed, in Sade's pornography, experiments performed on animals in European medical clinics are transformed into acts of torture performed on human females in the name of sexual pleasure.

To Griffin, the association of female flesh with eros helps explain why we find so many genres of pornography degrading women's bodies in an effort to preserve emotional distance from them. Sonia

Johnson gives a most graphic description of such scenes: "There we are, our beautiful, powerful, mysterious bodies tied and bound and gagged in degrading positions, helpless, being sodomized, gang-raped, raped by animals, hanging from meat hooks, machetes or rifles or broomsticks bristling with razor blades being rammed up our vaginas, pincers tearing the flesh off our nipples."[104]

Griffin finds a paradigmatic example of this brutal and ritualized mastery over feeling in *The Story of O*, a classic pornographic text that she likens to a case study on autism or schizophrenia.[105] To Griffin, *The Story of O* is a mirror image to the story of Renée, whose autobiography on madness we touched upon briefly in the last chapter. Renée's autobiography depicts her as increasingly alienated from her body and experiencing greater degrees of delusion before she is able finally to regain the feeling of her own body and thus rediscover not only her self but the world around her. In *The Story of O* exactly the opposite happens: O is made to unlearn all knowledge of her body; the animal spirits are systematically stripped away through commands the master reinforced by torture. Her master explains to O that through him all pleasure will vanish. She is "carefully schooled out of every bodily impulse," like Schreber's children, the Victorian hysteric, and Harlow's monster mothers. O is made too cold and then too hot; she is whipped, raped, and placed in tighter and tighter corsets; her anus is stretched by a series of tubing. She is portrayed as going mad by being prevented from drinking the "milk" of the male penis, for here, as in the politics of reproduction, it is the father who rebirths and feeds.[106]

Like the witches of the Middle Ages and the Hottentot Saartje Baartman, O is identified with animals and is shown copulating with them. O is portrayed as "a butterfly impaled on a pin," "spread-eagled," and as a "bird of prey." She is also made to wear the mask of an owl. But while the shaman who lives in an erotic universe is able to see with the eyes of an owl by wearing the mask of the owl, in this war of culture against nature the owl's mask is only meant to mock both the woman's body and the natural world. Initials are branded into her flesh, and a chain is placed through her vulva, making it perfectly clear that her body is no longer her own.[107]

Pushing the link between the denigration of women and nature as far as it goes, we find an entire genre of pornography dedicated to presenting females as "fresh meat." In these films and photographs female bodies are portrayed as a collection of parts made ready for butchering—legs, breasts, thighs.[108] Carol Adams reminds us, in *The Sexual Politics of Meat,* that the title of the magazine *The Hustler* was first the name of a restaurant in Cleveland specializing in beef. With a woman's buttocks on the cover, its menu proclaimed, "We serve the best meat in town."[109] An advertisement for the restaurant was a chart of a woman's body portrayed as cuts of meat, and the first uniforms designed for its waitresses were bright red with a cattle brand on the left buttock.[110]

As these examples make abundantly clear, when we socialize males in our culture to associate feeling with weakness, we teach them two very dangerous things: to deny their own feelings and to perceive anyone identified with feelings as weak, thereby closing off the possibilities of empathy and intimacy. Serial killer Jeffrey Dahmer represents as well as anyone the extent to which someone who is able to achieve sexual satisfaction only by mastery will go. According to his father, Dahmer's way of being in his own body changed dramatically as he entered adolescence: he developed a rigid posture and walk and a masklike stare and spoke in a monotone. The elder Dahmer remarks, "How could a teenage boy admit, perhaps even to himself, that the landscape of his developing inner life had become a slaughterhouse?"[111] Dahmer was addicted to pornography, but he needed to experience absolute control over his sexual partners in the flesh, not just on the page or the screen. According to his own account, Dahmer only achieved sexual satisfaction after—and not while—killing his victims, that is, only after he had stripped them totally of their subjectivity. He began sexual relations with a mannequin, moved on to drugged bodies, and then to dead bodies. The dead bodies were perfect for sex as far as his taste for intimacy was concerned, but they had the side effect of rotting. He needed his sexual partners to be alive enough not to decay but dead enough not to respond. His solution was to create zombies, his own kind of wetware, by pouring acid into the holes he drilled into their brains. When this and attempts at refrigerating entire bodies failed, Dahmer tried to keep his victims with him by preserving a few body parts—a head, a heart, a biceps—and consuming what he could.

Horrifying as they are, such actions can perhaps only begin to be comprehended as a solution to the most desperate kind of isolation. Like the "zoophagous" Renfield, in *Dracula,* who absorbs as many parts of other life forms as possible, eating "cats that have eaten mice that have eaten spiders that have eaten flies," Dahmer represents a distorted vision of the erotic reality that we are the relations that compose us.[112]

Culturally induced feeling disorders should act for us as canaries in the mine, clues to the extent to which we become paralyzed, morally and otherwise, in societies that fail to take eros seriously. G. S. Rousseau observes that in the twentieth century "hysteria" affects both genders and that our struggle with feeling is now found in the tattoo and piercing parlors, SM dungeons, weight rooms, cosmetic surgery and diet clinics, and shopping malls: "the places where modern hysteria—which our vocabulary calls stress—has learned to disguise itself *as health.*"[113] We take these concerns into the next chapter, along with Griffin's insight that purchasing sense at the price of insensibility can never lead to health but only to more addiction.

As long as part of us remains insensitive, the circling of the flesh will be short-circuited. Opening up to both pleasure and pain freed of their associations with immorality and weakness may be the only solution that creates somatic markers which preserve erotic sensibilities. Morris concludes about Sade, "Sade shows us that a truly just society would need to construct a new understanding of pain: an understanding that did not disavow but rather accepted and transformed the tendency in pain to isolate the individual and to plunge every human value into uncertainty."[114] But as we have seen in our examination of pornographic and sadistic touch, only in truly erotic space, where we are not seduced by the gaze that objectifies the body of the Other, can we reclaim our bodies as the home of intimate relations.

4

MASOCHISTIC AND ASCETIC TOUCH
Body as Instrument

> Our instincts salute the incommensurability
> of pain by preventing its entry into worldly
> discourse. The result of this is that the very
> moral intuitions that might act on behalf of
> the claims of sentience remain almost as inte-
> rior and inarticulate as sentience itself.
>
> —Elaine Scarry, *The Body in Pain*

We know that the somatic life of individuals is inextricably woven into the way the environment "matters" upon each of them. All species find social, sexual, and other adaptive behaviors easier to acquire when they are raised in a landscape similar to the one of their evolutionary history. But for human beings, evolution carries with it the implications of biocultural feedback. The environment that molds our sentience is continually transformed through culture into new material and social realities that in turn alter the environment in which we (and all other animals) live. This karmic cycle becomes particularly evident in modernity when the human transformation of nature, a transformation that began in earnest with the industrial revolution, now leaves no part of the earth untouched by humanity. The more we interact with our environment in unreflective ways, the smaller this biocultural feedback loop becomes, the quicker and seemingly more determinative the transformations. Yet as we move headlong into this humanly constructed, cyborg universe, we have failed to take into account the fact that we are transforming ourselves when we alter our environment. And, of course, ignorance of our own transformations finds its way back into the worlds we are constructing. The somatic effects of our present landscape, I will argue in this chapter, are expe-

rientially closer to the dynamics of Natalija A.'s influencing machine than to the dynamics of Temple Grandin's squeeze machine,
and thus we are well on our way to fulfilling Foucault's description
of "the bourgeois body [as] a descent into the empty site of a dissociated ego."[1]

As we have seen in the first three chapters, hypersensitivity to
feeling, loss of feeling, and controls over feeling intertwine and are
equally dangerous distortions of eros, equivalent in practical and
moral terms to Polanyi's example of the blind man walking with a
cane, the feel of which in his hand replaces his being in touch with
the world. The most consistent way we lose this sense of being in
touch is by means of violence enacted against us. Child abuse and
domestic violence rank among the greatest threats to erotic morality, along with war, poverty, malnutrition, and environmental toxins, all of which create physiologies associated with post-traumatic
stress disorders. Racism, sexism, and heterosexism are also threats
to erotic morality not only because they poison those who hate
and motivate them to violence, but also because of the internaliza-
tion of prejudices by those who are targets of their hate. And anyone who is fortunate enough to escape these threats to the erotic
life still has to contend with the conditions of modern life, which
increasingly produce versions of nineteenth-century hysteria by
transforming our nervous systems into pendulums that swing between the extremes of hypersensitivity and numbness. Thus, for a
variety of reasons, all of which cluster around what Marx referred
to as "breaches in sentience," those of us living in privilege in developed worlds, if honest, would have to answer "no" to the traditional greeting of a rural Cameroon villager, "Are you in your
skin?"[2] Instead, we are coming to share the biochemical and behavioral characteristics of people with damaged and nonadaptive
nervous systems—autistics, schizophrenics, people with frontal
lobe disorders, and the growing number of people with post-traumatic stress disorders.

Self-destructive behaviors, addictions, and obsessions, such as
eating disorders, drug use, compulsive exercise, and self-mutilation,
are ways to regulate psychological and biological equilibrium when
nervous systems have been affected by stress, trauma, or social isolation. While the results are more subtle than the paralyses of older
forms of hysteria, stress-deadened nervous systems are nevertheless

lured into rituals equivalent in function to Grandin's rocking or Williams's "whizzies" because these rituals shut out the world and calm sensory chaos. Bombardment by excessive sensory stimuli is a technique used during the brainwashing and torture of prisoners because the unpredictable and intrusive nature of stimuli leads to feelings of isolation, fear, and disorientation. Similarly, the chaos that bombards us daily creates sensory and emotional fragmentation, divorces our inner and outer worlds, and produces hypervigilant somatic states as well as sensory shutdowns. And it is this drive to find tolerable levels of stimulation that leaves our attractions and repulsions open to manipulation by a variety of culturally created influencing machines.

Stress suppresses and distorts sensory and emotional feeling while encouraging addictive tendencies, symbolized in our culture by the polarity of bulimia and anorexia. Flip sides of the same coin, both excess and deficiency draw us away from the development of our inner lives and responsible choices. By damaging perception and working memory, chronic stress can contribute to impulsive behavior and the failure to consider the consequences of one's actions.[3] Under stress we pay little attention to our own pain or that of others, and we are more likely to perceive erroneous information about the environment and therefore react unreflectively. Like obsessive-compulsive behavior, where rituals replace meaningful action altogether, stress can also lead one to become paralyzed by reflection on endless possibilities. Made hypersensitive or numb, we are alternately withdrawn and violent, angry and depressed, sadistic and masochistic.

Richard Sennett suggests that the psychological effects of disregarding eros in public life have been profound. He describes the loss of communal feeling in modern society—a loss we have been moving toward for more than a century—as enforcing a closure around the individual psyche. Our self-absorption is thrown back at us as a persistent and haunting dissatisfaction: "If only I could feel more, or if only I could really feel, then I could relate to others or have 'real' relations with them. But at each moment of encounter, I never seem to feel enough."[4] The loss of ways to express feeling together leaves us less and less responsive to stimuli necessary for involvement in the present and confused with regard to relationships and the future. Cut off from erotic, intersubjective life, we have come to reproduce autistic behaviors such as collecting things, treating others as objects, and using rituals or habits to protect us against change and intimacy.

When we are displaced from a public sense of eros, even those of us with the best of intentions hold convictions unrelated to our actions—eating food sprayed with pesticides, building communities on earthquake faults, burying nuclear waste on top of aquifers. These breaches in sentience are reinforced by the capitalist abstraction of exchangeable commodities and by modern technologies where visual media replaces face-to-face contact with panoptic forms of imagery. Capitalism becomes the economic equivalent of *The Story of O,* with consumerism placing us in pseudo-control of a material world stripped of sense, drawing us farther and farther away from each other and from feeling. In this, John Watson, the founder of behaviorism, may have been more correct in his assumptions about humanity than the Enlightenment thinkers who imagined that autonomous individuals would choose individuality and freedom rather than the numbing conformity of Wal-Mart. Remarking that the consumer was to the manufacturer as the green frog was to the experimental physiologist, Watson left academia to apply behaviorism to marketing, which for him held greater potential for manipulating human desires and preferences.

Actions taken under conditions of stress, like those borne from trauma, are particularly stubborn in their rigidity, their learned helplessness, their tendency toward obsession, and their blindness to consequences, all of which work together to limit self-reflection, promote addiction, and prohibit changes in consciousness. Even when designed to promote health, daily habits used as protective devices or to alleviate anxiety can take on the paralyzing qualities of learned helplessness and thus close us off from the possibility of erotic engagement. As reactions to stress, our daily habits can be used to block feeling and awareness in more subtle and pervasive ways than we realize.[5] This is certainly why Schreber controlled every detail of the daily lives of his children—by controlling their bodily life, he was also controlling their imaginations and emotions. However, it is precisely because body and mind are one that the alteration of daily habits and the attention to bodily feeling also have the potential to liberate consciousness and heighten awareness. It is this alternative that we will explore by considering the moral posture of the ascetic living in the desert or other natural space, where survival depends upon life lived in one's own skin, with "constant attentiveness to exterior and interior landscapes alike."[6]

Traditional Western views of asceticism are of religious personages who fear or despise the body and thus try to harness it through sadomasochistic forms of discipline. We find these strands of asceticism generally in dualistic religious traditions bent on transcending the body and feelings in the name of moral and spiritual purity. Hence, Audre Lorde in her essay on the power of the erotic refers to the ascetic "who aspires to feel nothing."[7] However, in all of the world's religions there are nondualistic ascetic traditions that use the body as an instrument to transform awareness precisely by producing a heightened sense of being in the flesh. These are the same traditions that seek to deepen the inner life along with the freedom and the authority of the individual. Ascetics who embrace the flesh remain less well known to us because they are not well suited to the political hierarchies and external authorities of dualistic civilizations. Recent scholarship on the Christian desert fathers and mothers as well as the female mystics of the Middle Ages proposes that the lessons of asceticism are broader and more interesting than the idea of simply deadening the flesh. Adherents describe mystical practice as a science of the inner life based upon the use and transformation of erotic energy. If one already lives in a state of awareness, any somatic state could be used to extend consciousness and awaken eros, but for those who do not have a well-developed capacity for awareness, the body can be trained to become an instrument of awakening.[8]

Leading scholars on asceticism, including Belden Lane, Caroline Walker Bynum, Peter Brown, and Margaret Miles, believe that ascetic practice, even in its masochistic forms, is undertaken to gain direct experience of how intricately body and mind are one. Generally speaking, asceticism uses the bodily acts of our daily lives to alter consciousness. Practices such as fasting and taking a vow of silence remind us that the development of an inner life can be enhanced by changes in daily behavior and in the environment in which we live. This is why we often find ascetics in silent retreat in the desert and in the mountains, where the power of the landscape to affect consciousness is most evident. Ironically, ascetics who have been stereotyped as hating the flesh report that when the senses are stripped of their trained habits of aversion and attraction, they undergo a renewal that results in the most ordinary and even repugnant objects becoming almost unbearably appealing.[9]

By means of guided spiritual practices, our relations to our bodily needs and desires can heal breaches in sentience and promote circlings of the flesh to nurture us and open us to feelings of compassion and empathy. Because ascetic practice focuses attention on the acts of daily life, it has the potential to use the body's own erotic energy to expand rather than inhibit awareness. Ascetic practice has the potential, in other words, to deconstruct the mental, social, and physical habits that imprison us, thereby making new perceptions, emotions, and modes of mutuality possible. As such, ascetic acts are central to the religious quest that Joseph Campbell described as seeking "an experience of being alive, so that our life experiences on the purely physical plane will have resonances within our innermost being and reality, so that we actually feel the rapture of being alive in our bodies."[10]

TWENTIETH-CENTURY HYSTERIAS

We have seen how the body as sensory agent is composed moment to moment out of the situation in which it finds itself. Drug overdoses, for example, frequently occur not because the person has taken a larger dose of the drug than usual, but because the drug was taken in unfamiliar surroundings, causing the body to respond with lower levels of tolerance. Persons who meditate know that rooms used consistently for meditation (or prayer) are not simply places to escape outside disturbances, although they are certainly that. After meditating in one specific place over a period of time, the body knows the context and begins to alter awareness as soon as the place is entered, prior to the actual act of meditation.

Likewise, the adaptive behaviors of an organism do not work when the biology of the organism fails to mesh with its environment. In *The Biology of Violence*, Debra Niehoff gives several instructive examples of how animals that are adapted to a particular kind of environment develop nonadaptive behaviors in an environment that does not suit them. Border collies love to herd sheep by using intensive eye contact, and do so with remarkable enthusiasm and skill when a trainer develops this genetic propensity. Allowed to run for miles each day, these dogs make wonderful pets, but when confined in urban environments, the same strengths that make Border collies excellent herding dogs work against them. In the wrong environment, their need to run, to listen keenly, to make eye contact, and to respond to external stimuli with absolute attention causes the dogs to manifest destructive behaviors such as excessive barking, digging, biting, and self-mutilation.[11]

Niehoff also considers the "lesson horse," an animal often considered to be unresponsive, stubborn, and defiant. Whereas horses are born attentive and highly responsive, horses used to give lessons to novice riders often learn to shut down. People who don't know how to ride jerk hard on the reins, the equivalent of screaming rather than speaking to the horse, and then when the horse is listening intently for a clue, the rider fails to provide one. All the attributes that would make the horse a steeplechase winner work against it because the rider communicates only "meaningless chatter." Thus the lesson horse develops a "hard mouth," the equivalent of ceasing to listen.[12]

In our everyday lives, we can be just like these animals, our sensitivities becoming hardened by the chaos of stimuli that surround us. The combination of deadening to present stimuli and hyperactivity to make up for it is a central characteristic of the nervous systems of people with repeated criminal offenses. Researchers speculate that when our emotional responses to the environment are underaroused, we fail to learn how to anticipate the consequences of our actions, especially with regard to aggression or risk. Like Elliot, the underresponsive fail to learn from their behavior because they do not register any somatic markers that attach their emotional lives to others. The physiology of some sociopaths, batterers, and serial killers appears to be calmed by violent acts: heart rate and blood pressure fall as the violence escalates. Sociopaths, for whom empathy and other emotions are largely impossible, often show no galvanic skin responses, even when they are about to receive an electric shock.[13] As far as moral agency is concerned, neither hyposensitivity nor hypersensitivity produces adaptive somatic markers. The neurochemistry of unresponsive, antisocial individuals too slowly and too weakly connects stimulus and response, while, in contrast, the neurochem-istry of overresponsive, hypersensitive individuals—for example, people with post-traumatic stress disorder—makes the connections too quickly and too strongly. Both are examples of "neurochemical survival strategies gone haywire."[14]

Turning Our Adaptive Responses against Us

Stress is a good example of how bodily attributes adaptive to or-ganisms in one environment can be turned against them in an-other. Bodies and nervous systems don't evolve at anywhere near the speed at which humans have come to change the landscape in which we live. Because the fight-or-flight defenses perfect for hu-man survival during the Pleistocene era have survived into the modern world, our natural defenses have come to work against us. One leading researcher on stress observes that we can go through all the physiological changes meant in evolution to help us escape a hungry predator just while running late for a critical appoint-ment. In *Why Zebras Don't Get Ulcers,* Robert Sapolsky argues that we have created an environment in which, biologically speaking, we are living every day as an emergency and paying a heavy price for it. Walter Cannon, who defined what we now call the fight-or-flight response, referred to the equilibrium necessary for survival as homeostasis. A stressor is anything that throws the body out of homeostatic balance, and the stress response is the body's attempt to restore that balance.[15] Being late to an appointment is a stressor that the body responds to by pumping adrenaline in the attempt to maintain equilibrium appropriate to external conditions.

Stress is debilitating to short-term memory and promotes heart disease, strokes, immune deficiency, ulcers, and even types of obesity. It overactivates the cardiovascular system, blunts pain, in-duces insomnia and hypertension, and makes us more likely to eat fatty foods and drink alcohol. To the body, stress appears as an emergency, and thus the brain pumps the body with adrenaline, making us more and more reactive to the environment and less and less in control of what is happening to us. Moreover, the neo-cortex's prefrontal region, which normally tries to refine the amyg-dala's level of threat by allowing us to reflect before we act, can actually create the physiological responses of an emergency when we just sit around worrying. This is why, according to Sapolsky, we have ulcers but zebras do not. We can transform fear into a real enemy as far as the body is concerned, our thoughts alone convincing the rest of our brain and body that an emergency is actually happening. The same structures of the emotional brain, structures that improved our chances in evolution by their capacity to ingrain and extend memories, turn out also to be highly problematic in a fragmented, highly competitive society like ours because those structures hold onto every single confrontation and traumatic event.

Stress works against moral agency because prolonged or chronic stress makes it difficult to determine, much less focus upon, what really matters. Robert Kugelmann describes the experience of stress as equivalent phenomenologically to the experience of the astronaut who is suspended in space and bombarded by stimuli and information but cannot make bodily contact with the world. Under stress, the present is overwhelmed by the future, while the space one is in continually falls away to the next space one must occupy, resulting in a kind of erotic homelessness. Kugelmann also reminds us that "stress" is a metaphor that applies equally well to machines—and like a machine, when one is stressed the heart pumps and the tape in the head whirrs but there is little sense of flesh-and-blood animation.[16] In a stressed state, people appear to be objects on pasteboard scenery. Elaine Scarry describes the pain of torture as producing a similar sense of the world's insubstantiality. Perhaps this is because stress is its own form of pain—a persistent trauma that numbs us to the very things that might ordinarily sustain us.

Researchers find depression, the second most disabling ailment in the Western world next to heart disease, to be at least partially caused by stress-related emotions. PET scans show that the more depressed one is, the more blood flows away from the prefrontal cortices to the amygdala, increasing fear, dread, and negative perceptions. Since the amygdala presents reality in general rather than specific terms, in a depressed condition almost everything can begin to look hopeless and dreadful. Neural circuitry fails to generate positive feelings and fails to inhibit negative ones. Stress also manipulates the organization of emotional memory so that the most painful memories are given prominence while positive memories retreat.[17] Cognitive life is affected so profoundly and perceptions are distorted so radically as to make some researchers describe depression as a disorder of thought rather than emotion, once again showing how mind and body are one. Symptoms of depression include lack of energy, sleeplessness, loss of interest in food and sex, the inability to experience pleasure, the inability to see alternatives, and impaired short-term memory. Depression is chemically equivalent to the effects of violent trauma.[18]

While many important lessons can be drawn from this about moral agency, one of the most important things to realize about the relationship between depression and stress is that these bodily states have been tied in research to the phenomena of "learned helplessness." Recall that Elliot, Damasio's patient, could not produce adaptive behaviors because his inability to experience pain made it impossible for him to learn from loss. Something similar happens to animals exposed to unpredictable psychological stressors in pathological amounts. Sapolsky cites the work of psychologists Martin Seligman and Steven Maier, who used sporadic noise and electric shocks on rats to induce a condition very like human depression. Rats given identical shocks in predictable patterns had no trouble thereafter learning to avoid a shock that was then given on only half of the floor grid and only after a signal. However, the rats experiencing noise and electric shock in an unpredictable manner never did learn to avoid the shock that was applied on only half of the floor grid and only after a signal. Like the lesson horse with a hardened mouth, the rats that experienced helplessness may have learned not to bother paying attention at all. If so, this means that they could not take advantage of being given the freedom to alter their situation. Sapolsky points out that the opposite is also true—organisms rewarded in an unpredictable manner never learn coping behaviors. In addition, persons with a strong sense of inner life appear to be less affected by stress and trauma than those who need to feel accepted by external authorities.[19]

Compulsion and Addiction: Punishing Karmic Cycles

Nervous systems under stress will prompt organisms to take flight, fight, or freeze. While Niehoff points out that the differences between these choices might be important for society, nervous systems don't care: "All are stressful [responses], and all will perpetuate the steady erosion of mental and physical health, the fatal attraction to unacceptable responses."[20] We lose many moral agents to stress because, beyond limiting options and compromising empathy, stress attracts us to unhealthy solutions, that is, solutions that are comforting in the short term but unacceptable in the long term. Seeking relief from what Niehoff calls "the numbing discomfort of a stress-deadened nervous system" leads to compulsive, unproductive, or even self-injurious or masochistic behavior.[21] Stress leads to such nonadaptive behaviors in large part because it produces a loss of flexibility in neurological structures, creating a dependence upon everything staying exactly the way it is. Antidepressants such as Prozac work to restore the plasticity necessary to move beyond fixations and are often prescribed for anxiety and depression, the two bodily states most likely to lead us into destructive behaviors.

Addictions are ways of regulating psychology and biology when the normal equilibrium has been disturbed. Although many addictions are the result of an abusive childhood, stress contributes to addictions as well. Given the fact that stress produces nervous systems that are both hypersensitive and numb, it is no accident that our legal drugs of choice as a society are nicotine, alcohol, and food. Nicotine is a highly rewarding, mood-altering substance that mimics a tranquilizer in stressful situations and a stimulant in depressive ones. The chemicals in nicotine as well as those produced by binge eating chemically mimic the brain's own neurotransmitters, including acetylcholine, serotonin, and dopamine. Alcohol provides similar feelings of calm, euphoria, and anesthetization to pain by inhibiting neural cell conduction and neurotransmitter release. Food eaten in too little or too large portions brings with it many of the consequences of alcohol, including addiction and lack of awareness about the consequences of present actions. Bingeing acts as a stress reducer, relieving muscle tension as well as emotional anxieties.[22]

Addictive behaviors provide a brief, although false, sense of being in control and can end up increasing the original feelings of powerlessness that gave rise to the addiction. Linda Hess says about her compulsive eating in "Craving," "I'm trapped inside this puffed-up, dead-surfaced body. I want to avoid contacts with people. . . . What gets liberated when I don't eat is love."[23] When asked if she ate out of a fear of feeling, one compulsive eater reported that "it wasn't as if she had feelings and then ate to get rid of them. That would assume that she had feelings to begin with. That would assume some kind of connection."[24] Another gave up compulsive eating, she said, because she did not want her daughter to know her as someone "disconnected from the world."[25] Yet another observed, "I didn't feel anything. I mean, if—if I had felt something, I wouldn't have had an eating disorder."[26] These kinds of addictions can substitute anesthetizing behavior for encounter and intimacy. In a punishing biopsychological feedback loop, substances used to manage pain often end up mimicking the original stimulus that led to their use. Substance abuse can become like Donna Williams's persona Willie, a dictator of feelings and behaviors, one that takes the place of the original abuser rather than providing freedom from that abuse.

Self-mutilation is another addictive solution to sensory chaos and emotional distress. People drawn to self-mutilation cut themselves either when they find the senses flooded or when they find themselves too numb and detached from the world. Like nicotine and binge eating, mutilation is a stress response that answers the needs of both hypo- and hypersensitivity. Self-injury acts as a "regulator valve" so that when one is feeling overwhelmed by the world, cutting reduces the stimuli, allowing reconnection with the self; when one is feeling too detached, cutting sharpens the senses, helping to reconnect to the world.[27] Most self-mutilators, like most bulimics and anorexics, are female; however, self-mutilation is on the rise in male prison populations in response to restricted environments. Some people who cut themselves speak of bringing the skin to life, of being able to affirm their existence by seeing their own blood.

Nicotine, alcohol, dieting, overeating, and self-mutilation all affect the pleasure system: the dopamine pathways in the limbic brain create, however briefly, a sense of euphoria or calm and well-being. The pleasure centers of the brain are those that have been tagged as deserving reward in our evolutionary history by being associated with activities related to our survival. Eating, having sex, taking pride in a job well done, and solving problems all lead (or should lead) to pleasurable feelings. Researchers speculate that direct access to the brain's reward system by outside sources such as nicotine, alcohol, and too much or too little food is totally accidental; that is to say, it is nothing that would be designed by natural selection. The steady use of cocaine, for example, creates changes similar to those found in frontal lobe disorders and can induce symptoms identical to paranoid schizophrenia. Alcohol affects our capacity to estimate the consequences of action, lowers the signal for danger, and leaves us craving immediate reward. Nevertheless, when alcohol or other drugs do break into the centers designed for survival, the experience is recorded by the brain as pleasurable and the phenomenon of craving is set in motion no matter what the consequences.

At the same time the brain craves these new levels of pleasure, it also creates higher levels of tolerance. Thus the addict is left needing more and more to feel less and less. Even after breaking the addiction, the brain continues to overcompensate for the dopamine abuse by demanding greater levels of dopamine for any small taste of pleasure—the addict now must contend not only with withdrawals from the drug but with the absence of life's most simple pleasures.[28] This is extremely difficult because, like traumatic experience, opiates are tied to the limbic brain and come with very strong emotional memories. Just visiting a place that has been frequented for drug use can create sweats and the taste of the drug in the back of the mouth.

The Commodification of Feeling

Addictive and compulsive behaviors turn the body into an instrument under the influence of something external, and that external source appears to offer the only sensory and emotional realities worth pursuing. Distancing ourselves from the world's flesh-and-blood reality is not only the goal of nervous systems under trauma and stress, but part of everyday life when bureaucratic systems and technologies of mass production take us away from the sources of our material existence and therefore the consequences of our actions. To the dissociated ego of the bourgeois world, pain does not exist, and the consequences of action appear insubstantial. Affluence itself, along with the pseudo sense of power and control that attends it, easily creates an atmosphere of a world populated with ghostly commodities. Consumers stand outside of the flesh, living in a vast commodification of reality, one that eventually turns their own bodies into things in need of modification and perfection.

We know that the idealized American lifestyle is destructive to the environment, to workers, to personal relationships, and to our own health; yet our society goes to great lengths to hide the true costs of overconsumption. Overeating, for example, costs billions of dollars in health-care expenses for diabetes and other obesity-related diseases. Yet the need for immediate gratification, the principle of bigger is better, and the decision to buy now and pay later are considered to be badges of success rather than symptoms of moral weakness. Bingeing on consumer goods has become a cultural form of stress relief, the symptoms of which include a massive credit-card debt. Here capitalism combines with biology and psychology to construct an influencing machine that acts with extraordinary power to create artificial needs to be satisfied at whatever cost—including the stress that leads to more consumption. Rather than an expression of subjective life, desire is part of an external system objectified in capital—the central influencing machine of our era—and sanctified in the idea of progress.

The vicious circle is complete when the resulting stress created by the need to consume is relieved only by more consumption. In *The Overspent American,* Juliet Schor argues that shopping has become a form of "retail therapy." We give ourselves gifts to lift our spirits, convinced that we deserve them for working so hard. Increasingly, we consume "to fight the blues, to savor a happy moment, to reward [ourselves], to enhance self-esteem, or to escape from boredom. Indeed, consumerism is so pervasive that 'retail therapy' is a response to just about *any* mood, state or psychological problem."[29] Of course, like other addictions, this kind of therapy actually ends up creating more problems than it solves by tying us to stressful jobs, mortgages, and mounting debt, all of which serve to make our lives feel more determined and the world feel more threatening—and less nurturing—than it would otherwise be. Capitalism is designed to extend the needs created by stressful lifestyles while it works to create more stress. We are relentlessly bombarded with messages about upgrading old products and buying new ones. The list of what we think we need grows longer, as does the cost of keeping up with the pace of the lives we are living—child care, private schools, gated communities, take-out foods, house cleaners, accountants, recuperative vacations, massages, and health clubs—and we imagine all the while that we can get around the problems of society simply by spending more money.[30]

The media is quite literally an influencing machine in forming our expectations of what we think we need to be whole and complete. Nearly half of our population reports not being able to buy the things they really need, and according to Schor, this is not the poorest half. Her studies show that we are working harder and longer hours; yet many of us feel that we are barely making it and are fearful of losing ground. Since no one really knows how much money it takes to survive into old age or to raise our children well, we continue to hoard and consume rather than live more simply, and we remain stubbornly apathetic about the consequences for others and for the planet. Schor suggests that in fundamental ways we have become our things, our clothes, our cars, and our houses. We go all out for brands likely to be seen and therefore admired by our friends, while skimping on "invisibles" such as insurance, retirement, health care, and public services. Kids and adults flock to the "cool" brands to establish an identity and to express themselves. Not surprisingly, one's ability to be seduced by media images appears to be in inverse proportion to the development of inner life, self-esteem, and a sense of belonging.[31]

The distance between available commodities for consumption and our needs as sentient beings is enhanced, perhaps not coincidentally, by technologies that act as pimps to our consumption and open us to the experience of mass marketing by presenting the world as a virtual reality product. Media images make it possible to turn each viewer into an infinitely reproduced mass for which products can be developed for universal consumption. Those same products can then come to act as substitutes for our ability to feel together. Under the conditions of mass consumption, it becomes possible to replace feeling together with feeling the same. Aldous Huxley (in *Brave New World*) and the behaviorist Watson both understood that when individualism is tied to mass consumption a new form of totalitarianism becomes possible. Through the manipulation of stimulus-driven desire and response, one can create a mass experience of submission more powerful than any form of fascism because it is a subservience that feels like both freedom and belonging. Universalized images are designed to evoke the same feelings in everyone, and therefore belonging can be reduced to feeling whatever it is the imagery is designed to evoke.

Kitsch art uses canned laughter and predictable sentiments to induce everyone to respond the same way to the same things. Feelings themselves begin to seem packaged and reproducible, as are the commodities that television and computer screens reduce the world to. Similarly, emotional binges tied to "event-grief," such as the murder of JonBenet Ramsey, the death of Princess Diana, or the latest school shooting, witness to our hunger to feel something together. But, as Glen Mazis argues, kitsch is a substitute for real e-motion because nothing is moved through it or by it: kitsch operates by formula and demands nothing from its audience but passive consumption.[32] Kitsch helps to present the message of consumerism: we are to become individuals by feeling the same, looking the same, and desiring the same things—preeminently, youth and perfection. The taste for kitsch art also means that we come to see provocative, potentially transforming art as morally and politically threatening.

EROS AND THE MASOCHISTIC CONTINUUM

Disciplined approaches to distancing ourselves from the flesh, such as diet and exercise, are the most acceptable ways to use the body as an instrument of control over feeling in our culture because they are consistent with both puritanical forms of morality and the drives of a consumer society. To Susan Bordo, the ultimate irony of living in a culture in which we are being constantly fed with new desires is that the models used to feed us those desires are not allowed to look as if they desire anything. It is no accident that the anorexic, literally "without desire," is the premier image that advertising agents dance before us, the image Bordo calls the "heroic chic." Reminding us that "consumption" was the name of a disease long before it was the answer to all of our problems, Bordo describes the "heroic chic" as having the depression-and-death-are-cool look that model Kate Moss epitomizes.[33] Models appear to be not only emaciated, but cold and detached, as if caring about and needing nothing. That form of indifference is as attractive as sensationalized violence to a culture suffering from excess and aesthetic impoverishment. The fantasy at work in the model's mannequin-like body purifies, and she offers up desirelessness as an atoning public sacrifice for all of us as every kind of obsession is paraded before us. Body fat and softness come to symbolize a lack of discipline and character, while emaciation and indifference work to build character by purifying our cultural bulimia.[34]

The New Puritans: Pain as Discipline

Our contemporary purity systems not only are unconscious forms of guilt about overconsumption, but are rooted in centuries of religious philosophies suspicious of the desires and physical vulnerabilities of the flesh. Anorexia and bodybuilding are two examples of modern purity systems that function in our culture much as the body-hating practices of ascetics in dualistic religions that regard the flesh as tainted. These New Puritans, as Bordo calls them, see denial as an end in itself.[35] As it was for Kant and Schreber, control over natural and spontaneous bodily pleasures is not viewed as masochistic but as a virtuous display of the moral law within. And, as we have seen, once freedom and pleasure become associated with absolute control and obedience, it is a short distance from Kant and Schreber to Sade. This puritanical heritage also helps to explain why we are slow to recognize the pathogenic nature of desire when it comes to us from the media and other capitalist engines of consumption, but quick to do so when desire actually comes from within the flesh, especially whenever desire defies taboos related to gender, race, class, or sexual orientation.

For anorexics, compulsion cloaks the masochistic nature of the behavior by providing the illusory experience of empowerment and invulnerability. Fifteen percent of anorexics die; yet even when extremely close to death, they feel on top of the world, their brains flooded with opioids. As long as the body remains an instrument of the will, its submission is the anorexic's passage to freedom—like Kant, one is nurtured by nothing other than one's own obedience. In an essay on her life-threatening bout with anorexia, Jenefer Shute reports that even though she could not stand without fainting and her hair fell out in dry hunks, she never felt as strong and pure. As her reflex responses ceased and the electrolytes in her brain became unbalanced, she thought, "Fine with me. I don't want any involuntary responses. Soon, in this body, everything will be willed. . . . One day I will be pure consciousness, traveling unmuffled through the world; one day I will refine myself to the bare wiring, the irreducible circuitry of the mind."[36] Shute felt that every loss made her stronger until her only interest in nourishment was resisting it. Thin came to mean "just the bones, no disfiguring flesh, just the pure, clear shape of me. Bones. That is what we are, after all, what we're made of, and everything else is storage, deposit, waste."[37] Fasting, as religious adherents know, produces hyperacuity or a vivid sense of one's interior life. The strong sense of identity and physical euphoria work together to convince the anorexic that this is the appropriate path to enlightenment.

Anorexia reminds us that food matters, that in more ways than we would like to imagine we are what we eat, or what we don't eat. Without food, the skin of the anorexic dries up, her extremities become cold and blue, her body temperature drops, and menstruation ceases. Eventually she becomes disoriented about whether sensations are coming from within her or from the outside world. Her distance from food doesn't stop there but extends itself into the desire to find distance from all physical proximity, including touch.[38] Divorced from the world of emotion and her own sensuality, she begins to live in a way that denies any sense of being nurtured, warmed, or comforted, both psychologically and physically. Overpowering the needs of the body sets her free, but dealing with the world leaves her irritable, demanding, arrogant, neurotic, and depressed. In short, the obsession with food replaces intersubjective relations and becomes the sole measure of value. Just as Kant measured his character by having one cup of tea and not desiring another, what the anorexic does or does not do with food determines whether she is good, bad, greedy, or lazy. It is a small moral universe, but easily measured, an extension not only of the restrictions of desire put upon women, but also of our confusion of character with bodily discipline.

Bodybuilding is another contemporary form of purification in which the body is used as an instrument to construct a world in which mind is proven master over matter. Bodybuilding is a multimillion-dollar industry and one of the most demanding purity systems in our culture. Stephen Moore, in *God's Gym*, likens bodybuilders to a priesthood in their all-consuming obsession with perfection.[39] The discipline, self-control, and appearance of strength central to the sport are especially attractive to a culture of external excess and internal deficiency. Bodybuilders put themselves through brutal physical abuse that leaves muscles feeling not just tired but injured after a good workout. Adherents follow a diet regime as pure as the anorexic's, weighing and measuring proteins and carbohydrates while injecting steroids and diuretics. In this sport, the skin becomes a living testament to the discipline of the muscles and lack of fat behind them; indeed, the skin can become so devoid of fat that it takes on a transparency, like parchment.[40] Female bodybuilders lose the fat in their breast tissue, and the gender politics of the sport have led a majority of contenders (up to 80 percent) to seek breast augmentations that the judges consider necessary flesh replacement.[41] Like anorexics, bodybuilders see imperfections in their bodies as a form of laziness or character failure, with life reduced in moral and intersubjective terms to their physical structure. A good workout means one is a good person. Discipline is total control and absolute obedience to precise, externally measured standards.

Since value is truly skin deep, illusion plays a very important role in achieving the ideals associated with gender perfection. The perfect-looking female ceases to menstruate, while the use of steroids leaves the perfect-looking male literally impotent. Religious ascetics intent on punishing the flesh have also sought these conditions, but their motivation was to free themselves from the restrictions of sexuality rather than to achieve the perfect look. The female ascetic is said to become more spiritual as her fasting causes the menstrual cycle to cease, and with it her ties to nature. Male purity in dualistic ascetic practice was gained through forced celibacy, sometimes by means of castration. Male bodybuilders talk of being "less of a man" and "actually more of a woman," and they develop the so-called "bitches tits" even though they look like the epitome of power. As a Mr. International confided to Alan Klein, "By the time we reach the stage, we are more dead than alive. The dieting is too extreme; the anxiety, the dehydration all cause problems."[42] More than one contender has dropped dead on stage, and others have been taken directly from the stage to emergency rooms.

Anabolic steroids mimic the male hormone testosterone and have the ability to convert everything, including fat, into muscle and energy. It is not unusual to add up to fifty pounds of muscle in six months as the body incorporates rather than excretes an extra six thousand to ten thousand calories daily. In women, steroid use causes facial hair, an enlarged clitoris, and loss of breast tissue. Both men and women suffer liver damage from the use of steriods. Klein believes that there is an inversely proportional relationship between the mastery sought over one's body in the gym and energy used in other aspects of life such as relationships and work. The gym becomes a kind of sanctuary where contact with the world is broken and security is produced by what amounts to a monastic regime.

Some studies have found that women learn to be active rather than passive agents through bodybuilding. This is most likely due to the fact that women in the sport may be engaged in acts of cultural resistance, trying to break out of the molds that have imprisoned their bodies. (A song favored in women's performances has been Janet Jackson's "In Control.")[43] Thus some female bodybuilders appear to be redefining cultural norms by presenting themselves as physically powerful, while male bodybuilders appear to be overcoming insecurities by embodying the cultural ideal of male strength and perfection.[44] In either case, the danger is that workouts can escalate into obsessive-compulsive behavior in which the body becomes more machine than organism. Because bodybuilding is consistent with purity systems built on the need for control and perfection, bodybuilders, like anorexics, describe themselves using mechanistic images. Arms become "guns" and legs become "pistons," leading Pamela Moore to describe bodybuilders as cyborgs without prostheses.[45]

Novid Parsi's description of "Sam" in his essay "Don't Worry, Sam, You're Not Alone" provides many excellent examples of how obsessive forms of exercise can turn the body into an instrument to create distance rather than intimacy. Sam gives eloquent and insightful descriptions of his life as a bodybuilder: "The more I grew, the more I felt protected, *insulated* from everything and everyone around me." The better he looked, he says, the worse he felt, and the more he dissociated from his body. "I watched almost as a spectator as my body operated beyond my control."[46] Sam describes everything in the gym as being about isolation: isolating muscles and dividing the body into objectified parts as well as isolating himself from others. Steroids help complete the break by inducing an adrenaline-like conviction that nothing else matters. Pain is considered to be weakness leaving the body. The desire to rule the body was in Sam's case partially motivated by his failure to come to terms with his own homosexuality. He says that he "hated the flawed, weak, vulnerable nature of being *human*."[47]

> But once I'd manufactured all the muscles and the puffery, I felt trapped inside this colossal frame. . . . In the end, "the Walk" I did, the being I had become, felt stifling, limiting, claustrophobic, far from liberating. . . . To keep from feeling bad, I kept myself from feeling anything at all. Nothing penetrated my muscular armor. I had descended completely into a world of my own. . . .
>
> Everything I'd done for the last four years had been an effort to keep the world at bay, to find a place in which I wouldn't have to react or think or feel. . . . But this shell that I created wasn't meant just to keep people at bay. After all, a can of Mace can do that. No, this carapace was laboriously constructed to keep things inside too. The physical palisades and escarpments of my own body served as a rocky boundary that permitted no passage, no hint of a deeper self—a self I couldn't bear.[48]

Sam looked like the epitome of male power (although even walking hurt because no pads of body fat were left on his feet), but the larger and physically more powerful he became, the more he felt his true self shrink, until he feared that he would not even find his reflection in the mirror. In the end Sam left bodybuilding for the same reason he says that he came to it—to feel alive rather than made of iron.

Both the male bodybuilder and the female anorexic exhibit a self-control that reflects our culture's insistence on hyper-individualism and dependence on no one. But it is interesting how the dualistic conceptions of both anorexia and bodybuilding become self-defeating. The male bodybuilder finds in his image of perfect strength mostly weakness, which is taboo in traditional images of masculinity, whereas the anorexic female finds complete independence from her own flesh and reproductive capacity, taboo in traditional images of femininity.

Performing Masochism: Pain as Feeling

In our contemporary culture, according to Roy Baimeister's argument in *Masochism and the Self*, the most important thing we seek in the experience of physical pain is escape from the psychological stress of an overwhelmingly mental world.[49] Responding to this stress, on the one side of the continuum, are those who, like the New Puritans, use physical discipline to distance themselves from their bodies and feelings. On the other side are those who use sadomasochistic practices to reconnect with their bodies and feelings. Lynda Hart describes sadomasochism as the opposite of the dissociative process by which the mind vacates the body, a reversal of Plato's cave in which the body leads the self back into the physical world and the mind obediently follows. As one "bottom" says of her submission, "When I get there, I get real."[50] SM, or sadomasochism, is described by some adherents as being more about peeling off false identities and increasing awareness of the subtle dynamics of control and power than about finding pleasure in pain. For example, the "top" in sadomasochistic sex appears to be the active agent in administering the "discipline," but plays the role of passive slave to the one receiving pain/pleasure. Passivity is therefore experienced by the person being disciplined as the feeling of being in control.

Many SM practitioners say that the most important element in the whole drama is consent and trust and that it is this mutuality, along with the highly ritualized elements of the performance, that allows the pain to be cathartic and transformative. Besides the fact that SM draws the mind back into the body, people are drawn to consensual sadomasochism in the attempt to relive their past, often recreating the pain of being abused but under ritualized conditions in which their subjective lives are left intact and therefore become stronger. Pain denied repeats itself in very tight feedback structures: sexually abused children are drawn to abusive relationships as adults, and young men beaten by their fathers are drawn to SWAT teams, the border patrol, or the military. Bringing pain into awareness is the therapeutic part of SM. As Robert Stoller argues in *Pain and Passion*, the etiology of sadomasochistic practice is pain experienced previously, particularly in childhood. The more severe the pain experienced as a child the greater the need to relive it in a conscious attempt to overcome its attraction.[51] Says one adherent, "[SM] cauterizes our hurt, mends our shame, helps clear out the psychic basement, undo memories of the past."[52] By reliving the original pain under controlled circumstances, one can begin to break up established patterns so as to no longer unconsciously follow stimulus with response without regard to consequences. One can become no longer bound to doing to the self what has been done to the self in the past—pain expressed is an opening to freedom. As if softening the hardened mouth of the lesson horse, the body connects its powerful emotional memories to painful stimuli and responds by opening up to awareness and feeling.

Performance artist Bob Flanagan explains the masochism he portrays on stage as related to the pain he endured as a child from cystic fibrosis. Flanagan reproduces his childhood experiences of physical suffering in his performances, for example, the experience of being restrained while needles withdrew mucous from his chest. Flanagan says that he learned to transform pain into pleasure as a child when he suffered horrible stomachaches and tried to find relief by rubbing his body against the bedsheets. Eventually, the rubbing became pleasurable and he began to masturbate, blending the sensations of pain and pleasure, along with the loving care given to him while he was ill, with his own erotic energy. Lynda Hart sees Flanagan's life as a testament to Theodore Reik's definition of masochism as "pleasure and discomfort welded into simultaneity."[53] Flanagan's partner, Sheree Rose, describes his "supermasochism" as a process of bodily manipulation that propels him to a different state of consciousness. Flanagan concurs, adding that when he went to Catholic catechism as a child he immediately connected his own physical suffering to the Passion of Jesus. Identifying his pain with the Christian atonement, Flanagan began to flagellate himself using the song called "Trial before Pilot" on the album from *Jesus Christ SuperStar.* Linda Hart also notes that due to the traditions surrounding the saints many Catholic adherents of SM are drawn to suffering as a means to experience spiritual freedom.

Performance artists Orlan and Ron Athey have also found impetus for their public displays of pain in the martyrdom of the saints. The French performance artist called Orlan—herself a play on images and reality—says that she used her latest art project to increase consciousness in society about the impossibility and absurdity of the search for physical perfection. Since 1990 Orlan has undergone a series of surgical operations to reconstruct the features of her face using artworks said to capture the "perfect feminine"— for example, the forehead of Da Vinci's Mona Lisa, the chin of Botticelli's Venus, the lips of Boucher's Europa, the nose of Gerome's Psyche. The surgeries are televised and include Orlan's own commentaries along with those of physicians and philosophers. She says that the reconstruction of herself through deliberate acts of alienation is empowering because her body provides a mirror for women to see their own alienation. Having dubbed herself "Saint Orlan," she now sells vials of her liquefied flesh and blood, drained off by liposuction, during her "Carnal Art" performances. These "relics" help pay for her transformation and secure the parallel to the saints, whose bodies were said to contain healing powers. Drawing the connection to the saints is Orlan's tribute to Bernini's sculpture of Saint Teresa; she understands the sculpture to be the first postmodern artwork in Western history because of its combination of pain and ecstasy.[54]

After her "reincarnation" through the series of surgeries, her assumed name—Orlan—will be discarded for one chosen by an advertising agency, thereby completing the artist's message that it is impossible to find one's identity in physical perfection. Dubbed the "diva of dissection," the "biomorph queen," a "one-woman slasher film," the "doyenne of divasection," and an artist doing "cutting edge" work, Orlan has become a talk-show hit in France. While her constructions of identity cannot escape charges of self-promotion and sensationalism, she claims that her wounds are shamanic in the sense that the wounds in her body manifest the sicknesses of a society that overvalues eugenic ideals of physical perfection.[55]

Ron Athey is a controversial performance artist who likewise attributes his spiritual and political liberation to his encounters with the religious iconography of the saints and to his own masochistic practices. Raised in a strict Pentecostal setting by a virgin aunt who was convinced that she would bear the second coming of Christ, Athey was addicted by age fifteen to Valium prescribed for his hyperactivity. Since the hyperactivity may indicate an underresponsive nervous system, it is not surprising that Athey began experimenting with pain, including placing tweezers in a light socket, as a way to "free his mind" and overcome his boredom. After becoming a heroin addict with a criminal record, Athey discovered the martyrdom of the saints and began to map out his life by covering his entire body with what he calls "warrior markings." Gay and HIV positive, Athey inserts hypodermic needles into his arms during performances and uses a knitting needle to puncture a "crown of thorns" in his forehead. He says that the altered state of consciousness induced by physical pain exorcises the psychological demons that plague him, and that his performances are meant to communicate on a visceral level his struggle with self-loathing, suffering, healing, mortality, and redemption.[56] Like Flanagan and Orlan, Athey understands himself as transforming his masochism into a political statement and as channeling his pain and violent impulses into spiritual awareness.

EROS AND THE ASCETIC CONTINUUM

One key to whether the deliberate infliction of pain on one's own body is an escape from self-world or a means of entering into intimacy is the meaning of the wounds to the individual and to the community. Both pain and pleasure can be seen as serving erotic morality when they signify personal transformation, communal connection, or spiritual power. But as with all rituals, one person's power to transform or affirm the self through pain may be another's obsession or learned helplessness. We find both extremes in our society and also in religious asceticism, and they can be described as opposing ends of a continuum. Erotic approaches to morality judge attractions to pain and to pleasure not by the external act, or by rules about sensations being good or bad, but by whether they provide an opening to intimacy and compassion. Ascetic manipulations of the senses, even to the point of self-abuse, may be able to place one into the feeling body and thereby into connection with intersubjective being.

What distinguishes spiritual practice from merely masochistic or stress-induced behavior is not the act itself but the ways the body joins with consciousness during the act and the meanings given to the act. For example, the ascetic and the compulsive person may both sweep. The difference is that people sweeping compulsively will likely have no memory of picking up a broom and will reply, if asked, that they have no idea why they are sweeping, they just must. By contrast, the trained ascetic sweeps as a conscious and internally motivated act undertaken in the present moment. Every part of the body-mind is in touch not only with the broom, but with the ground, the wind, the sun, the birds, the garden. For the ascetic, the ritualized act of sweeping can be a trained expression of erotic connection from the inside out, extending sentience and empathetic feeling so as to place the individual within the world: it is the "touch-touching" of Grandin's squeeze machine. Rituals born of stress or trauma rarely are able to confer such meaning, or even any lasting emotional catharsis, primarily because the connections that weave our embodied and intersubjective lives remain unavailable when sensory expressions become palliative rather than instructional, or when they produce only private meaning.

It is not always easy to determine the differences between acts that deaden the flesh and remove the self from moral choice and acts that do the opposite, that is, correspond to Campbell's description of religious experience as feeling "the rapture of being alive." Context makes an extraordinary difference, and lines are not easily drawn between merely protective responses and active resistance to social pressures. This is why Julia Kristeva sees in the Victorian hysteric not only a victim but a rebel, a woman in the process of actively resisting the pressures on females to conform to society by taking on the symptoms of physical paralysis. Similarly, the anorexic might be seen as a victim who despises female flesh or as one who mocks the Western dualistic idea of mind over body, her skeletal frame a direct response to body-as-astronaut, a symbol of how removed we are from the body of the earth.[57]

When fasting becomes an act of resistance, it can be understood as a way to defend the needs of the flesh rather than a way to punish desire or achieve distance from the embodied self. As Gandhi's fasts for better treatment of the *harijans* (untouchables) illustrate, fasting as a moral and spiritual practice can connect one profoundly to the suffering of others and motivate one to alleviate it. Likewise, an act of self-mutilation performed alone in one's room in an effort to mask one's emotions is not the same as a similar act performed in the context of a tribal ritual signifying one's passage into adulthood.

Fakir Musafar, founder of the Modern Primitive movement, says that he practiced body modifications in deep isolation and shame for thirty years. His spiritual liberation came with the discovery of American Indian and Hindu cultures that associated forms of self-mutilation with states of grace rather than illness. Musafar has since been put into a Hindu Kavadi, a frame with ninety four-foot steel rods that pierce the upper chest and back. Dancing for hours with this fifty-pound load, he describes the experience as bliss. Musafar also pierced his chest with two large hooks and was suspended in the style of the Lakota Sioux Sun Dance in an experience that he describes as transformative: "I lifted out of my body, drifted up to a white light that radiated incredible love and understanding."[58] The indifference shown to pain in these acts and the experience of pain as transcendence is, he says, empowering. This experience is sought annually by 200,000 people in Penang, India, 500,000 in Kuala Lumpur, and 250,000 in Singapore.[59] This is the other side of both Kant and Sade, the home of the saints, the Christ, and the bodhisattvas, where eros is passion rather than pathology.

We have seen that on one end of the ascetic continuum is control over the flesh as represented by Augustine, Kant, and Schreber, with the intent of replacing sinful animal spirits with purified, culturally transmitted forces. This kind of asceticism shrinks morality into control over sexual behavior, often reducing it to a list of illegitimate pleasures identified with persons who, on the basis of their gender, race, class, or sexual preference, are especially given to lascivious behavior. I have argued that this intent to punish the senses is dissociative in nature because it is dualistic. Dissociation from the body and emotions leads to morality measured by duty and to laws dictated by an external authority assumed to guide culture from someplace outside of nature. Many of these obsessions with discipline are driven more by compulsion than compassion and have an unconscious determinism that leads the abused to become abusers. One truth of behaviorism, one that needs to be taken seriously for moral agency, is found here: to paraphrase Alice Miller, it is the absurd and hidden logic of addiction to do unto the self that which has already been done to the self.[60] Practices driven by repressed pain and fear of spontaneous feeling fail to nourish and can even subvert the human capacity for empathy, as we saw in chapter 3. Since the entire goal of this form of asceticism is to place controls on feeling equivalent to the mind's control over matter, it is always dualistic and in direct conflict with erotic forms

of morality. Moreover, this end of the ascetic continuum can eventually lead to fascism, especially when it fails to take seriously the
extent to which desire is the other side of the law. Many sadistic
kicks have been had here by authorities parading their pornographic forms of purity under the banner of religious morality.

Body as an Instrument of the Will

Saint Augustine's control over his sexuality bears all the markings
of obsession or compulsion. He referred to the "sin in his member"
as if the sexual organ were not part of him but manipulated by an
external other. He spoke of sexuality as if it were an illness and of
being frightened by the way sexual partners devour each other. His
behavior with food was also compulsive, and the lack of control
that he experienced with regard to both sex and food led him to
despise his own desire for pleasure and ultimately his own body.
Augustine called his obsession with sex a "disease of the flesh" and
appealed to images of slavery and bondage when attempting to understand it.[61] Instead of finding ways to take responsibility for his
desire, Augustine had all females removed from his presence. That
scapegoating allowed him to project responsibility for his insatiable appetite upon the women in his life and to project the responsibility for all human sin upon womankind in written works
that would guide Christian theology from the fourth century to
the present.[62]

Augustine's attempts to control his sexual urges led to noctur-
nal emissions and with them the enduring sensation that his body
was other than himself: "Like death, the onset and culmination of
sexual sensation mocked the will."[63] Because this failure of will was
in conflict with his image of himself, Augustine concluded that
sexual desire pointed to a breach in the human condition created
at the Fall of humanity in the Garden of Eden. Prior to the Fall, in
a "prelapsarian" condition, Augustine argued, the body was thor-
oughly subject to the will and purified of all desire. Adam sowed
his seed as he did any other mechanical operation. In the garden
prior to the Fall, sex was much less pleasurable than it is now, Augustine explained, more like vomiting or farting, which some men
can do at will even now.[64] As a consequence of sin, sex fell from
this purely utilitarian state into lust and thus "was itself responsible for the mindless continuation of a damned humanity, through

the act of intercourse."[65] Since there is still hope for salvation, Augustine reasoned, it would be better not to engage in sex and let the species die out than to seek this mindless pleasure. It may be helpful here to recall that passion (or pathos) was described in Greek culture as the meeting point between eros (bodily love) and thanatos (bodily death). Passion signified the most intimate moment in embodied love, where there is a death of the self in meeting the other—indeed, it is this moment that Augustine seems most to have feared.[66] Therefore, for Augustine passion could only be purified insofar as it completely shed eros and affirmed the death of the physical body, as it did in the sacrificial death of Christ, the only Passion that really matters.

A good contemporary example of the self-hatred and world indifference engendered by body-fearing religion is the cult called Heaven's Gate. Its leader, Marshall Applewhite, underwent castration (and recommended it to his followers) in order to deal with the (homo)sexuality which he could neither accept nor ignore. Applewhite used the idea of spiritual ascension to complete the divorce of mind from body, inserting into Darwin's theory of evolution the dualistic theological idea that one could evolve to a spiritually higher plane by leaving the shell of the body behind. Deliverance from the body looked easy, even somehow beautiful, as the thirty-nine "spent containers" lay peacefully in Rancho Santa Fe, one of the most elite communities of Southern California. There was nothing for them here, as they said, because life was much too ugly. Applewhite had come to understand our world as under the control of aliens, cosmic influencing machines from outer space programming all of us "human plants" to blindly follow meaningless normalcy.[67] But rather than engage in the serious and difficult business of transforming meaningless normalcy into effective agency, the members of Heaven's Gate chose to take flight to another world.

In similar fashion, leaders within the Christian church found it easier to think of the Kingdom of God as somewhere other than in the here-and-now rather than take up the task of social criticism as Jesus appears to have called people to do during his passionate, highly tactile ministry. There is no historical evidence that Jesus of Nazareth ever engaged in acts of deliberately punishing the flesh or viewed bodies as evil. If anything, according to the source called Q,

Jesus was accused of being "a glutton and drunkard" when compared to the ascetic John the Baptist.[68] The ministry of Jesus was steeped in healing forms of touch, and he consistently adopted the ethic of resisting unjust social structures rather than faulting the victims. Not surprisingly, those who adhere to the side of the ascetic continuum bent upon controlling the pleasures of the flesh understand the wounds of Jesus as a ticket for otherworldly redemption and an everlasting life unencumbered by the demands of the body. They are wounds that purify rather than bind us. On the other end of the ascetic continuum, if one takes his suffering in the context of his life, his ministry, and his Jewishness, the wounds of Jesus can be understood as they are by liberation theologians— as signifying the price of social justice, that is, pain endured for the sake of transforming society here and now, pain endured so that crucifixions will be eliminated, not emulated. His death is then viewed as a *kenosis,* or emptying, by which all forms of dualism are overcome and the Divine is made incarnate in the present.

Body as an Instrument of Feeling

On the side of the ascetic continuum that affirms rather than denies the flesh, we can distinguish ascetic practices that use pleasure and/or pain for the express purpose of bringing people back into their skin and in touch with the world. By amplifying the senses, ascetics seek to break out of numbing habits and the self-absorptions those short-circuitings of the flesh engender in order to feel, as Joseph Campbell put it, "the rapture of being alive." We find practices amplifying pain and pleasure in the traditions of Tantric Buddhism and in some forms of Christianity—the saints inherited a long-standing history in which pain was a primary means of making the suffering of Jesus a present and internal reality. Pain inflicted on the body was said to bring one closer to God by means of humbling the ego and focusing awareness. If we consider the intentional infliction of pain on one's own body as an avenue to erotic morality, then I would argue that it needs to be consciously performed in ways that bring about personal and social transformation. Such an example might be found in the self-immolation of Buddhist nuns and monks at the height of the Vietnam War, since their acts were intended to be communicative and socially transformative rather than simply suicidal expressions of hopelessness. Rather than attempts to end all feeling, their acts were attempts to express it.

Desert ascetics also belong to the erotic side of the continuum through their recognition that attention to and alteration of daily habits can transform consciousness. These monks and nuns are escaping not the world or their bodies, but the compulsive nature of the ego and the false images it projects. This is particularly true of ascetics who left urban Christianity after Constantine, when the church aligned itself with the forces of economic and political power in the Roman empire and thereby became caught up, like our own Christian right, in "the anxious, self-interested preservation of the world-as-it-is."[69] The desert into which these ascetics were drawn is the archetype of simplicity, the empty space where one can enter most deeply into the life of the senses. Thomas Merton has written that the sparse desert landscape has the capacity to "reject completely the false, formal self, fabricated under social compulsion in the world."[70] Through spiritual practices based upon the body's own erotic energy, ascetics learned to act rather than react by paying attention to sensations and emotions that were disclosed by altering habits of eating, sleeping, and speaking. Rather than being preoccupied by sin, the desert ascetics found ways to affirm the world as holy and escape the confines of the ego by attending to their own sensory attractions and repulsions as clues to the masks worn by the ego.

Many religious teachers have warned against engaging in ascetic practices in a way that separates the self from the world. According to the teachings of some rabbis, fasting when done obsessively increases pride, replaces good deeds, and damages one's relation to the community. They therefore recommended balancing fasting and feasting, with both acts done in moderation, that is, for only limited periods of time. The ascetic texts of early Christianity also expressed concerns about the isolation that ascetic acts can lead to, and so they recommended restricting fasting to not eating meat and not eating to satiety. One should always leave a meal, said John of Lycopolis, liking to eat a little more.[71] According to Belden Lane, in *The Solace of Fierce Landscapes,* through detailed attention to everyday acts, the desert ascetics practiced *apatheia,* or apathy, to things that did not matter so that they could focus on the things that did. This is why John Climacus called his ascetic practice the "tomb before the tomb," because it is the recognition of death in life that makes life precious and worth living.[72]

Pleasure and Pain as Openings to Intimacy

It is precisely the intimate moment that Saint Augustine feared, the death of the self in the meeting of the other that traditions which use pleasure and/or pain to affirm the flesh await. Where food and sexuality are viewed as sacraments, passion is affirmed as a way for the self to become part of a larger whole. Sexual climax has been valued by some spiritual traditions on the erotic side of our ascetic continuum because it is understood as a release from the need to be in control as well as a means to move away from the dominance of conceptual thought. One Christian theologian who sees sexual fulfillment as essential to nurturing human goodness describes being sexually aroused as "a biophysiological condition" that "breaks down egoism which otherwise confines the individual," thereby engendering responsiveness to others.[73] The same perspective is taken by Tantric Buddhism, known for its embrace of passion as central to the process of religious self-transformation. Tantra, from "tan," meaning to weave, is a form of Buddhism that arose in India as a protest against the privilege and scholasticism of religious leaders.[74] Tantric practitioners affirm the desire for sexuality and for food and the expression of emotions as spiritual ways to produce mutuality and reciprocity. Seeking to own their desires by immersion in them, Tantrics use ritual feasts with sacraments of meat and alcohol, poetry, dance, song, and yogic sexual postures to create the kind of intimacy that breaks through self-absorptions to unite self and world: "When the breath, fluids, and subtle energies of the yogic partners penetrate and circulate within one another" enlightenment can be found.[75] Tantrics say that release from habitual, narcissistic responses to life is found in that literal fluidity of boundaries, in this passionate circling of the flesh.

Sexual images are found in almost all forms of religious mysticism, where nondualistic images of ravishing and rapture, simultaneously gaining and losing, living and dying to the self, are given moral worth. Sexuality and feasting are affirmed in Tantric practice because the whole goal of ritualizing ordinary life is to break down dualistic thought, to experience the world in the mode of acceptance as it is, in its entirety, as "intrinsically pure and innately perfect."[76] But in other traditions it is possible that this same kind of theological ecstasy may be found through pain. For some female Christian saints, pain provided a more acceptable outlet for passion than pleasure in a theology that connected the sexuality of women with sin and evil. The connection between pain, pleasure, and spiritual transport portrayed in Bernini's sculpture of Saint Teresa of Avila captures her simultaneously in pain and in orgasmic rapture, the unification of immanence and transcendence making it impossible to say where pain leaves off and bliss begins. Saint Teresa wrote of her experience of God, "The pain was so great that it made me moan, and the sweetness this greatest pain caused me was so superabundant that there is no desire capable of taking it away."[77]

Many Christian saints had an obsessive fear of bodily contact and of hunger and thirst, perhaps reflecting their traumatic backgrounds as well as Church teachings that the enjoyment of bodily pleasures would make them captive to the sins of lust and gluttony. Touch and taste were seen to be particularly powerful and interrelated forces. Saint Basil, for example, linked the touch that occurs as taste with touch of the genitals. As if anticipating the Kate Moss image, Basil described the bodies of virgins as "dead"; a virgin's soul is so pure that she becomes "a sculpted image, unmoved by the assaults of the senses and unstimulated by thoughts and fantasies of pleasure."[78] Sins were confessed in the Middle Ages by addressing each of the five senses—considered windows through which evil entered the world—in the following manner: I saw, I heard, I smelled, I tasted, I felt.[79] Mary of Oignies is said to have feared her own pleasure so much that she prayed to have her sense of taste removed.[80]

But while many Christian saints lived on patrol of the senses with regard to pleasure, they seemed unconcerned about the use of pain to produce states of passion. Mary of Oignies mutilated herself according to the wounds of Christ out of guilt for breaking her fast during an illness, thereafter only eating black bread, which tore her throat and made it bleed. Catherine of Sienna's "joyful suffering" in which she ate only the Eucharist is said finally to have killed her, but it also took her to the heights of mystical passion. Female saints of the Middle Ages hacked at themselves until the blood flowed, using knives to make their bodies resemble the "bleeding meat they often saw in eucharistic visions." They wore hair shirts, bound their flesh tightly with twisted ropes, rubbed lice into self-inflicted wounds, thrust barbs and nettles into their breasts, and rolled in broken glass.[81]

Caroline Walker Bynum understands the masochistic behaviors of the female mystics as ways of expressing the body rather than controlling it, the goal being to realize the *"opportunity* of physicality."[82] If so, such acts would work to extend or heighten the senses while having the added value of appearing to others as a means of restricting them. Bynum thinks that medieval women used their bodies harshly for the purpose of developing an inner life and an internal sense of agency, as many contemporary women may be doing. To endure self-inflicted pain is to have power over the source of one's pain, a form of safety and freedom rarely allowed the oppressed. The female mystics of the Middle Ages found ways to place their ascetic activities in a schema of meaning that was neither self-absorbed nor capitulating to society, and they managed to do so, argues Bynum, in a tradition that found the passion of women highly suspect and almost supernaturally powerful. They took on pain in the context of a religious leader who is reported to have said, "This is my body which is broken for you."

As we have seen in our investigation of the masochistic and ascetic continuum, people who engage in some forms of masochism and in some forms of religious asceticism have found a powerful means of transformation and healing in pain. Like the desert landscape, pain has the capacity to shatter the ego, leaving us empty and open to fulfillment. To the shaman and the saint pain provides a vehicle for passage between worlds. The almost universal use of pain by tribal people in rituals and sacrifices signifies the association between pain and passing over from one form of life to another. This passage is most clearly seen in puberty and initiation rites where pain demarcates a new way of being, often with a visible sign of that commitment, such as scarring or tattooing. It may be the proximity of pain to death that gives pain transformative power. Pain forces a death of the self without literal death, and from this one emerges fundamentally altered.

THE SAINTS, HYSTERIA, AND
TRANSUBSTANTIATION OF THE FLESH

Pain is especially useful in reaching the emotional brain, since the memory of the limbic system with the amygdala as sentinel takes pain very seriously, and therefore pain has the power to regulate changes severe enough in consciousness to alter one's entire being. But if one is working out of harsh or oppressive conditions, as were many female mystics, the limbic brain could only be reached by seeking stimuli more painful than anything that had been experienced previously. In *Postmodernism and the Saints*, Edith Wyschogrod suggests that, far from practicing desirelessness, the female saints of the Middle Ages practiced unrestrained and excessive desire.[83] What contemporary scholars of ethics might find of value in the behavior of these women is the interpretation of their wounds and those of others as signifying the transformations that need to be made in society to release all of us from suffering. Their wounds tied them to the human condition instead of allowing them to transcend it, and thus their actions might be interpreted as supporting an ethic of resistance that takes embodiment seriously.

What made the saints saints was not that they engaged in deliberate acts of suffering, but that they transformed their suffering into care for the world, just as they believed Christ did. Learning to transform pain and pleasure into moral action is the heart of emotional intelligence and moral wisdom. The most literal way they transformed suffering into care in their bodies was through the transubstantiation of matter; this was said by hagiographers to occur as a result of their fasting. It is helpful in this regard to recall that in the Christian story Jesus is condemned to death around noon on the day of preparation for Passover, the time of the slaughter of the lambs by the temple priesthood. Jesus is offered up and later is referred to by writers of the New Testament as the "lamb without sin," his flesh and blood becoming the food that must be eaten to bring one into the presence of the holy. Indeed, the body of Christ was said to be so much a part of the body of the believer that one archaic meaning of "prosthesis" is the place in the church where the Eucharist was prepared. The Eucharist was the primary sacrament through which the Divine found vivid and visceral expression, Christ making their flesh new by assimilating it into his. They referred to the assimilation as being eaten by God, the moment of being eaten referring positively to the moment of pathos, in which the self is lost in the fluid intimacy. In the same way that the transubstantiated body of Christ nourished his followers, so, in eating only the Eucharist and suffering Christ's pain, the flesh of the saints was itself nourished and took on healing powers. Through fasting, their bodies were able to feed and heal those around them. As an affirmation of immanence, the saints "met God as flesh taken into, *eaten by,* flesh."[84]

Some medieval female saints "exuded milk, oil, or sweet saliva" that healed, according to hagiographies that explicitly connected their "failure to eat ordinary food or excrete ordinary fluids with exuding extraordinary liquids."[85] Catherine and Ludwina drank the nurturing sacrament from each other's breasts, just as Christ's blood that emerged from the wounds in his side was said to be transformed into the milk of the world. This is not stripping the material world of its sensuousness—the pathos of thanatos divorced from eros—this is a passionate extension of the senses in touch with both life and death, defying every breach in sentience. Transubstantiation is a prosthesis of eros that restores rather than depletes the world of its Being. It is also very like the way we come to our first meal, through the breast of the mother who endured the pain of birth for us, as Christ is said to have endured his Passion for the rebirth of humanity.

Understood in a nondualistic manner, transubstantiation is, first and foremost, not a ticket to life after death or a paid debt that allows us to continue to live in mindless patterns of overconsumption and self-absorption. Rather it is fundamentally erotic, an archetypal symbol of the role the redemption of the flesh can play in the transformation of culture. "If I grow thin from labor in the fields, my flesh becomes wheat. If that wheat is used for the host it becomes Christ's flesh," wrote Simone Weil, referring to her lifelong commitment to economic and social justice for workers as well as her revolutionary struggle against oppressive political regimes.[86] Such an embodied extension of the flesh circling in the here and now was admittedly not on the minds of the early Christian Church Fathers, who were suspicious of bodies and worked hard to separate the flesh of Jesus from our own by claiming it to be of a different ontological order. Mark Taylor has likened the

Christological reflections of the early Church Fathers to Gordon Gekko's reflections on greed in the movie *Wall Street*. Tertullian, for example, described the transubstantiated body of Christ as a mixture of gold and silver that can buy us a place in the heavenly kingdom. The material product of the resurrection, said Tertullian, was "electrum," the material out of which the first coins in the Western world were made, and the church later literalized the analogy by stamping insignia on Eucharist wafers to make them resemble metal coins or tokens that could be redeemed for life everlasting.[87]

For the female saints transubstantiation does not purchase a transcendence of the flesh in the next world but rather a transformation of the flesh in this world. A similar transformation can be found in the Mahamudra Chod, a meditation exercise taught by Machig Labdrön as part of an eleventh-century renaissance of Buddhism in Tibet, a renaissance that she helped to accomplish. The Chod, or "cutting," is a ritual meant to cut attachments to the individual ego by producing respect for the transitory nature of existence and the relational nature of our being. In the exercise the practitioner, or Chodpa, visualizes consciousness leaving the body through the top of the skull, forming an image of a *dakini*—a wrathful creature with a crescent-shaped knife—who cuts off the top of the head of the practitioner. The top of the head, or skullcap, then becomes a cooking bowl, suspended over a flame, into which is placed the rest of the practitioner's body, cut into pieces as one would any meat. The flesh and blood of the practitioner transforms itself into a nectar which is then fed to every existing being and satisfies all of them completely. Like in the Eucharist, each participant in the ritual is taken up into the whole and fulfilled. The Chod is meant to convey an understanding that there are no boundaries in the fulfillment and suffering of existents, that what is life to one of us is death to another, and that even though our lives are ephemeral we can help to nourish and create bliss in each other.[88]

Other religious practices have been undertaken for similar purposes and stand, as does Chod, in marked contrast to the masochistic forms of bulimia and anorexia with which we are more familiar. For example, Hindu ascetics are guided by a meditative exercise, found in the Upanishads, that seeks to connect one's self to the universe as one contemplates eating the universe, piece by piece, until there is nothing left. "Hunger is our food," say the Sufi, recalling how the search for wholeness is part of the erotic life force.[89] In the *Jakarta Tales,* the Buddha is said to have offered his body many times on behalf of those in need, including a lioness so hungry that she would have eaten her own cubs had he not made an offering of his own body by throwing himself off a cliff above her.

The power to transform matter into a sacred and nourishing presence was recapitulated by the saints in their self-inflicted wounds, stigmata by which these women emulated the Christ. They bled from the nose, the mouth, the hands and the feet, anywhere but from the vagina—still too much a symbol of the power of women and nature, the cyclic worldly incarnation that in its capacity to create life through birth seemed to threaten the power of the Christian sacrifice. The suffering of these women, in other words, had to transcend femaleness to be affirmed. Since according to Christian tradition the most carnal and insatiable women were those who were independent of males, the nuns of the Middle Ages were only for a brief time accorded the authorization of power in the transformation of matter. Some scholars find increased male scrutiny of these women partially responsible for the cultural linking of women with witchcraft and then later with hysteria, as women became scapegoats for the repression of feeling.

As diagnosed retrospectively by Charcot, Freud, and Janet, Saint Teresa of Avila was the first to be called a hysteric due to her description of the experience of God as simultaneously blissful and painful. Similar diagnoses followed for Catherine of Sienna and the more contemporary Simone Weil. Like Catherine, Weil died of malnutrition and tuberculosis, a "holy anorexic" accused of starving herself in working to bring about a more just world.[90] In response to the diagnosis of hysteria, Simone de Beauvoir wrote that Saint Teresa of Avila was not in bondage to her nervous system but inspired by "the immediate presence of God as lover" and an intensity of faith which "penetrates to the most intimate regions of her flesh."[91] Following de Beauvoir's lead, French feminists Julia Kristeva, Luce Irigaray, and Hélène Cixous have also struggled to affirm women's mixing of pain and pleasure without reducing it to the charge of masochism.

Rather than reading the passionate excesses of the female saints as symptoms of illness, it is possible to read them as manifestations of personal and social transformation. Here Foucault's description of how physicians of the nineteenth century viewed the origins of hysteria may be instructive: "One fell ill from *too much feeling;* one suffered from an excessive solidarity with all the beings around one . . . one was the victim of everything which, on the surface of the world, solicited the body and the soul."[92] The hysteric was, in other words, a victim of erotic intimacy, the moment in which the self discovers its own fluidity in relation to others. It is this form of hysteria that befell the female saints and the desert ascetics as well as bodhisattvas and the Christ, moral exemplars who take on the suffering of others for the sake of their redemption.

5

MINDFUL TOUCH
Body as Awareness

> If one really knew how unhappy it is making
> this whole planet that we all try to avoid pain
> and seek pleasure—how that was making us so
> miserable and cutting us off from our basic
> heart and our basic intelligence—then we
> would practice meditation as if our hair was
> on fire. We would practice as if a big snake
> had just landed in our lap.
> —Pema Chödrön, *When Things Fall Apart*

A udre Lorde wrote in her cancer journals that there was a terrible clarity of vision that accompanied her illness and that she found to be empowering when faced directly. The cancer in her breast meant that there was no longer a time of waiting, that life had become filled fully with the present, the "now" pushing everything else away. What remained was the urgency to reclaim the visceral awareness of her ephemeral physical nature. She described this new consciousness as a "burst of light," leaving the words of Simone de Beauvoir echoing in her ears: "It is in the recognition of the genuine conditions of our lives that we gain the strength to act and our motivation to change."[1] The end of things as we have known them often carries the force necessary to break us out of our comforting habits with their thick physical and psychological enclosures. In whatever moment those enclosures begin to crumble, we sense that it is the impermanence and fragility of life that makes it precious and real. Both pain and pleasure have the potential to force awareness of our own indeterminacy—and that recognition may lead us to acknowledge that the world is no more determined than we are.

I want to conclude this analysis of our embodied lives by suggesting that the Buddhist practice of mindfulness may be a way for us to be in touch with erotic sensibilities through forms of awareness which can act, like a diagnosis of cancer, to clarify the richness and fluidity of life lived in the present. By providing techniques through which we can literally come to our senses, mindfulness uses the present—the unique moment of immanence in which all the concrete particulars and interconnections of life are available—as the means to bring us into intimacy. Radical immanence is an embodied form of transcendence through which the self gains a more inclusive sense of being by finding release from the more narrow cravings of the ego, cravings based largely on what is absent rather than present. Along with eye contact and comforting touch, the practice of living in the present is one of many "squeeze machines" made available to us by enhanced bodily awareness, the temporal home of erotic morality in which we feel sustained rather than assaulted by the myriad of things. In mindfulness we become fellow travelers with Temple Grandin, Donna Williams, and all of those recovering from the effects of isolation, stress, trauma, and addiction in their efforts to find the resources to feel the sensory, emotional, and intersubjective connections of ordinary life.

To clarify the conceptual dynamics and practical utility of erotic morality, we must find ways to enter the squeeze machine ourselves. Therefore, I want to conclude this investigation by addressing spiritual practices that are the physiological and psychological equivalents of embodied, tactile love. Understanding the body as prison, object, other, and instrument has helped bring to attention the dynamics that weave our sensory and emotional lives into somatic postures and potentialities. Those somatic states regulate the thresholds of sensory and emotional touch and thus help to construct the physical, moral, and spiritual health of the individual and the society. Lived in mindfulness, our daily acts can open up and extend our sensory lives in ways that allow us to feel cared for, capable of change and empathy, in short, empowered rather than victimized by erotic intimacy.

For a society living largely in a state of denial and insensitivity, mindfulness training, such as *vipassana* (or insight) meditation, is a hopeful solution. Vipassana cultivates detailed awareness of sensory, emotional, and mental processes. The practice begins with mental and bodily calm and proceeds as an act of attention to the sensations we are experiencing in each moment. The philosophy behind this sensory investigation is that the experience of one's own somatic states as they arise provides direct evidence about the nature of the self, prevents dissociation by yoking mind to body, and restores free will by breaking down habitual conditioning which otherwise portrays itself as freedom. The recognition of feeling as it happens is the touchstone of emotional intelligence and in many ways captures the essence of the dharma, or teachings, of the Buddha. The attention is less on what is being done than on having full awareness of what one is feeling in the doing, providing a visceral sense of consequences, value, and meaning. The goal of mindfulness—like that of the *apatheia* practiced by the desert ascetics—is to become open to what is valuable and closed to what is trivial, creating belonging through awareness of one's being in the world as it is, not as one would like it to be or as it might have been in the past. Meditation can move us toward moral action by eliminating the frivolous, defined by Tibetan teacher Chögyam Trungpa as "the extra and unnecessary mental and physical acts with which we keep ourselves busy in order not to see what is actually happening in a situation."[2]

Since monitoring the body in its relationship to the world is very likely the first function of the neocortex in evolution, mindfulness provides a way that reason can be trusted to have epistemological and moral integrity. Through sustained attention to the body, mindfulness builds upon and extends the adaptive qualities of our evolutionary history rather than feeds the dissociative tendencies that separate us from nature. Detached from the ego's cravings but in no way divorced from the body, mind-body is no longer open to dualistic constructions that turn the body into object or other. The restoration of the subjective life of one's own body serves to place the self in the world with other subjective bodies. In touch again with intersubjective life, the mind can now once again serve the body rather than attempt to rule it, bringing awareness, knowledge, creativity, and imagination to the cultivation of freedom and wisdom. James Austin's exhaustive study, *Zen and the Brain*, proposes that meditation and the daily practices that accompany it act to "help release basic, preexisting neurophysiological functions" and thus have the potential to "gradually reshape brain and body, behavior and attitudes, consciousness itself."[3] Meditation, he argues, is so attuned to the structures of our neurology that it provides another way for us to understand how the human brain works. The opposite of the flight-or-fight response, meditation has been shown to reduce stress, anxiety, and depression, increase perceptual acuity, enhance academic and athletic performance, and help people break the addictions of substance abuse. It restores connections of the amygdala to the prefrontal cortices and breaks down reactions triggered by habits, thereby helping to cultivate openness to new possibilities.[4]

Though any nondualistic spiritual practice may be helpful to integrate mind and body, self and other, and culture and nature, for our purposes Buddhism is an important path to consider because of its explicit use of the body as a spiritual teacher. As suspicious of the undisciplined mind as Christianity has been of the undisciplined body, Buddhist traditions have a great deal to teach us about the need to face suffering directly and the points at which desire becomes pathogenic. Buddhism has the further advantage of asserting a fully relational or nonessentialist ontology consistent with erotic intimacy in its notion of the self as "empty" or composed of relations. Meditation can also act to break down behavioral conditioning, the thick skin and rigid musculature that prevents choice and responsibility. Ann Klein describes mediation as "consciously seeking a more spacious way of experiencing embodiment" with the goal of remaining open to the world but inwardly free.[5] In contrast to the physiology of the Border collie confined in a tiny backyard, meditation has been described in physiological terms as "giving a huge, luscious meadow to a restless cow."[6]

A form of sensory consciousness, mindfulness can be performed as a seated meditation or through practices that include movement—walking, breathing, chanting, eating—or "the simple experience of being physically present to oneself, others, and the physical elements" (for example, just paying attention to the flavors and textures of food in your mouth is mindfulness).[7] Exercises that include the motion of the body seem to attract people with high cognitive anxiety and low somatic anxiety—the focus on the body acts to take them out of their heads by lowering the center of gravity. People who feel their anxiety more in the body than in their cognitive lives seem drawn to seated meditation.[8] Yet even in seated meditation such as Zen, the popular stereotype of meditation as a means to escape rather confront reality is rejected. The practitioner of Zen is drawn into immediate sensory experience and even e-motion by the use of tangible objects, such as a bell, a statue, a flower, or the stick of the Zen master who, with one strong whack across your flesh, brings you into your body and the present.

What we find in mindful attention to our embodied being is the erotic life that Kant and Schreber were obsessed with escaping. As we have seen, they used the stick to deaden rather than awaken the flesh. Mindfulness, in its detailed attention to and discipline of the body and acts of consumption, can be likened to the practices of both these men, except that it is designed for the opposite purpose, namely, to break down rather than build up our sensory defenses. If performed correctly, mindfulness should increasingly move one toward what Ruth Denison, a teacher of vipassana meditation, calls "tactile consciousness." Denison is known for her ability to help the practitioner bring the flesh of the world to life by investigating the sensations of one's own body bit by bit—the neck, throat, tongue, nostrils, lungs, shoulders, hands, buttocks, thighs, feet. Tactile consciousness is the visceral experience of what Buddhists call emptiness, a burst of light so profoundly in touch with the dynamics of our existence that one's own cells reverberate with the sentient truth of impermanent and interrelational being. What occurs in the depth of that awareness is the resurrection of one's own flesh and with it the sweet and abiding compassion for all likewise embodied beings. Sandra Boucher describes precisely the same experience I had at one of Denison's retreats at Joshua Tree, California, after several days of meditation: "Soon I began to experience the flesh and bone of my body as living tissue, as cells vibrating with a life of their own and participating in the constant flow and change of all life. . . [with it arose an] all-inclusive compassion for one's sister beings, animal and human."[9]

Tactile consciousness is the highest level of eros available to us. In feeling one's own flesh as vital and vulnerable, the flesh of the world is made present and with it the gift of life itself. Buddhist monk Thich Nhat Hanh describes the perception of one living cell as a sentient form of grace because "the presence of one cell implies the presence of all the others, since they cannot exist independently, separate of the others."[10] No one cell could exist apart from the emptiness in which we "interare," thus one cell ultimately implies the existence of the whole of organic life on earth with a five-billion-year evolutionary history. Everything is as it is due to its relations, or as the Buddhist doctrine of dependent co-arising states, "This is like this because that is like that." When our own incarnation is affirmed through mindfulness, the ontology of emptiness strikes us like the stick of the Zen master: you are here, alive, perceiving, breathing, drinking, and eating with an entire biosphere to support you. Nhat Hanh turns to the central Buddhist scripture on dependent co-arising, the *Avatamsaka Sutra*, to explain the meaning of emptiness as "interbeing." Using a sheet of paper as an example, he explains that to say the paper is empty is to say that it is composed of non-paper elements: "A cloud is a non-paper element. The forest is a non-paper element. Sunshine is a non-paper element. The paper is made of all the non-paper elements to the extent that if we return the non-paper elements back to their sources, the cloud to the sky, the sunshine to the sun, the logger to his father, the paper is empty. Empty of what? Empty of a separate self. It has been made by all the non-self elements, non-paper elements. . . . Empty, in this sense, means that the paper is full of everything, the entire cosmos."[11]

If tactile consciousness can allow us to feel kinship with the myriad of things that create, sustain, and nourish us, then that feeling of being comforted may provide us with the moral strength to give that care back. Morally, everything changes with the experience of emptiness because one's incarnation as interbeing and impermanence creates a consciousness of gratitude and responsibility. When we cease to be lazy about perception, perception can become a form of grace. Or, to paraphrase Rachael Carson, the more attention we pay to sentience the easier it will become to actively resist indifference and to lose our appetites for frivolous, addictive choices. Because mindfulness can teach us to maintain healthy thresholds of sensory and emotional feeling while at the same time extending rather than withdrawing from intersubjective life, it can provide a subjective form of materialism, or a materialization of subjectivity, that is erotic rather than either behaviorist or eugenic in character. As such, mindfulness is political because the restoration of the senses is also a restoration of our ties to the material world and to the consequences of our actions. Buddhist emptiness, as seen in the example of the cell or the paper, is reminiscent not only of Darwin's theory of evolution, but of Marx's materialist understanding of labor and the products of labor as composed of their relations. Tactile consciousness connects us with the extended network of our biological and economic lives. In so doing, rather than creating new moral systems, it creates a subjective life attuned to bodies—or, to use Marx's language, a materialism that takes subjectivity seriously.

SANCTUARIES AND PRISONS: CREATING PERMEABLE SPACE

It is said that the Buddha grew up in an artificial environment not unlike our own. The young Siddhartha Gotama was provided every form of excess in a luxurious estate surrounded by high, impenetrable walls meant to shelter him from illness, aging, death, and ascetic life. His father's elaborate palace—both sanctuary and prison—was constructed to keep Gotama from witnessing the sights of suffering prophesied to draw him into a spiritual quest. Upon his inevitable escape from the confines of the palace, Gotama is described in Buddhist scripture as making his way into the countryside until he comes upon a landscape that "matters" upon him with a force that reverberates the entire sentient condition: "There he saw the soil being ploughed, and its surface, broken with the tracks of furrows, looked like rippled water. The ploughs had torn up the sprouting grass, scattering tufts of grass here and there, and the land was littered with tiny creatures who had been killed and injured, worms, insects, and the like. The sight of all this grieved the prince as deeply as if he had witnessed the slaughter of his own kinsmen. He observed the ploughmen, saw how they suffered from wind, sun, and dust, and how the oxen were worn down by the labor of drawing. . . . He then alighted from his horse and walked gently and slowly over the ground, overcome with grief. He reflected on the generation and the passing of all living things, and in his distress he said to himself: 'How pitiful all this!'"[12]

In response to this experience, Gotama left his life of mindless pleasure and began to punish the flesh. He gave up eating as if he were personally responsible for every plowed furrow that ever existed. He punished his body severely until finally, on the edge of his own annihilation, he recognized this suicide as equivalent in its narcissism to his former overindulgence. Intent on finding ways to affirm life within the midst of suffering without indulging the ego, he decided to eat in moderation and nurse himself to health. His teachings explore the interplay between desire and suffering as part of the human condition, the urges to exist and not to exist pulling us back and forth in ways that create dissociative, addictive, and sadomasochistic behaviors in all of us.

Trying to understand our failure to respond compassionately and creatively to a world filled with suffering, Mary Kay Blakely remarks, "Certainly, future historians studying the arms race, global pollution, our immune-system dysfunctions and the whopping world debt will think it odd we didn't 'know' what was going on."[13] Hiding behind our own walls, many of us remain bystanders who end up, by default, perpetuating a world filled with victims and perpetrators. As in Grandin's slaughterhouse, the sadists take the kill chutes and almost everyone else looks the other direction. Blakely is intrigued, however, by the few who are able to engage in political action in spite of the immensity of the pain and complexity of the problems that they encounter. She speculates that people who can act in a painful world with compassion must have some kind of "damping apparatus" that prevents them from "being swamped by the unbelievability of life as it really is."[14]

Blakely became interested in the damping apparatus that protects compassionate agents when, struggling with her own lack of such protection, she was sent by the editor of a national women's magazine to investigate the outbreak of agoraphobia that occurred soon after the nuclear incident at Three Mile Island. Agoraphobia is traditionally called "the housewife's disease" because most of the people afflicted are women; symptoms include panic attacks, elevated blood pressure and heart rate, and fear of imminent danger and open spaces. The cases Blakely was sent to investigate appeared within months of the nuclear accident when vans combed the streets warning people to shut doors and windows and telling women not to breast-feed infants due to the possibility of radiation poisoning. Her research showed that psychologists find agoraphobics to be imaginative, intelligent, and creative, "but extremely uncooperative when it [is] time to 'come back to reality.'" She concluded that the reason these women no longer wanted to face reality was because "reality wasn't all that appealing to the Three

Mile Island women anymore—they were depressed, and their breasts hurt. After spending time with these highly articulate, self-imprisoned women, [Blakely] came to think of them as the canaries in the coal mines of suburbia, the first sensitive casualties in a toxic environment that would eventually affect us all."[15]

Searching for a positive angle for her story, Blakely eventually found at Three Mile Island a group of agoraphobics who had joined a local environmental organization. These women were motivated by rage, pain, and compassion to leave their houses, find each other, and enter public, political space. They used their illness and pain to touch the same world that had, without their consent, touched them quite cruelly with its interbeing. Turning pathos into a force for resistance rather than death, they realized that their healing had to come from the same source as their illness: they could only treat themselves by treating society. Their aching breasts and feelings of imprisonment made them ready to address the pathology, and they recognized that it lay not within them but in societies filled with people who feared and hated each other enough to give birth to the poison that is nuclearism—a magnificent example of how destructive our protective mechanisms can become.

Blakely's editor refused to accept her story for publication. He said that she had confused the psychological with the political and that the story was far too depressing for their readers, who just wanted "to feel happy."[16] This, she notes, was also the response of *Time* to Rachel Carson's *Silent Spring*, which detailed the biomagnified circling of the flesh that accompanies the use of DDT. Perhaps guided by Kant's dictum that morality requires us to be cheerful, the editors of *Time* concluded that *Silent Spring* would frighten readers. Those who measure the bottom line by profit or by the status quo would rather we all stayed locked up in our palaces, experiencing life through the prosthesis of the computer screen or television. Better to diagnose these women as ill or otherwise individually deficient than to suggest that what affects one of us affects us all. Erotic morality requires us to stop pretending that our walls cannot be penetrated or that devising impenetrable walls is what we really need to make us healthy. Since the monsters we create in isolation follow us into our cells, our nervous systems, our bloodstreams, and our neighborhoods, remaining open to the world and in dialogue with our monsters may be the only way to prevent our being consumed by them.

Clinging to the illusion of impermeable boundaries provides a sense of comfort, but too often the same defenses we use to prevent being touched also prevent us from receiving what we need to care about ourselves and others. Because we can feel supported only to the extent to which we let our defenses down, we must work to soften the rigid parts of us that hold the world at a distance. As we have seen, even for autistics living in a closed system is overwhelming. But for those of us who are not autistic, life lived as if it ends at your own skin creates a restricted environment that leads to self-destructive behaviors not unlike those exhibited by the monkeys in Harry Harlow's sadistic experiment. Therefore, part of moral practice should be to look for the places that we are rigid or stuck, as partners do when they face off in the playful "push-hand" exercises of T'ai Chi. Standing face-to-face with feet firmly planted, partners use their hands to gently push the bodies of each other in a fluid dance. Any rigid places discovered are mutually revealed to be the places that leave us vulnerable when pressure is applied. I push at the place where you will not give, disrupting your balance—and you do likewise to me. One wins at pushhands by relaxing into one's own flexible strength, giving when pushed, and by using the other's rigidity as leverage to push him or her off center. The lesson is one that any good masseuse knows well. The painful parts of us, although rigid and hardened, ironically act to make us vulnerable because the protections we construct around them to prevent being touched also keep us from the possibility of being healed.

At the same time, living within permeable space does not mean eliminating the protections we need to keep from feeling overwhelmed. What we need as moral agents is a squeeze machine that takes us into our own inner lives and those of others, but with a damping apparatus that keeps us from becoming paralyzed by the pain we find there. I feel quite certain that Grandin would not take her squeeze machine into the slaughterhouse, certainly not into a hoist-and-shackle operation, which, even with the emotional protection her autism provides, leaves her with nightmares. To do so would compromise the equanimity that allows her to function in painful conditions while remaining compassionate. To be morally healthy, all of us need worldly relations that open and close like the membranes of cells, themselves vast and intricate ecosystems which create appropriate exchanges between the inner and the outer. Eros lives there, in the midst of exchanges on the borders, providing passageways between the inside and the outside, like the doors of our houses and our skin itself.

Joan Iten Sutherland helps us imagine the kind of permeability we need when she describes the effects of an illness that left her immune system out of balance. Her immune dysfunction meant that in some areas of her body her protective systems shut down entirely, leaving her utterly vulnerable to infection. In other areas her body developed autoimmune reactions in which her protective systems attacked healthy parts of her body.[17] In both ceasing to protect and in attacking itself, her body became a meditation on the kind of defenses that fail us and the sadomasochistic responses produced by them. By contrast, a healthy immune system recognizes all parts of the body as its own. By leaving no cells totally vulnerable and by not allowing other cells to grow out of control, healthy immune systems maintain a porous and balanced sense of relatedness. One might say that borders are constructed responsibly. According to Ann Klein, this is also what the dharma prescribes, that we "understand our physical boundaries as selectively porous in ways that allow us to receive what is helpful and release what is not." If we can create permeable borders in this selective manner, then "the space through which we understand ourselves to move is expanded."[18] The space Klein has in mind is neither the outer space of the astronaut nor the inner space of the narcissistic ego—the isolated spaces that Hannah Arendt said defined the twofold flight from responsible relations in the modern era. Rather Klein is talking about space that is empty and therefore replete with interbeing: self-other, culture-nature, body-mind, composed in "a system of countless nets intertwining in all directions in multidimensional space."[19]

Erotic forms of homeostasis may originate and be maintained within this selectively porous space; however, determining what is helpful to take in and to release in such a fluid system is a highly complicated matter. Since each of us are as empty as Nhat Hanh's piece of paper, taking in what is good for me is partially unique to me and also has to occur in relation to what is good for many others. Indeed, it could be argued that in such an organic system, one's skin stretches as far back into the past as the first cell and as far out into space as the biosphere and the energy that sustains life on this planet. Evolution witnesses to all our previous existences, says Nhat Hanh: look around and you will see them—rock, gas, mineral, plants, animals, and trees.[20] Because this is nondualistic space, we find ourselves trying to take in what is helpful and release what is not in the midst of an ontology in which everything in the world somehow touches everything else, the butterfly's wings flapping in Beijing contributing to the weather next month in New York City. Boucher implies as much when she interprets the practice of taking refuge in the dharma as "a friendly, accepting relationship with the 'world out there' and the 'world in here.'"[21]

Our permeability must therefore address many of the same issues Donna Williams addressed when she struggled to determine the boundaries of her own skin, including learning how to balance openness to the world with the world's ability to consume those who are open to it. Williams understands the dilemma quite well, explaining that she was "born alienated from the world" but later came to realize "that the world also makes nonautistic people that way. Perhaps in some strange way I started at the end and tried to work my way back."[22] Williams worked her way back into her own skin and porous, extended relations by waging battles to join the world and battles to keep the world out. She applied her own kind of mindfulness that included taking refuge from chaotic environments in order to reclaim her own sensory experience. She also recognized when her sanctuaries became prisons and responded preeminently by killing Willie—the persona she created to escape painful encounters. These are things that we too must do.

Pema Chödrön guides our construction of a viable damping apparatus by recognizing that the places where we touch the world are home to both our neuroses and our wisdom. Chödrön is a practitioner of *tonglen* meditation, which she describes as meditation for difficult times. Once associated with lepers, who obviously know a great deal about skin, touch, pain, and boundaries, tonglen is part of Tibetan mind or heart training. The practice is meant to awaken compassion by finding and then breaking through all the places we are stuck, that is, the places where we turn to denial, control, or apathy rather than to compassionate awareness. The basic idea is to create permeable relations by reversing our inclination to turn away from pain. Since our neuroses and our wisdom are both products of our erotic lives, we need to use heightened sensations and emotions as teachers. Instead of running from moments that scare us, Chödrön recommends that we "lean into the edge," allowing our most intense sensations and emotions to become somatic markers able to guide and transform us. If we shut down to our most intense feelings—the most frightening, the most irritating, the most infuriating—then all of our other feelings begin to pale, leaving us feeling vaguely unreal and using our senses as markers only for preference rather than for insight and transformation. Right there, in the most chaotic, anxious, or repugnant moments, "in that inadequate, restless feeling is our wisdom mind."[23] Or, as Audre Lorde puts it, "The erotic is a measure between the beginnings of our sense of self and the chaos of our strongest feelings."[24]

Tonglen constructs a damping apparatus by using the model of the wounded healer and the belief that it is precisely the things we run from that have the power to cure us. As a breathing meditation, Tonglen asks us to breathe in everything we find fearful and painful, and then breathe out the happiness and joy that we would rather keep. By going against the grain of our habitual life, which has long associated pain and pleasure with punishment and reward, the practice pokes holes in the armor around our hearts, making possible the beginning of awakening. Such a practice, Chödrön argues, can create a more open landscape and a less restricted heart, in essence, extending the selectively porous nature of our skin.[25] Sitting still with one's basic energy softens one up, allowing freedom from patterns set upon tightening and pushing away. Alice Walker says of tonglen that one can actually feel the heart respond physically to the practice, meeting the constriction with relaxation, opening to the world.[26]

Chödrön suggests that the most efficient way for us to awaken compassion is look at pain directly, without averting our eyes. Looking away from pain creates confusion, guilt, and anger. If we can learn to keep the heart open in situations when it usually shuts down, our falseness will be stripped away, leaving us able eventually to experience a more genuine sense of joy. Machig Labdrön, Tibetan teacher and master of the Chod, gave her students the same advice she learned from her teachers: "Approach what you find repulsive, help the ones you think you cannot help, and go to places that scare you." Everyone must start from where they are, and no one but the most advanced practitioner, the one who takes the vow of the bodhisattva, can take in the pain and remain compassionate toward all sentient beings. Joanna Rogers Macy suggests using the apocalyptic vision of nuclear war or nuclear accident as a reference for meditation on the world's beauty and fragility in relation to human fear, unawareness, and the political work to be done. Chögyam Trungpa, Chödrön's teacher and founder of the Naropa Institute, used the experience of once having witnessed boys stone a puppy to death as the touchstone of his meditation on how our failure to acknowledge emptiness creates suffering for others and for ourselves. Beldon Lane finds the moral equivalent of the ascetic's desert landscape—sensitive to both our inner and outer worlds—in the oncology waiting room, the AIDS hospice, or inner-city neighborhoods. Seen in this light, it is less surprising that Grandin says she learned to care in the slaughterhouse and less surprising that the sages predicted Gotama's spiritual path would begin only if he had a taste of suffering. My own practice, such as it is, began with the death of my father, when I spent the last ten days of his life being present to the moment in acceptance and compassion. The nondualistic perspective, in which one attempts neither to recoil from pain nor to squeeze the life out of pleasure, is also in line with the moral analogy of the immune system. Immunity can actually be weakened by taking too much medication, as the proliferation of antibiotic-resistant bacteria reveals, while immunity is actually strengthened by absorbing minimal doses of the disease one is trying to prevent, as in the case of vaccines.[27]

Because we are each the sum total of relations that are unique, there are no clear rules for finding permeable space. Chödrön therefore likens the moral task to a koan. Learning what it means to shut down and to be open is, she says, "the path of the warrior." The path of the warrior is the path of compassionate vulnerability and begins with the realization that the extent to which we fail to accept who we are and what we feel is the extent to which we either shut down, hurt ourselves, or project our pain onto others. Morally, the difference between a prison and a sanctuary is that prisons are enclosed spaces that, whether mental or physical, work to deaden eros and strengthen neuroses through isolation, addiction, and violence. Sanctuaries provide enough open space for us to awaken to our erotic lives and come to use them in the service of wisdom. Paradoxically, we can only reduce our own suffering and that of others by finding the cracks in the armor of our defenses.[28]

Lorde took the path of the warrior. Deeply in touch with her own body, she was appalled by the presumption of hospital caretakers that she would never know the difference between her own sensuous breast and the pink one made of lambs wool that she was given to hide the fact that her breast was missing. Told to wear the prosthesis when she came to the doctor's office because without it she would depress other patients, Lorde refused. She saw the artificial breast as one of many masks we wear to pretend that social problems are nonexistent. Lorde had a strong damping apparatus and little patience for denial or numbness, both of which she explicitly associates with pornographic sensibilities. Like the agoraphobics who left their houses, she used the place that the world had touched her most cruelly to create meaningful resistance. She imagined all the one-breasted women in America marching on Washington, sans prostheses, warriors in the tradition of their ancient Amazon sisters, who cut off their right breasts to exercise greater finesse with bows and arrows. In mass, they would demand that the use of carcinogenic, fat-producing steroids and hormones in beef be outlawed and that the American Cancer Society make available research concerning the connections between eating animal flesh and breast cancer as it had done with tobacco and cancer of the lungs. Her wounds, like those of the shaman and the saint, were taken as teachings about the nature of wisdom, openings through which to touch the world and heal it. Lorde says, "For me, my scars are an honorable reminder that I may be a casualty in the cosmic war against radiation, animal fat, air pollution, McDonald's hamburgers and Red Dye No. 2, but the fight is still going on, and I am still a part of it. I refuse to have my scars hidden or trivialized behind some lambswool or silicon gel. I refuse to be reduced in my own eyes or in the eyes of others from warrior to mere victim, simply because it might render me a fraction more acceptable or less dangerous to the still complacent, those who believe if you cover up a problem it ceases to exist."[29]

NEUROSIS AND WISDOM: COMING TO OUR SENSES

To dwell mindfully in permeable space we need first to bring our senses back to life in ways that enhance our capacity for erotic connections to the world around us. Reclaiming the sentient awareness to promote circlings of the flesh necessary to our physical, psychological, and moral well-being demands healing the places we have become numb or hypersensitive to touch as well as softening rigidities of body and ideology. These are the places that produce nonadaptive, neurotic behaviors by imprisoning us in the nonrelational space in which bodies become objects or other. As we are increasingly coming to realize, the product of life lived in closed systems is erotic life degraded, with our failures at intimacy reborn into the world as pollution, violence, poverty, and disease. Buddhist analysis of the interplay between our sensory and psychological lives can help us understand how eros stands at the borders where we construct the openings and closures to the world in healthy and unhealthy manners.

Habitual conditioning creates one place where desire begins to become pathogenic because it leaves us desensitized, open to addiction, closed to present experience, and therefore inwardly less free. The loss of plasticity leaves us out of touch with our inner lives and open to control by external authorities and forces. From a Buddhist perspective, the way the individual ego constructs false identities is clear in multiple personality and dissociative disorders, but those pathologies are only exaggerations of the ways we construct identities around fixed borders by means of habitual conditioning. The moral problem lies not in our senses, but in the ways our mental lives insert themselves between us and our feelings, much as the persona Willie did for Donna Williams. Asked to explain from a Buddhist perspective what is reborn, since the self is considered empty, Trungpa unhesitatingly answered "neurosis," because what is reborn in the strongest way is our propensity to mindlessly repeat the past, especially to repeat the ways we learn to shut down to pain, change, and intimacy.[30]

In Buddhist thinking, the senses in and of themselves are neither moral nor immoral, producing no karma to bind us. We are born attuned to sensation as pleasant, unpleasant, or neutral, and, in itself, this is completely adaptive. It is not our senses but our reactions to them that produce karma, that is, the consequences that bind us and others to our action. Staying true to its nondualistic ontology, Buddhism denies both the immortal soul and the materialist claim that the "self" ends at death. Instead, Buddhism emphasizes that what is reborn, moment to moment, is the fruit of this act and every other.[31] What is reborn is the propensity or inclination that led us to the act as well as its effects, rippling out into the world like a stone cast into the water. What is born is the seed of the tree, not a reincarnated tree, the consequences of one's life, not oneself. Thus the heart of karmic conditioning in one's own life, and, by extension, through one's actions into the lives of others (and from their actions into one's own life), works by means of a psychophysiological magnification, somewhat like Rachel Carson's description of how toxins like DDT move through the food chain. Karma extends in every direction and multiplies vastly. Dependence on initial conditions matters, and whatever enters a system comes out magnified many times over. The karma we are born with is the embodiment of organic evolutionary history as well as the acts of everyone who preceded us. This is not original sin, but the recognition that, in each case, "This is like this because that is like that." Such a heritage both lessens and intensifies our moral burden by freeing us from individual guilt and blame while at the same time placing us within a web of extended relations in which even the smallest acts make an enormous difference as they reverberate throughout the whole.

In many ways we are born with skin as permeable as that of the frog, who breathes everything in the water through the pores of its skin. Frogs absorb their environment so profoundly that biologists consider them a "sensitive indicator species" for the health of the environment. Human infants also are born open to the world with highly permeable skin and a heart-mind ready to embrace what comes to them. As Chödrön argues, we are born in the state of original vulnerability or softness, responsive to whatever we encounter.[32] The biochemical mechanisms used to negotiate the world become habits set in basic synaptic wiring and imprinted on our sensory system. Based on those conditioned patterns of sense, the brain gives us clues about when to feel good and bad, and our emotional lives construct themselves around sensations already interpreted as attraction, repulsion, or indifference. The Buddha did not use the language of synapse and biochemistry, but he did teach that in accordance with dependent co-arising, conditioned patterns of sense group, disband, and regroup in our perceptual and sensory lives. We then go on to build mental compartments and ideologies around these conditioned likes and dislikes, loaded with concepts of right and wrong, good and evil, beautiful and ugly, self and nonself.[33] The adaptive reason to link neurological structures to feeling states is to create somatic markers. But those markers are no longer adaptive when they blind one to the reality of the present or to the possibility of new experience. Apart from mindfulness, we respond simply to what we have in the past found pleasant, unpleasant, or of no interest. Our neurology works with our erotic life as if to stitch body suits out of experience, and the power of the body-mind to hold onto the past is strong enough to leave us caught there in sensations that are already conditioned.

The price we pay for our initial openness is the same price paid by the frog: the possibility of inhospitable environments turning our openness against us. Habits become particularly engrained when developed under conditions of trauma. As witnessed in post-traumatic stress disorder or in the tragic karmic cycle by which the abused becomes an abuser, violent stressors increase our defensiveness and reduce empathy and erotic sensitivity. For those who find the world too painful, the self develops, as we say, thick skin, taking on forms of rigidity that are manifest not only in the skin and musculature, but in repeated, self-defeating actions.

Developing healthy sensory and emotional lives in our society is impeded further by chronically overstimulated nervous systems that only serve to reinforce habitual conditioning. As we have seen in earlier chapters, the fight-or-flight reaction can be a double-edged sword, warning us of immediate dangers but also creating false alarms and unnecessary stressors. Under conditions of stress, assessments of risk are compromised and empathy becomes impossible. Instead, with the amygdala on edge we become anxious and fearful about the boundaries of the self and we also lose the input of the prefrontal lobes in assessing our situation. We find ourselves consumed by acute problems or minor irritations and remain oblivious to the potentially disastrous consequences of a host of chronic environmental and social problems, such as extinction of species, global warming, deforestation, overpopulation, malnutrition, and escalating violence in our communities. In this we are also like the frog: when placed in hot water, the frog jumps out, but when placed in water growing hotter by increments, it sits there until it is dead. As Neihoff says, "A brain tied to a program is at the mercy of the outside world; a brain responsive to the environment can work around it."[34]

From a Buddhist perspective, self-absorption is part of the human condition, and thus the tendency to get stuck in neurotic behaviors applies to all of us. However, in an unjust society that self-absorption can be magnified in ways that poison our erotic lives. Traditionally understood as greed, hatred, and ignorance, the Three Poisons of Buddhist doctrine lie at the center of our determined behavior, eclipsing moral and spiritual possibilities as the body is reduced to a stimulus-response mechanism. Depending upon the extent of poison in our systems, what we find attractive leads to craving and then to addiction. What we find repulsive leads to hatred and then to violence. What we find neutral renders us indifferent, or even nihilistic, about areas of life that we find neither attractive nor repulsive, shutting out vast areas of life as unworthy of attention or value. (As is the case for people with slow skin conductance, indifference also encourages us to seek thrills and take counterproductive risks.) The behaviorist-turned-marketing-strategist John Watson recognized along with the Buddha that habitual conditioning is the part of us most open to manipulation. The difference is that Buddhism proposes to break the stimulus-response connection by engendering awareness, whereas marketing strategies and media (such as hate radio) work to reinforce it.

The Buddha recognized his own attraction to excess as indicative of the human condition in which craving leads to numbness as well as to repeated patterns of needless suffering, but he could not have anticipated what Marx saw about the ways capitalism uses sensations and emotions to feed the ego. Efforts in philosophy to apply Marx's analysis of capitalism to our psychic lives have turned to schizophrenia as an example because marketing works like influencing machines to manipulate our sensations and responses. Though he did not live in a capitalist society, the Buddha recognized that once the object of desire had more power, value, and reality than the subject doing the desiring then all forms of addiction, illusion, and suffering become possible. The degraded forms of desire produced when one becomes addicted to attractions turn one's erotic life inside out: craving creates numbness rather than passion, empathy serves cruelty rather than compassion, and doing what one wants becomes the least free thing to do.[35] This is why, according to Nhat Hanh, free will exists only in direct proportion to how well we practice mindfulness.

One of the assumptions of the practice of mindfulness is that we can discover, enter, understand, and alter patterns in our emotional and mental lives by means of directed attention to our sensory lives. That our skin may provide access to our inner life seems less far-fetched than it might when one considers the effects of the squeeze machine on Grandin or the lack of skin conductance in sociopaths and people with frontal lobe damage, such as Damasio's Elliot. It also helps one understand the needs of those who feel compelled to mutilate their skin in the attempt to prove to themselves that they are alive. One reason meditation allows us to reclaim our erotic lives and feel at home in the world is because it reproduces in biological terms what loving touch does to an infant, leaving the skin vibrant and responsive, with defenses and openness properly balanced. That balance registers not only in the brain and the nervous system, but also in the skin, which vipassana meditation treats as central to erotic life. From the perspective of Buddhist analysis the loss of that vibrancy has to do with expectations constructed by the ego through habitual conditioning. The more that vibrancy is lost, the more the brain becomes tied to a program dependent upon repeating behaviors associated with past attractions, repulsions, and indifferences.

The connection between the vibrancy of the skin and other parts of the body and our openness to whatever comes in life can be found not only in vipassana meditation but also in kundalini and tantric yogas, Taoist philosophy, Chinese martial arts such as *qigong* and T'ai Chi Ch'uan, and health practices such as acupuncture or massage therapy. As a nondualistic system, Chinese medicine is based on the principle that health is a matter of having full and continually flowing energy in the body, called *qi (chi* or *ki),* sometimes translated as breath or life force. The traditions of China teach that the body's energy becomes maladaptive when we become stuck or inflexible. Qi is said to become sluggish under a hard shell, such as the muscular rigidity that accompanies anxiety and fear of spontaneity. When qi is sluggish or blocked, the organism is said to fall into states of imbalance and disease, as the qi fails to flow within the body as well as between the body and the environment. According to the theory of qi, both the inner life and one's relationship to the world are affected by blockages of energy that occur with decreased vitality of the skin: "When the outside is hard, the inside rots."[36] This is part of Taoist philosophy as well, which, by associating flexibility with life and rigidity with death, recognizes that health and well-being demand a fluid and balanced mind-body in harmony with a balanced culture-nature.

Qigong moves energy throughout the body either as a seated exercise using visualization or as a moving exercise using bodily postures and gentle motions to approximate a self-massage. Qigong brings an immediate sense of vitality to experience and is often described as the physical equivalent of a trip to the mountains or the desert because of the restful sense of connection and space that the exercises provide in either their still or moving form. In China, this way of health by means of moving energy was also seen to be the way of nature. The martial arts explicitly recognize the vitality of the body as tied to the struggle with the ego and with prejudices creating unhealthy borders. What is at stake in the martial arts is the restoration of fluidity that places body-mind in touch with the world in the present. As one teacher writes, "In the dojo we are looking to shed old skin for new in a constant process of physical, mental, and spiritual growth."[37] The bodily postures of qigong and T'ai Chi are intended to emulate the supple, graceful strength of the natural world: the bear, the crane, the snake creeps down, and carry the tiger are thought to have their origins as animal dances of the ancient Chinese shamans. Kenneth Cohen traces the use of masks, skins, and animal postures to the cave paintings of the Zhou Dynasty (1028–221 B.C.E.).[38] To become like animals is to be vital and aware, to regain a more natural, spontaneous, and balanced sense of motion. T'ai Chi names the center of agency the *tan tien,* a point four inches below the navel, a center much more rooted to our animal natures and our gut feelings than the head, emphasized in most Western philosophy.

One Western philosophical movement at turn of the century in Europe is worth mentioning, however, as it proposed achieving spiritual and moral health by means of awareness through motion. Proponents of the study of kinesiology, preeminently Moshe Feldenkrais and Matthias Alexander, argued that behavior could be transformed through yogic postures and stretching exercises integrating physical and moral development. In response to mechanistic forms of bodily movement brought on by the industrial revolution, both men developed techniques evoking conscious awareness though postures meant to integrate mind and body. Alexander's students included Bernard Shaw, John Dewey, and Aldous Huxley, all of whom were convinced that people were becoming imprisoned in bodily habits, thus preventing spiritual change and freedom. Alexander believed that cultivating awareness through walking, talking, breathing, and handling objects would break people out of their habits in adaptive and moral ways. As if to echo the Taoist on qi, or the Buddha on mindfulness, Dewey wrote, in his introduction to one of Alexander's works, that lowered sensory appreciation led to maladjusted psychophysical organisms. By contrast, enhancing sensory appreciation through bodily movement would enhance emotional lives, bringing the confidence, happiness, and equilibrium needed to act in contingent surroundings.[39] (Sadly, the elder Schreber may himself been have affected by the philosophy of kinesiology, but the gymnastics and pedagogy composed by him were based on using motion to control rather than extend sensory awareness.)

Acupuncture rests on the same understanding of energy and health as qigong and, like skin conductance measurements, provides a good example of the connection between our physical and our emotional lives. Indeed, the same meridians and flow of energy accessed by qigong and T'ai Chi from the inside are accessed by acupuncture with needles placed on the outside of the skin. Acupuncture uses the skin to unblock and activate qi in order to improve digestion and respiration, enhance the functioning of the immune system, and treat depression and addiction. Yuasa Yasuo's work on qi suggests that emotions may themselves be composed of flowing qi energy that uses a meridian system unique to the living body and therefore elusive to medical techniques based on dissection. The physiological functions of the meridian system are apparent in galvanic skin response tests, which Yasuo describes as allowing the skin to be used as a window into the unconscious.[40]

His speculations may eventually find support in Western medical research showing the emotions to have material manifestations in the form of strings of amino acids called neuropeptides. Message molecules and receptors for the biochemistry of emotions are found in cellular structures on monocytes that also read messages from the immune system. The two memory systems—the brain and the immune system—may communicate through the bio-chemistry of the emotions, helping to explain why emotions such as happiness and sorrow are able to affect our immunity.[41]

Both anecdotal and scientific evidence points to connections between a healthy and rich inner life and the vitality of the periphery of the body. Massage, for example, has been reported to help people deal with both the emotional and physical effects of smoking and other addictions, conditioned patterns somehow more easily broken by means of physical touch and the release of muscular tension. Like acupuncture, massage is part of traditional medical practice in China performed by licensed medical physicians in the service of moving qi along the meridians to cope with disease. Heightened conductivity of electrical charges in the skin at the acupuncture points is measurable during and after qigong exercise. Skin conductance and low-frequency muscular vibrations show an increase in electrical charges at the same points where practitioners feel warm and tingling, for example, in the center of their palms.[42] In my own experience of qigong and T'ai Chi exercises, I have felt that energy along with the perception of a closer, more vibrant, colorful, and beautiful world.

In search of more than anecdotal evidence, Mark Epstein's team went to Dharamsala and by the use of skin conductance tests, EEGs, and rectal probes discovered that through meditation the monks were able to get inside their involuntary nervous systems and gain control of the peripheral body, including control of the temperature of the skin and extremities. Through meditation the monks were able to direct the external temperature of their skin by tapping into the autonomic nervous system. Monks recruited from out of the foothills of the Himalayas by the Dalai Lama were able to increase the temperature of their fingers and toes by as much as 8.3 degrees centigrade.[43] It is interesting in this regard that Julie Henderson, a bodyworker who provided massage therapy for a Tibetan high lama in the category of *tulku* (the embodied presence of the Buddha), claims that, given twenty years of observing the tissue of thousands of human beings, she is confident that the tissue of the lama differs from our own. She describes his flesh as "open, spacious, formed without being bound. Presence without pattern," whereas the bodies she normally massages she describes as "full of pattern, story, attitude, preference, expectation, hope, and fear. Just as we are."[44] One would expect that if the flesh of an enlightened body-mind differed from one's own, it would do so in exactly this way, by embodying the equanimity that comes with transcending the controlling ego. Totally in body-mind, attuned to the present without unencumbering expectations, able to draw on the past but not be bound to it, tulkus may exemplify in their openness to touch the transformation that James Austin describes as a natural, habitual, neurophysiological response in which one is fully aware yet totally detached from cravings and aversions.[45]

Meditation has adaptive and moral significance because those who practice it show measurable results: they actually feel their own sensations more acutely. Erotic lives that approximate that of the tulku may therefore help us respond to the chronic issues that plague us. The skin conductance of experienced meditators registers both an opening and a closing: they are able to shift between a very high skin conductance, indicating that the senses are wide open, and very low skin conductance, showing the senses are shut down. This means that the tulku, while present and open to intimacy, has a damping apparatus that shuts down to harmful stimuli. Meditation creates an extremely sophisticated selective permeability, a measurable tactility that, like a healthy immune system, preserves health and well-being by knowing when to open and when to close to the world.[46] Such a selective permeability can prevent us from both absorbing pain and projecting it onto others. As the Dalai Lama has pointed out, Tibetan monks and nuns trained in meditation have coped amazingly well during incarceration and torture by the Chinese military, showing no signs of post-traumatic stress disorder even under the most abusive treatment.[47]

The erotic life constructed through meditation permits both empathetic and self-protective space by sensitizing the same neurological structures enhanced in the development of infants who receive loving touch. Defenses and openness properly balanced relax restrictions of the heart, render plasticity to the brain, enhance perception of somatic markers, and, perhaps most importantly, build a strong inner life connected to the inner lives of others. Treatments for recovery from stress as well as trauma and addiction involve providing a calm, comforting environment which can help to slow down the brain's hair-trigger responses and prevent strong emotional memories from leading to self-defeating patterns of behavior.[48] While never a substitute for a safe and nurturing physical environment, meditation attempts to provide the internal conditions of sanctuary anytime, anywhere and also helps to disrupt patterns associated with an overstimulated amygdala. Herbert Benson, a physician at Harvard Medical School, refers to the body's response to meditation as "the relaxation response" because it quiets the sympathetic nervous system responsible for the biochemical changes that produce the fight-or-flight response. Meditation provides an equilibrium that does not compromise the body's ability to become aroused when necessary but excludes overreactions to the trivial stresses and chaos of daily life.[49] Walter Cannon, who defined the fight-or-flight response, saw it as a paradox of evolutionary history that the only things that could truly be stable were those that were capable of change. He called adaptation "the essence of homeostasis," referring to the equilibrium between inner and outer as necessary to respond to contingent conditions.[50]

As far as erotic morality is concerned, finding the equilibrium to calm the amygdala and engage the prefrontal cortices is a necessary first step, but the relaxation response cannot alone create morality. Both Williams and Grandin were driven to rituals such as rocking, spinning, or staring at patterns in objects in an effort to reduce sensory overload rather than as a way to relate to others. Without the benefit of spiritual training we may find a similar sense of peace or even belonging but not the sense of community or of interbeing necessary for social and political action. In *Bodied Mindfulness*, Winnie Tomm argues that dance is able to provide the emotional-spiritual balance required for enacting social change. But it is not the motion of the body or the biochemical states produced by the body that lead to spiritual transformation. Rather it is the capacity of dance to awaken our inner lives and produce a deep stillness within that helps us to know ourselves and overcome maladaptive fears.[51] Dance is thus a spiritual practice only when, like the martial arts, tonglen, or vipassana, it grounds consciousness in ways that lead to compassion and healing. Casey Hayden captures this sense of stillness in motion or inner awakening when she talks about her political activities as moments of mindfulness, moments that reminded her of giving birth, the body acting in wisdom to cut through any falseness. This is stillness completely unlike that of the frog sitting in the heating water because it is stillness grounded in emptiness or full erotic engagement. Hayden says, "I remember when I was dragged from the courtroom in Albany, Georgia, for sitting in the black section, how calm I was. I was actually completely present there in that body, willing it to stillness, devoted to that practice. . . . This commitment to the action, regardless of result, is seeing the oneness of cause and effect. I recall saying at the time of the sit-ins that if I knew not a single lunch counter would change its policy as a result of my action, I would still do it. One is simply being the truth with one's body."[52]

CULTIVATING MINDFUL TOUCH:
EMBRACED BY THE MYRIAD OF THINGS

The goal of mindfulness is to practice awareness in daily life. Coming to our senses in the present can help us learn to use discipline in the service of freedom. Equanimity is not indifference but a passion for life that comes from gratitude rather than the need to control.[53] In vipassana training, the beginning practitioner is encouraged, as a minimum, to attend some form of retreat once a year, to meditate for twenty minutes a day, to live one morning a week mindfully, and to eat one meal a week in mindfulness. However, mindfulness can be practiced anytime, anywhere, even while we wait in stalled traffic or in bank lines, in otherwise aggravating moments that can blind us to the richness of life in the present. Above all, mindfulness is a practice—thinking, talking, writing, or reading about mindfulness is not the same as being mindful. Creating a space to stop the endless round of mindless activities that make up our lives is the first step. As Thich Nhat Hanh says, "Stopping and seeing are very close." Nhat Hanh, the first scholar to write about the Vietnam War from the perspective of Vietnamese Buddhism and the person most responsible for convincing Martin Luther King Jr. to stand up against that war, recommends that to

change civilization we need to take slow, mindful walks and practice breathing.[54]

Sensations as Mindful Touch: Killing Willie

The observation of sensation constitutes an entire foundation of
mindfulness as found in the *Satipatthana Sutra,* indicating that the
Buddha found sensory awareness significant in determining the
path toward wisdom and compassion. Sensations are the ground of
desire and provide the foundations of emotional and mental craving. Practitioners are first taught simply to observe their sensations, whether pleasant, unpleasant, or neutral, without judging or
trying to control them. However, the first thing that becomes clear
to everyone who attempts to meditate is that the mind has a life of
its own. The mind chatters incessantly, as if to avoid at all costs the
possibility of feeling and simply being. Buddhism sees everyday
thought as obsessive, the mind always intruding, inserting the past
and the future into the present, and in a variety of ways trying to
control the flow of lived experience. As soon as one stops, one sees
that the mind is completely unreliable, jumping around everywhere, as Hindus say, like a drunken monkey stung by a bee. This
is a helpful moral lesson as many of us who have never experienced the undisciplined nature of the mind assume it to be a fair
judge and a wise leader.

Taking a vow of silence is a very good way to perceive how the
mind works. Because the mind names and judges primarily
through the instrument of language, one finds that silence opens
up permeable space and creates conditions of intimacy that exist
beyond language. One also becomes aware of how easily others get
pushed away by snap judgments and self-serving prejudices. Listening is a form of erotic touch because it grounds perception in silence, opening one up to and preserving the being of the other.
James Austin says that silence reflects the neurophysiological fact
that when we are in the process of truly experiencing the world,
the impulse to chatter drops away and the world does the talking.[55]
Southeast Asian Buddhism uses twenty-one different words for
silence, including the silence of a focused mind, the silence between thoughts, and the silence of awareness.[56] The most extreme
version of silence in meditation is absorption, when all sensation

disappears and the mind, having nothing to hold onto, reaches complete repose.

For those learning to meditate, the mind often takes at least three days to exhaust itself and return to the body. This is why anyone who has not practiced for some time or who is only beginning to practice should start with a period of retreat long enough to allow the mind to wear itself out—the mind is the most insidious influencing machine we face, and it is a formidable task to turn it off. In meditation, thoughts eventually become more like passing clouds than dictators, and when that happens sensations are heightened, along with feelings of fragility and gratitude, because one feels embraced by existence itself. Developing what Denison calls tactile awareness, one discovers the richness of the present moment where life exists. One begins to listen, look, and feel "as though all one's pores were open and receptive. The senses seem to stretch out to close the gap between stimulus and perception," a gap once filled by judgment.[57]

With the judging mind in retreat, one can relax into sensations and begin to use them as teachers, doing the work of insight or vipassana meditation. The first thing that needs to happen during vipassana is to feel sensations and own them. The next is to let attachments to them go. Like many things in life, this is a paradoxical process. You can only give up attachment to what is yours. The more distanced we are from sensations and emotions, the more control they have over us and the more they appear to come from outside of us. We have seen this in the philosophies of Plato, Augustine, and Kant and in the schizophrenic's influencing machine. Through the observation of sensations without judgment or reaction one comes to realize that sensations and emotions are not independent entities which exist somehow outside of us, and this realization restores one's internal sense of agency. It is not that anger overcomes me, but that I get angry. Not that hunger and lust overcome me, but that I do hunger and lust.[58] Recognizing what one is feeling is essential to every treatment for violence, abuse, and addiction, not to mention purposive action and moral agency. By using observation to erode conditioned responses, feelings cease to be triggers and become somatic markers, points of reference signaling danger and promoting health. The more we become comfortable in the ownership of sensations, the more sensations

too become like clouds instead of dictators, mind and body working together to find relief from the obsessions that plague them in
separation.

Watching sensations come and go is a lesson in impermanence
with the power to teach us to stop clinging or pushing away. We
are to pay single-minded attention to what is experienced in the
moment, registering just the bare facts, with the goal of learning
eventually to separate raw sensations from our reactions to them.
Feeling sensations without reacting to them is the first step to being released from habits reinforcing our narcissistic propensities.
By experiencing pleasure without strangling the life out of it (attraction), by staying with pain from which we would normally recoil (repulsion), or by paying attention to what is normally
considered unworthy of attention (indifference), a sense of personal freedom and responsibility is renewed. Through cultivating
awareness of the short-lived nature of sensations apart from habitual response, meditation has the power to alleviate the anxiety
that creates neurotic patterns, opening us to the possibility of
changing them.[59] People with highly determined patterns of behavior have found relief in the practice of vipassana—for example,
a prison inmate in North Seattle found that vipassana helped her
to see that she was responsible for her actions, once "the rattling in
[her] brain got put to sleep." Another who had given birth to two
crack-addicted babies, one of whom died, sat through her meditation with welts from slashed wrists. She said that she learned about
internal freedom by letting an itch pass without scratching it—the
first time she remembered not being controlled by a sensation.[60]

Meditation retreats are filled with people in tears. Meditation
is like being in therapy or recovering from addictions; many
people who meditate report that they have learned for the first
time what it is to feel. Whether one is moved by touching pain
long denied or by the feeling of being nourished by life, intimacy is
restored and the sense of being stuck recedes. As Mark Epstein puts
it, meditation restores "the capacity for connection from the inside."[61] The feeling of being connected and motivated from the inside is enhanced in meditative practice by considering how
emotions build upon sensations and lead to mind states like happiness or dissatisfaction. Emotional intelligence developed by
means of meditation should be able to inform us when attraction

becomes compulsive or addictive, when repulsion becomes fear or hatred, or when indifference makes us bystanders whose acquiescence contributes to the injustice and suffering of others.

Breathing and Eating as Mindful Touch: Entering the Squeeze Machine

Most meditation practices, including vipassana, begin with breathing exercises. Breathing falls under the contemplation of the body in the *Satipatthana Sutra,* along with contemplation of parts of the body, such as flesh, bones, limbs, torso, and organs; contemplation of the way the body relates to the elements of the earth, such as flesh to soil and breath to air; and cemetery contemplations on the body as corpse. Breathing is considered a bridge between mind and body and is important enough to Buddhist practice to have a sutra of its own, the *Anapanasati Sutra.* Breathing connects the self to the world and the body to the mind so intimately that it can be considered a reciprocal form of touch. Yasuo speculates that it is the focus on the breath during meditation that forges a connection between the cerebral cortex and autonomic functions of the central nervous system, strengthening the prefrontal, amygdala circuit crucial to the establishment of functional somatic markers.[62] Oxygen nourishes the cells of our body as carbon dioxide nourishes the plants that breathe with us in a continual circling of the flesh. Breathing puts one in touch with rain forests and the biosphere. We share the resource of air with most other beings, recalling, in our meditation as we breathe, that the flower is breathing too. Breathing is an act of purification, releasing what is toxic to us but nourishing to others, taking in what is nourishing to us but toxic to others. To breathe is to be in touch with the metabolic workings of one's own body and the body of the earth, so much so that "the meditator no longer breathes, but *is breathed,* slowly and quietly."[63]

While practicing vipassana on retreat, I found myself waiting for the gap, the space between breaths, which felt to me both sacred and scary. Waiting for breath was a form of dying to control, allowing the intimacy necessary to be embraced by something larger than my own will. I came to apply the Buddhist precept "do not steal" to this moment, because rushing the next breath, as if there would not be another, felt like stealing the gift of the breath. Waiting "to be breathed" not only created a sense of gratitude and dependence but helped keep my impatience and desire for immediate gratification in check. I have since learned that Indian yogis refer to this moment as the "turning of the breath." It is a time of deep, inner stillness, a place of recalling birth and anticipating death, our first inhale and last exhale framing the lifetime we are given. What is found between the inhale and the exhale of the breath is what Tantric practitioners say is found also in orgasm: "the state of nondual awareness," the permeable space opening us to the mystery of the intermingling of self and world.[64]

Physiologically, the breath is an interesting place to center one's practice because breathing is both voluntary and involuntary. Autonomic and motor nerves govern the respiratory organs, and both voluntary and involuntary muscles are attached to the lungs. Austin's work on the brain and Zen describes breathing as a primary example of the intimate relation of mind and body and therefore a reliable index of how our emotional life influences rhythmic workings of the brain stem. For example, we all know what it feels like to take a deep breath to settle down or to release frustration. Mindful breathing feels like an extension of that centering process. By contrast, when we are anxious or fearful we tend to hyperventilate, sigh, or stop breathing entirely, lengthening and then holding onto the inhale. Under these conditions we breathe from the chest, engaging the sympathetic nervous system, home of the stress response. Meditation and martial art exercises teach breathing from the diaphragm (as infants do), engaging the parasympathetic nervous system, which results in rest and relaxation.

People trained in meditation are able to slow their breathing to four to six breaths per minute—two to three times slower than most people breathe at rest. Beyond slowing the breath, and thus the metabolism and the central nervous system, meditators increase the time spent exhaling, the exhale coming to assume three-quarters of the respiratory cycle. Austin believes that deep exhaling is conducive to feelings of tenderness; like turning the breath, it is a moment of allowing. In general, breathing in causes nerve cells to fire, while breathing out, as in meditation and chanting, quiets the brain, including the amygdala and the hippocampus. The central nucleus of the amygdala measures fewer firings of brain cells when exhaling is prolonged, contributing to the feeling of emotional and psychological peace.[65]

Breathing puts us in touch with sentient life on the planet and restores our own vitality, literally as well as emotionally. By focusing on the breath, one begins to move through the breath into the present, the only place life actually exists. In the present, we can feel the energy of the breath flowing through us as our skin comes into the pink and blood revives limbs that may have come to feel artificial. Breathing, we know ourselves as organisms rather than mechanisms, dependent upon the intricate interworkings of the biosphere rather than servants of external authority. Breathing opens the heart as well as the mind, pulling back the sentinel patrolling our borders and opening a space for us to feel again.

Mindfulness can be practiced in any action that connects us as embodied, sentient beings with other beings and the world around us. Besides breathing, eating is one of the most fundamental ways in which we touch the world and the world touches us. Like breathing, eating, at least in a society like ours, is so taken for granted that we often eat a meal without any awareness of what we have just eaten. At the vipassana retreat I attended at Ruth Denison's Dhamma Dena in the California desert, we were taught simple exercises in mindful eating, such as putting down utensils between bites of food in order to break the habit of taking another bite without awareness of the bite of food that is already in the mouth. Like not scratching an itch, taking time between bites of food is an important exercise in present-mindedness. It is an excellent reminder of how much we miss in life by not paying attention to what we already have.

During the retreat we were also taught to chew each bite of every meal slowly and in complete mindfulness, to be aware of taste in relation to the body's hunger and desire. I was reminded of Aldous Huxley's *Island* utopia, where he imagined "grace" as the first bite of a meal chewed mindfully. In mindful eating one becomes aware of the tastes and textures of food as well as the involuntary and voluntary actions of the tongue, the jaw, the throat, and the complex event of swallowing. In mindful eating we also become aware of the labor and the elements of the earth that are part of what we are consuming. Just one bite of food eaten in awareness each day could act as a reminder of how well we are nourished by the extended network of life that surrounds us and how our actions have consequences ultimately for the entire planet.

In the classic tea ceremony of Zen Buddhism we find another good example of mindful consumption. During the ritual the practitioner is aware that each action is to be undertaken as if it were the last. The body, like the cup that holds the tea, is both finite and fragile. The care and attention to detail expressed during the ritual create the time and space to taste and feel the warmth of the tea in the richness of the present moment as well as to reflect upon what has gone into the production of the tea. This is not the discipline of Kant's one cup of tea instead of two, but rather the experience of gratitude for what one has. Parallels can be drawn between the Zen tea ceremony, the Christian ritual of the Eucharist (which literally means "thanksgiving"), the Tibetan Chod, and Jewish kosher rituals as practices of presence and gratitude. Several Jewish writers have been interpreting kosher practices in ways that make them explicit exercises in social justice and ecology.[66] Jewish dietary law for centuries has witnessed to the use of mindful food preparation and eating not only as a means to create and sustain strong human communities, but also as a way to maintain awareness of all life as sacred.

Similarly, in many religious traditions both fasting and feasting can become occasions for mindful awareness of our bond with other beings on the planet. Feasting is a way of reminding ourselves of the joy of abundance and the pleasure of coming together as a "full-filled" community, while fasting can be a visceral way of identifying with those who don't have enough to eat as well as a recognition of our dependence on other forms of life for what we eat. In the case of fasting and other ascetic practices, however, these rituals are exercises in mindfulness only if they do not involve denial for the sake of denial since, as the Buddha recognized, denial can easily lead to narcissism. By contrast, the desert ascetics can show us how spiritual practices of self-denial can serve to awaken senses and feelings numbed by living unmindfully in the midst of abundance. As the *Tao Te Ching* puts it, "Colors blind the eye. Sounds deafen the ear. Flavors numb the taste. Thoughts weaken the mind. Desires wither the heart."[67]

Mindful Consumption: *Feeding the Hungry Ghosts*

Audre Lorde asks of her new life that began with the diagnosis of her cancer, "What do I eat? How do I act to announce or preserve my new status as temporary upon this earth?"[68] If we have come to our senses in mindfulness, then these are the questions we too will be asking. When the burst of light makes us empty enough to feel truly connected, the implications of our patterns of consumption become very real. Consumption is part of sensual, material reality and should be considered a form of touch that allows us to feel sustained by and responsible to the myriad of things. If we are to create erotic modes of morality, not only breathing and eating, but each act of consumption needs to be placed in the context of the circling of the flesh. Eating, like breathing, provides a good example of permeable boundaries because what we take in becomes part of us and leaves again in a form that is nourishing in a correctly functioning ecosystem. Food is closely tied to what nourishes us spiritually and emotionally and to our companions, literally those with whom we break bread.

The slaughterhouse would not be a place most of us would wish to make the focus of our awareness; however, I believe it is crucial for us to apply the practice of mindfulness to factory farming and the consumption of animal products in the way we have begun to do with tobacco products and firearms. If we can see the sun or forest in a piece of paper, then we can also see the deforestation, destruction of habitat, and the resulting extinction of species in a McDonald's Happy Meal. If we apply the practice of mindfulness to what we know about factory farming, then what happens when we contemplate eating a typical American breakfast of ham and eggs? Seeing "ham" in its emptiness, we become aware of hogs layered three and four stories high, locked in cages too small to move in, suspended over metal grates into which their waste flows. In an egg, we see several hundred million hens locked in dark, cramped cages, where they are fed antibiotics which force them to lay eggs for their entire lifetime as if they were machines.[69] Profit and demand, both of which are rising, establish the rate of kill; and, as Grandin says, killing animals in a way that respects them as sentient beings is impossible at the rate we now consume them. Manufacturers kill an average of twenty-two million chickens a day, and in each slaughterhouse anywhere from 1,350 to 1,500 cattle in eight hours. Calves are butchered in full sight of their mothers. Of their cries of agony, Upton Sinclair wrote years ago in *The Jungle*, "Seeing their fear, seeing so many of them go by, it had to remind me of things no one wants to be reminded of anymore, all mobs, all death marches, all mass murders and extinctions."[70]

Factory farms, like prisons, often exist in the poorest communities, where people are paid a minimal wage to work in abhorrent conditions. Placing socks over their hands and faces to prevent being clawed, men and boys are paid one dollar for each crate of three hundred live chickens gathered up in a time of two to four minutes. If lucky, a worker can leave at the end of a night with a hundred dollars, having captured and thrown thirty thousand live chickens into crates for transfer. The journey to slaughter for factory-farm animals can last up to seventy-two hours without food or water, in bitter cold or in blistering heat. Workers in slaughterhouses are surrounded by razor-sharp knifes, the sounds and smells of animal parts moving on hooks, drains and hoses used to wash down blood. Unable to interact while working, they get one fifteen-minute break and a thirty-minute lunch. Under these conditions, it should not be surprising that hog-farm workers were recently sued when an undercover tape revealed them beating and then skinning hogs alive. There is increasing evidence that, as with prison guards, the work follows these workers home, where they transfer the violence to their wives and children.[71]

Byproducts of eating meat include heart disease and high cholesterol for some people and hunger for others. Converting plant protein to meat protein in cattle takes twenty pounds of plant protein to produce one pound of animal protein, making millions of tons of plant protein unavailable for human consumption. An acre of land used for cereal production can provide five times more protein than an acre used for meat production, and legumes provide ten times more. A recent study argues that the typical North American diet, which derives 30 percent of its calories from animal sources, could only support two of the six billion people on the planet. In addition to grains, we feed animals the largest share of the world's fish catch. Six billion people could be nourished properly on a vegetarian diet if no grains were used for livestock; and because vegetarians consume much less grain than livestock, they also use less water, on average 330 gallons per person per day, as opposed to 2,500 gallons per animal per day. The beef we import takes plant protein from people in developing countries, primarily in Central America and Africa. For example, when people in Haiti grow feed for pigs that end up as sausages in the United States, they are obliged to clear mountain slopes to grow their own food, creating potential ecological disasters in the form of erosion, flooding, and loss of biodiversity.[72]

Pollution from the liquid and solid wastes of millions of animals should also be part of our mindfulness. Hogs in North Carolina outnumber citizens and produce more fecal waste than the human population of California. A study of meat-packing wastes in Omaha reported "100,000 pounds of grease, carcass dressing, casing cleaning, intestinal waste, manure and fecal matter from the viscera [spewing] into the sewer system and from there into the Missouri River each day."[73] Philip Kapleau estimates that the contribution of livestock to water pollution is ten times that of people and three times that of industry. While Kaplan's study is twenty years old, between then and now the numbers of animals consumed have risen steadily. Pork farms have dumped tens of millions of gallons of untreated hog feces into North Carolina's rivers, and that waste in combination with the drugs and hormones used to keep animals growing in their cages has lead to the presence of drug-resistant superbugs such as pfiesteria piscicida, a toxic microbe found in rivers and lakes. The pfiesteria piscicida can already change into twenty-four forms depending upon the species it is attacking (killing one billion fish in 1991 by dissolving their flesh). As Robert F. Kennedy Jr. concludes, industrial meat production, which has driven a million American family farms out of business and which subjects animals to a life of torture, "has escalated the karmic costs beyond reconciliation."[74]

But becoming mindful of the suffering that results from our current patterns of consumption is only of value if it leads us beyond privately held guilt and the moral paralysis that often accompanies it. In "The Zen of Eating," Ronna Kabatznick provides a good example of how we might respond differently by becoming more aware of the connections between our own pain and the pain of others. Kabatznick suffered from overeating and came to understand her insatiable hunger as a product of her desire to hold onto a world that is constantly changing. It is part of the most basic teachings of Buddhism—the first and second noble truths—that a certain kind of desire *(tanha)*, best translated as craving or compulsion, is often the cause of our suffering *(dukkha)*.[75] Freedom from such desire is possible, according to the third and fourth noble truths, by learning to live mindfully—in Kabatznick's case this meant starting Dieters Feed the Hungry, an organization which enables people with eating disorders to "feed" themselves by providing food to those who really need it. Kabatznick imagines a responsible society as one in which the food and diet industries support a circling of food between the overweight and the hungry rather than profiting by exploiting people's weaknesses.[76] This is a vision of justice based on emptiness, or the Buddhist vision of the fundamental interconnectedness of all beings, and, like the work of the agoraphobics at Three Mile Island, is a wonderful example of turning individual pathology into healing forms of resistance.

Another example of erotic circling of the flesh can be found in The Edible Schoolyard, a program begun by Alice Waters, the chef who created the California cuisine craze at her Berkeley restaurant, Chez Panisse. Waters began this program at Berkeley's Martin Luther King Jr. Middle School to help children appreciate what is really entailed in the creation of good food. Other schools have had vegetable gardens or cooking classes, but Waters combined them in order to show the whole cycle, garden to kitchen and back to the garden. Children work an hour every other week in the organic garden, pulling weeds and harvesting vegetables. They then take time in the school's kitchen learning to cook, to set a table, and to use a knife and fork. The children are given the opportunity to extend their palates beyond fast food menus and begin to recognize something valuable in one of the most basic activities of our lives. Waters's students had their first harvest in 1996, and since then the program has sought funding to be continued and has expanded to other schools.[77]

A third example of how to respond in mindful awareness and touch to some of the most basic problems we face is the Heifer Project, an international organization that runs WILD, or Women in Livestock Development. WILD empowers women living in poverty by donating a cow or other female farm animal to a woman who promises to give one female offspring to another woman in need. One dairy cow (a gift worth $500) can double or triple a family's income by milk sales as well as raise a woman's self-esteem, a husband's respect for his wife, and her place in the community.

The women are taught environmentally sound farming techniques, nutrition, community health, and business skills along with care of the animals, skills which can be passed down to their children.[78]

What makes these examples of erotic morality is that they take the flesh seriously enough that the karma produced by the action is healing and emancipatory. When one is in touch with the consequences of action, means and ends become one. Economist Robert Sardello's description of how erotic life might be restored to commodities is very much like the Buddhist notion of emptiness. Performed in awareness, the exchange of an apple for a quarter brings with it "[my] relationship to this store in which I stand, the clerk whom I face, the employer who paid my salary, the family budget which portioned the earnings, the desire which brought me to the store, the company which owns the store and the employees which it retains, the produce merchant who brought the apples in, the farmer who grew the apple, the tree from which it came, the earth from which it sprouted, the rain which moistened it, the clouds which shaded it, and the sun which reddened it."[79]

Similarly, economist Juliet Schor writes about the insidious nature of desire in the American economy, suggesting that we look "through" or deconstruct products rather than look "at" them. Looking through a pair of Nikes, through the successful "just do it" ads that pay women athletes handsome sums, we see the $1.60 a day paid to female Vietnamese workers who produce the shoes. Looking through the Jeep rolling over pristine wilderness, we see the smog, oil spills, and habitat destruction that accompany our dependence on fossil fuels.[80] Schor also suggests, as a Buddhist might, that we pay attention to how one desire leads to another, because when we do we will see that many of our desires are not based on wanting the next purchase, but on wanting itself. She suggests that if we create more mental space by concentrating on what really matters to our physical and mental well-being, we can put off purchases and watch the need disappear. Like having an itch and not scratching it, with every act of resistance our sense of internal freedom is strengthened. Her research shows that people who successfully simplify their economic lives have good educations and strong inner lives. Rich in what she calls cultural and human capital, they are able to find happiness by having more free-dom and time rather than more things.[81]

The alternative, continued mindless consumption, is evident in the fact that people have consumed as many goods and services since 1950 as all the previous generations on earth put together. Those who have the most wealth, the top 20 percent of the popu-lation, use 66 percent of the earth's resources and generate 75 percent of the world's waste, including 90 percent of chlorofluoro-carbons depleting the ozone and 96 percent of radioactive wastes. When consumption patterns are factored into population, the United States becomes by far the most populated nation on the planet, with each child the equivalent of thirty to forty consumers in less developed nations.[82] Moreover, these patterns of consump-tion do not appear to be helping us become more content or caring, nor are they helping us face aging, illness, and death. Instead, it seems that the more we have the more alone and vulnerable we feel.

Individual choices send consequences throughout a highly ex-tended network of relations, particularly in a global economy. By increasing awareness of those relations, I think we are offered an opportunity to heal breaches in sentience and become the true ma-terialists that Marx hoped we would be by taking sensuousness and subjectivity seriously. Marx wrote in his *Theses on Feuerbach* (the philosopher who said we are what we eat), "The chief defect of all hitherto existing materialism . . . is that the thing, reality, sensu-ousness, is conceived only in the form of the *object* or of *contempla-tion*, but not as *human sensuous activity, practice*, not subjectively."[83] Under the conditions of capitalism, the privileged are socialized to experience bodies from the outside in rather than from the inside out. The privileged have the economic and technological means to distance themselves from the body, particularly from bodily pain, while the poor do not. Thus the people with the economic power to alter existing social relations are not moved to do so because they become estranged from their own sentient life and open to manipulation by external forces. As Elaine Scarry explains, for Marx there is a "serious dislocation in the species itself, for [capi-talism] announces that the original relation between sentience and self-extension . . . has been split apart and the two locations of the self have begun to work against each other."[84] This breach in sentience creates a dysfunctional social body in which, like a dysfunctional immune system, the consequences of the actions of some begin to work against the whole. Capitalism creates two completely different groups of people: those bound in radical ways to embodiment—the poor, the ill, the elderly, the traumatized, and the addicted—and the privileged, who experience their bodies by means of objectification. To Scarry and to Edith Wyschogrod, among others, everything about awareness changes with this difference. The values of those who are bound to the body are ignored by the privileged, who, as disembodied subjects, fall prey to "a production process in which desiring-machines are both the agents and the final products of the process."[85]

For the affluent, mindfulness therefore needs to be considered as a means of resisting the deadening and cheapening influence of the marketplace as well as a means of entering into the bodies of those who suffer to make our privileged existence possible. Erotic forms of asceticism could be used in anarchistic ways to break through the social structures that cause injustice, much the way Paulo Freire used the "pedagogy of the oppressed" to educate peasants and workers about the economic and political forces that oppress them. Those of us who live in affluence can use mindfulness to create a sensuous, political materialism that extends our awareness to those upon whom our consumption depends. Wyschogrod suggests developing a "postmodern asceticism as a sort of pedagogy of pain, in which persons engage in acts of self-denial as a way of making a space in their own experience for compassionately identifying with the pain of the other."[86] As in the practice of tonglen, what makes a pedagogy of pain bearable is the recognition that it also restores our capacity to feel free and joyful. Indeed, part of what drives us into mindless consumption in the first place is the need to escape the knowledge that much of our pleasure is purchased by the pain of others.

Having captured in its original teachings the insight that craving leads to numbness rather than to passion, Tibetan Buddhism refers to people who seek fulfillment through material goods as Hungry Ghosts. Mere shadows of their erotic selves, Hungry Ghosts are blind to the counterproductive and insatiable nature of desire and so are pictured as creatures with mouths the size of needles, long raw throats, and huge bellies. Filled with desire, most especially with unfulfilled longings from their pasts, Hungry Ghosts can never have their needs satisfied because the tiny opening for a mouth and the thin, aching throat will never allow enough food to fill their stomachs. In the Buddhist psychological contemplations, the Hungry Ghosts exist beside those in the Hell Realms who believe that they are being tortured by outside forces over which they have no control. People in the Hell Realms are filled with rage and anxiety but fail to recognize that their torturers are products of their own minds. Both of these psychological profiles clearly speak to us. To the Hungry Ghosts, the Bodhisattva of Compassion carries a bowl filled with spiritual nourishment to fulfill their true hunger, which is psychological and emotional. And to those in the Hell Realms the Bodhisattva brings a mirror for them to see that the emotional states which torture them are of their own making.[87] Cultivating the practice of mindfulness can address our insatiable hungers and the fears that drive them. By becoming mindful of our sensations and emotions, past conditioning will no longer result in our ignoring or being overwhelmed by the alarms and beacons of our somatic lives. Dwelling in permeable space, no longer erotically homeless, we will have little need for tranquilizers or stimulants to distance us from sensual and emotional connections with others.

In a culture suffused with dualisms people are often repulsed by permeable space, the erotic center where borders are crossed and yang meets yin. Besides creating rifts within the self, dualisms carry the added moral burden that a high level of attraction must carry a equally high level of repulsion. This is what the mystics of all ages have perceived, that dividing the world into absolutes of good and evil is a very dangerous thing. Denying what is repulsive or painful often leads to more pain as well as a moral paralysis that prevents us from doing something about the pain caused by social injustices. Austin describes the practice of mindfulness as proceeding in an increasingly intuitive manner from the inner to the outer and back again: "So, on some brief occasions, paying bare attention will turn into an *out*flowing: a totally appreciative, sacramental approach to the wondrous commonplace events of the present moment. At other times, bare attention turns *in*ward. Now it functions to include *introspection and self-analysis.*"[88] These are precisely the rhythms we need to transcend dualisms and become self-

reflective, responsible moral agents who are nourished by reciprocal relations with others. As Winnie Tomm says, when one is present to the embodied self, an exchange of erotic energy occurs in
which "the inner subjectivity of each person reaches out to the
other." Mindful practice works like Grandin's squeeze machine because in mindfulness "each person transcends their own individual
boundaries, thereby expanding their subjectivities in the intersubjective exchange of energy."[89]

What we need to do is really quite simple, if radical: make the
time and the space to be, to breathe, to feel, to stay in mindful
touch with the consequences of our actions. Awakening to our
senses and developing the emotional intelligence we need to dispel
the Hungry Ghosts and our self-made hells can help us recover part
of the energy we now use escaping pain to live in ways that do not
harm ourselves or others. This is a resurrection of the body that
truly matters because it concerns not only the individual but the
whole body of the world.

Notes

INTRODUCTION

1. Audre Lorde, "Uses of the Erotic: The Erotic as Power," in *Weaving the Visions: New Patterns in Feminist Spirituality*, ed. Judith Plaskow and Carol P. Christ (San Francisco: Harper and Row, 1989), 208 and 210. Throughout this text, I am using the term *feeling* the way that I think Audre Lorde does, equating feelings with emotional connection. My use of the word *feeling* and also the word *sensual* implies a feeling for, and even a feeling with, that the words *sensation* and *sensationalism* do not.
2. Trinh Minh-ha, *Woman/Native/Other* (Bloomington: Indiana University Press, 1989), 90.
3. Sallie McFague makes this point when she suggests that touch might be a better category than vision for understanding ourselves as embodied and relational beings (Sallie McFague, *Super, Natural Christians: How We Should Love Nature* [Minneapolis: Fortress Press, 1997], 91–93). In an earlier essay, I argued that the eye can represent the entire sensual gestalt if one considers nondualistic or allocentric forms of vision. There I followed Maurice Merleau-Ponty's analysis of the artistic vision of Rilke and Cézanne and Evelyn Fox Keller's descriptions of geneticist Barbara McClintock as examples of touching the world. I called this form of perception "lateral transcendence" because it held onto the concreteness and particularity of the world's multiplicity of beings. See Linda Holler, "Thinking with the Weight of the Earth: Feminist Contributions to an Epistemology of Concreteness," *Hypatia* 5, 1 (1990): 1–23.
4. Diane Ackerman, *A Natural History of the Senses* (New York: Vintage Books, 1990), 301.
5. Daniel Goleman, *Emotional Intelligence* (New York: Bantam Books, 1995); Chögyam Trungpa, *The Myth of Freedom and the Way of Meditation* (Berkeley and London: Shambhala Press, 1976), 2.
6. Even technological questions are issues ultimately of attractions and repulsions for, as Edward Tenner has argued, in how we design our neighborhoods, our houses, and our front yards "what is most crucial and most uncertain is not invention and discovery but taste and preference" (Edward Tenner, *Why Technology Bites Back: Technology and the Revenge of Unintended Consequences* [New York: Knopf, 1996], 275).
7. There is some dispute within the psychiatric community concerning whether Asperger syndrome is a form of autism or another kind of syndrome in its own right. I

have been persuaded by the work of Uta Frith and Lorna Wing, who argue for an autistic continuum with severe autism (Kanner's) at one end of the continuum and high-functioning Asperger syndrome at the other end. Asperger syndrome then tapers into developmental disorders such as dyslexia and attention-deficit disorder (ADD). The new DSM-III-R criteria support such a continuum, with full autism at one end and ADD at the other.

8. Temple Grandin and Margaret M. Scariano, *Emergence: Labeled Autistic* (Novato, Calif.: Arena Press, 1986), 96.

9. Oliver Sacks, "An Anthropologist on Mars," *New Yorker*, 27 December 1993, 107. Grandin notes that her father had Asperger-like behaviors. Her sisters are visual thinkers like she is—one is dyslexic and said to be a brilliant decorator and another sculpts. Grandin's mother wrote scripts for documentaries on emotionally disturbed children prior to Temple's birth. She was alert to her daughter's intelligence as well as her sensory and emotional distress and helped direct her talents. Grandin's grandfather co-invented the first autopilot used on airplanes.

10. Donna Williams, *Somebody Somewhere: Breaking Free from the World of Autism* (New York: Times Books, 1994), 23.

11. Ibid., 76.

12. Ibid., 3–4.

13. Alison M. Jaggar, "Love and Knowledge: Emotion in Feminist Epistemology," in *Women, Knowledge and Reality,* ed. Ann Garry and Marilyn Pearsall (Boston: Unwin Hyman, 1989), 132.

14. Donna J. Haraway, *Simeans, Cyborgs, and Women: The Reinvention of Nature* (New York: Routledge, 1991). Sharon Salzberg is quoted in *Healing Emotions: Conversations with the Dalai Lama on Mindfulness, Emotions, and Health,* ed. Daniel Goleman (Boston: Shambhala, 1997), 66. In the dialogue with Salzberg, Goleman, the Dalai Lama, and others, Francisco Varela points out that the immune system functions for the body as a second brain and is equivalent in its responsiveness to the environment. Lymph organs, for example, include sensors that continually monitor one's relationships to the world.

15. For a description of an immune system doing precisely this, see Joan Iten Sutherland, "Body of Radiant Knots: Healing as Remembering," in *Being Bodies: Buddhist Women on the Paradox of Enlightenment,* ed. Lenore Friedman and Susan Moon (Boston and London: Shambhala, 1997), 3–4.

16. Lorde, "Uses of the Erotic," 212.

17. Charlene Spretnak, *States of Grace: The Recovery of Meaning in the Postmodern Age* (San Francisco: HarperSanFrancisco, 1991) and *The Resurgence of the Real: Body, Nature, and Place in a Hypermodern World* (Redding, Mass.: Addison-Wesley, 1997).

18. Adrienne Rich, *Of Woman Born* (New York: Bantam Books, 1976), 21.

19. Pamela L. Moore, introduction to *Building Bodies,* ed. Pamela L. Moore (New Brunswick, N.J.: Rutgers University Press, 1997), 1.

20. As Terry Bisson says in "They're Made out of Meat": "Thinking meat! You're asking me to believe in thinking meat?" "Yes. Conscious meat! Loving meat! Dreaming meat! The meat is the whole deal" (Terry Bisson, "They're Made out of Meat," *Shambhala Sun,* November 1999).

21. Maxine Sheets-Johnstone, *The Roots of Thinking* (Philadelphia: Temple University Press, 1990), 369, see also 288–300. I think Sheets-Johnstone would be critical of my use of autism and other feeling disorders to understand the importance of feeling, since she argues that one of Merleau-Ponty's greatest errors was to identify the normal body by looking at pathological ones. Sheets-Johnstone rejects such an approach partly because pathological bodies are exceptions to the rule in evolution, on which her epistemology is based. However, it is notoriously difficult to decide what is an exception in evolutionary theory. In some sense all mutations are exceptions, as Steven J. Gould has argued in *The Panda's Thumb: More Reflections on Natural History* (New York: Norton, 1980). I see no reason why we cannot learn about the interworkings of mind and body by referring to those whose organic dysfunctions provide exaggerated forms of what we might otherwise call dualism.

22. Ruth Ginzberg, "Philosophy Is Not a Luxury," in *Feminist Ethics,* ed. Claudia Card (Lawrence: University of Kansas, 1991), 132 and 133.

23. Ibid., 132.

24. Susan Griffin, *A Chorus of Stones: The Private Life of War* (New York: Anchor Books, 1992).
25. Robert Sapolsky, an authority on the effects of stress on human and nonhuman animals, says that the reason to do behavioral biology is to better understand Reinhold Niebuhr's Serenity Prayer: *"God, grant me the serenity to accept the things I cannot change, courage to change the things I can, and the wisdom to know the difference"* (Robert M. Sapolsky, *The Trouble with Testosterone: and Other Essays on the Biology of the Human Predicament* [New York: Scribner, 1997], 11, italics in original).

CHAPTER 1: AUTISTIC TOUCH

1. Ashley Montagu, *Touching: The Human Significance of the Skin* (New York: Columbia University Press, 1971), 218, see also 4–5.
2. For an elaboration of moral value as "fitting response," see my work on H. Richard Niebuhr as an example of a moral theorist working within a relational ontology: Linda Holler, "In Search of a Whole-System Ethic," *The Journal of Religious Ethics* 12 (fall 1984): 219–239, and "Is There a 'Thou' within Nature?" *The Journal of Religious Ethics* 17 (spring 1989): 81–102.
3. Ackerman, *A Natural History of the Senses*, 70–71. These metaphors are good instances of George Lakoff and Mark Johnson's hypothesis that language evolves from bodily experience outward. George Lakoff and Mark Johnson, *Metaphors We Live By* (Chicago: University of Chicago Press, 1980).
4. The image of autistics as profoundly retarded is better known to us because the first studies of this form of autism were done by Leo Kanner. Kanner moved to Baltimore from Vienna in 1924; there he became head of the Johns Hopkins clinic and wrote in English, thereby making his work immediately accessible. Hans Asperger stayed in Vienna, where both men were trained, and his work was not translated into English until 1991. Although they never met, both men described the same kind of disturbed child, during the same year (1943), and used the same term—*autistic*. Eugene Bleuler had previously used the term *autistic*, from the Greek, *autos*, to denote the schizophrenic's loss of contact with the world.
5. Uta Frith, "Asperger and His Syndrome," in *Autism and Asperger Syndrome*, ed. Uta Frith (Cambridge, U.K.: Cambridge University Press, 1991), 22. Digby Tantam interviewed sixty adults identified by psychiatrists as eccentric and socially isolated, forty-six of whom met the criteria for Asperger disorder. Tantam notes that while most of our behavior is conditioned by shared social conventions, they have none. See Digby Tantam, "Asperger Syndrome in Adulthood," in *Autism and Asperger Syndrome*, ed. Frith.
6. R. Peter Hobson, "Social Perception in High-Level Autism," in *High-Functioning Individuals with Autism*, ed. Eric Schopler and Gary B. Mesibov (New York: Plenum Press, 1992), 165.
7. Ruth C. Sullivan, "Rain Man and Joseph," in *High-Functioning Individuals with Autism*, ed. Schopler and Mesibov, 247.
8. Asperger quoted in Sacks, "An Anthropologist on Mars," 109.
9. John J. Ratey, Temple Grandin, and Andrea Miller, "Defense Behavior and Coping in an Autistic Savant: The Story of Temple Grandin, Ph.D," *Psychiatry* 55 (November 1992): 382–391.
10. Temple Grandin and Margaret M. Scariano, *Emergence: Labeled Autistic* (Novato, Calif.: Arena Press, 1986), 19.
11. Grandin quoted in Sacks, "An Anthropologist on Mars," 109.
12. Ibid., 118. Asperger's translator and interpreter Uta Frith remarks that "a dash of autism is not a bad way to characterize the apparent detachment and unworldliness of the scientist," and she goes on to attribute such "a dash" to herself, as Asperger did to himself (Frith, "Asperger and His Syndrome," 32).
13. Grandin and Scariano, *Emergence*, 112, italics in original.
14. Temple Grandin, "My Experiences as an Autistic Child," *Journal of Orthomolecular Psychiatry* 13 (1984): 167. See a simulation of Grandin's squeeze machine at http://www.autism.org/hugbox.html.
15. Temple Grandin, "Calming Effects of Deep Pressure in Patients with Autistic Disorder, College Students, and Animals," *Journal of Child and Adolescent Psychopharmacology* 2 (1992): 66.

16. Grandin and Scariano, *Emergence*, 96.
17. Ibid., 113, italics in original.
18. Ibid., 32.
19. Williams, *Somebody Somewhere*, 43.
20. Ibid., 59.
21. Donna Williams, *Nobody Nowhere: The Extraordinary Autobiography of an Autistic* (New York: Times Books, 1992), 169.
22. Ibid., 205.
23. Williams, *Somebody Somewhere*, 136.
24. Ibid., 97.
25. Williams, *Nobody Nowhere*, 202.
26. Oliver Sacks, *The Man Who Mistook His Wife for a Hat: And Other Clinical Tales* (New York: Summit Books, 1985), 42.
27. Williams, *Somebody Somewhere*, 232. As Grandin has pointed out, some of Donna Williams's experience seems atypical for autistics. Grandin mentions that people working in the field of autism are "somewhat perplexed" about Williams's "poetic, dreamlike descriptions" and that on the phone Williams "sounded completely normal with lots of affect." (To Grandin's ear she didn't have the classic autistic monotone.) Grandin concludes, "Possibly, her type of autism has a more normal mind trapped in a totally dysfunctional sensory system." Grandin thinks that Williams "may be an important bridge of understanding between the Kanner-type autism and so-called lower functioning autism" (Temple Grandin, "How People with Autism Think," in *Learning and Cognition in Autism*, ed. Eric Schopler and Gary B. Mesibov [New York: Plenum Press, 1995], 150–151). One reviewer of Williams's writings says that she would diagnose her as having a severe case of PDD rather than as autistic. But, in general, people in the field of autism believe that there are as many kinds of autism as there are autistics.
28. Williams, *Nobody Nowhere*, 103.
29. Williams, *Somebody Somewhere*, 132.
30. Ibid., 235. Upon gaining body awareness, one of the first things Williams realized is that she is short. Prior to that, she had assumed that she was the same size as whomever she was with at the time. Others were her external map, and through them she saw herself. She wonders if anything like this goes on with anorexics, who, in feeling fat, may have distorted body sense (Williams, *Somebody Somewhere*, 235).
31. The causes of autism remain mysterious, although heredity clearly is a factor. Families that include autistic individuals also tend to include sufferers of AS and are said to experience schizophrenia, manic depression, dyslexia, and attempted suicides more frequently than other families. Frith describes autism as a brain abnormality due to genetic fault, brain insult, or brain disease, either before birth or in early childhood (Frith, "Asperger and His Syndrome," 2).
32. Montagu, *Touching*, 10–13.
33. Ibid., 15–16.
34. Ibid., 19–27.
35. Ibid., 54.
36. Daniel Goleman, "The Experience of Touch: Research Points to a Key Role in Growth," *New York Times*, 2 February 1988.
37. Grandin and Scariano, *Emergence*, 110.
38. Goleman, "The Experience of Touch."
39. Grandin, "My Experiences as an Autistic Child," 150.
40. Ibid., 149–150.
41. Montagu, *Touching*, 87.
42. See Margaret Talbot, "Attachment Theory: The Ultimate Experiment," *New York Times Magazine*, 24 May 1998, 27.
43. Ibid., 30.
44. Ibid., 38.
45. Grandin, "My Experiences as an Autistic Child," 157–158; and Temple Grandin, "An Inside View of Autism," in *High-Functioning Individuals with Autism*, ed. Schopler and Mesibov, 114.
46. Marion Cleaves Diamond, *Enriching Heredity: The Impact of the Environment on the Anatomy of the Brain* (New York and London: Free Press, 1988), especially 3, 7, 52, 90, and 115.

47. Goleman, "The Experience of Touch"

48. Goleman, *Emotional Intelligence*, 226.

49. Temple Grandin, *Thinking in Pictures: And Other Reports from My Life with Autism* (New York: Doubleday, 1995), 118.

50. See Goleman, *Emotional Intelligence*, 204.

51. Ibid., 27.

52. Dianne Dunagan and Danni Odom-Winn, *"Crack Kids*" in School: What to Do/How to Do It* (Freeport, N.Y.: Educational Activities, 1991), 32.

53. Ibid., 54.

54. Grandin, "How People with Autism Think," 144. The cerebellum is found to be abnormal in the brains of autistics as well as in the brains of primates deprived of physical touch. Grandin is interested in the hypothesis that it might act as a kind of volume control on sensory experience, helping to filter out stimuli and focus attention. We know the cerebellum connects sensory input and output related to motion, but functions of the cerebellum are not completely understood. This "little brain" weaves so many neurons and connections together that its potential for processing information is comparable only to the cerebral cortex. Its circuitry may allow the brain to maintain an overall picture of what is going on, that is, to shift attention, to see cause-and-effect sequences, and to keep the comet's tail of awareness, thus providing coherence from one moment to another. Grandin's MRI shows her cerebellum to be 20 percent smaller than normal, but it has not yet been determined whether primary damage to the brain stem or cerebellar neurons could lead to dysfunctional development of limbic structures. The cerebellum receives signals from the brain stem, the cerebral cortex, the spinal cord, and each of the sensory systems. (The only other structure of the brain to receive input from all sensory systems is the prefrontal cortex.) Theories about the cerebellum's role in organizing sensory information vary and are recent. MRIs show the cerebellum to be most active when subjects are asked to identify (by touch) objects placed in their hands or when researchers rub objects, such as sandpaper, on their hands for identification. Eric Courchesne has been researching possible infectious and toxic causal agents for autism, finding a window of vulnerability during the fifth week of gestation when the kind of neurogenesis occurs that is lacking in autistics. His hypothesis is that the neurons for facial expression are not fully developed and may reflect part of the reduced size of the cerebellum. Since the cerebellum is involved in the sensorimotor schema, it is possible that normal infants encode facial expressions with emotional meaning, thereby coming into intersubjective life and emotional awareness. That step of encoding emotional states into facial motor output would be a key step missing in autistics, who have a near total absence of neurons in brain stem facial nuclei. See Eric Courchesne, "Brainstem, Cerebellar, and Limbic Neuroanatomical Abnormalities," *Current Opinion in Neurology* 7 (April 1997): 269–277.

55. Grandin, *Thinking in Pictures*, 44.

56. Williams, *Somebody Somewhere*, 45–46.

57. Williams, *Nobody Nowhere*, 46.

58. Grandin, "My Experiences as an Autistic Child," 166. Both Grandin and Williams are quick to point out that they do not experience hallucinations. They experience sensory and social confusion, but hallucinatory visions and voices are not part of AS.

59. Williams, *Somebody Somewhere*, 24–25.

60. Grandin, "My Experiences as an Autistic Child," 150.

61. Ibid.

62. Dunagan and Odom-Winn, *"Crack Kids*,"* 75.

63. Grandin and Scariano, *Emergence*, 89.

64. Grandin, "My Experiences as an Autistic Child," 167.

65. Grandin, "How People with Autism Think," 106.

66. Montagu, *Touching*, 123–124.

67. Grandin, "My Experiences as an Autistic Child," 156.

68. Williams, *Nobody Nowhere*, 206.

69. Eugene d'Aquili and Andrew B. Newberg, *The Mystical Mind: Probing the Biology of Religious Experience* (Minneapolis, Minn.: Fortress Press, 1999), 79–84 and 25–27.

70. Covert Bailey, *Smart Exercise* (New York: Houghton Mifflin Company, 1994).

71. Grandin and Scariano, *Emergence*, 25.

72. Williams, *Nobody Nowhere*, 3–4.
73. Grandin, *Thinking in Pictures*, 96–97.
74. Grandin and Scariano, *Emergence*, 180.
75. Grandin, *Thinking in Pictures*, 44.
76. Grandin and Scariano, *Emergence*, 110.
77. Ibid., 183.
78. Williams, *Somebody Somewhere*, 29. Also see Williams, *Nobody Nowhere*, 56 and 23–24.
79. Mary Bray Pipher, *Reviving Ophelia: Saving the Selves of Adolescent Girls* (New York: Putnam, 1994); Watson quoted in Liz Stephens, "Cutting Too Close," *San Diego Union Tribune*, 9 October 1997.
80. Grandin, *Thinking in Pictures*, 113.
81. Williams, *Nobody Nowhere*, 34.
82. Ibid., 12.
83. Ibid., 35.
84. Ibid., 6.
85. Williams, *Somebody Somewhere*, 67.
86. Ibid., 69 and 70.
87. Ibid., 44.
88. Williams, *Nobody Nowhere*, 189.
89. Williams, *Somebody Somewhere*, 133.
90. Ibid., 230 and 231.
91. Williams, *Nobody Nowhere*, 20.
92. Ibid., 67.
93. Ibid., 68.
94. Williams, *Somebody Somewhere*, 115.
95. Ibid., 6.
96. Williams, *Somebody Somewhere*, 104.
97. Williams, *Nobody Nowhere*, 170.
98. Williams, *Somebody Somewhere*, 116–117.
99. Williams, *Nobody Nowhere*, 202.
100. Grandin, "An Inside View," 109–110.
101. Grandin and Scariano, *Emergence*, 104. In his article on Grandin in the *New Yorker*, Oliver Sacks says that when he visited Grandin she showed him the squeeze machine, and when she entered it, he noticed that her voice became softer and her manner less rigid (Sacks, "An Anthropologist on Mars"). The attraction to pressure appears to be biological, since hyperactive children (with PDD and with Tourette's syndrome) are also calmed by it. Grandin mentions people who have constructed pressure suits from wet suits or inflatable life jackets or who wear tight belts, shoes, watches, and wristbands for the same purpose (Grandin, *Thinking in Pictures*, 114).
102. Dunagan and Odom-Winn, "*Crack Kids**," 43.
103. Grandin and Scariano, *Emergence*, 95.
104. Grandin, *Thinking in Pictures*, 92.
105. Ibid., 143.
106. Temple Grandin, "A 'Hog Slaughter' Commentary," *Meat and Poultry* 357 (August 1989): 26.
107. Grandin, "How People with Autism Think," 149–150.
108. Temple Grandin, "Behavior of Slaughter Plant and Auction Employees Toward the Animals," *Anthrozoös* 1 (spring 1988): 205–213.
109. Ibid.
110. Grandin and Scariano, *Emergence*, 130.
111. See Grandin, *Thinking in Pictures*, 206. Many kosher slaughterhouses still use the method of shackle and hoist. Waiting their turn to die, five or six cattle are left hanging upside-down by a leg (which often breaks), their nostrils clamped and necks stretched. Their necks are then cut, and they bleed to death. Grandin thinks it goes against the kosher ritual, which, in the Torah, explicitly includes respect for animals and their pain.
112. Grandin, "Behavior of Slaughter Plant," 205–213, 208–209; Carol J. Adams, *The Sexual Politics of Meat: A Feminist-Vegetarian Critical Theory* (New York: Continuum, 1990), 68; Grandin, "Behavior of Slaughter Plant," 210.
113. Grandin, "Behavior of Slaughter Plant," 210. The euthanasia of animals at the ASPCA

is also taking an enormous emotional toll on workers, most of whom were attracted to their jobs because they love animals. Those who, as a regular part of their jobs, have to kill hundreds of young, healthy animals that could be adopted as pets suffer grief, depression, and nightmares. The decision about which animals to kill is particularly unnerving and often quite arbitrary. (Since we have three black dogs already, this black dog must go.) One employee said, "I am tired of being responsible for society's carelessness" (Debra White, "It's a Dog's Life," *Psychology Today*, November/December 1998, 10).

114. Grandin, "Behavior of Slaughter Plant," 208.
115. Colin Wilson and Donald Seaman, *The Serial Killers: A Study in the Psychology of Violence* (London: W. H. Allen, 1990), 172.
116. Ibid., 173.
117. Marti Kheel, "From Heroic to Holistic Ethics," in *Ecofeminism: Women, Animals, Nature*, ed. Greta Gaard (Philadelphia: Temple University Press, 1993), 260.
118. Grandin, "Behavior of Slaughter Plant," 212.
119. Francesca G. E. Happé, "The Autobiographical Writings of Three Asperger Syndrome Adults: Problems of Interpretation and Implications for Theory," in *Autism and Asperger Syndrome*, ed. Frith, 211.
120. Ibid., 211. The quote reads thus: "One explanation for Temple's merging of human and animal data may be that she ignores or discounts the importance of our affective or emotional life."
121. Happé, "Autobiographical Writings," 213.
122. Ibid., 210.
123. Ibid. Grandin admits to being "very angry when Happé (1991) implied that [she] was not able to express emotion" (Grandin, "How People with Autism Think," 148).
124. This refers to a telephone conversation I had with Grandin in January of 1998. By self-diagnosis Grandin began taking 50 mg of Tofranil (imipramine) daily to calm her nerves, after which she felt that her panic attacks were 90 percent controlled. After four years she switched to 50 mg of Norpramin (desipramine) and had fewer side effects. The medication, she says, changed her life, helping to control stress and colitis. She uses drugs known to help with panic attacks and depression, but in doses much lower than those prescribed for depression. Using these drugs, she says, "is like adjusting the idle screw on a car's carburetor. Before taking the drug the engine was racing all the time. Now it runs at normal speed. I no longer fixate, and I am no longer 'drivin'" (Grandin, "An Inside View," 112).
125. Williams, *Nobody Nowhere*, 204–205; Stanley Milgram, *Obedience to Authority* (New York: Harper and Row, 1974).

CHAPTER 2: DISEMBODIED TOUCH

1. Peter C. Whybrow, *A Mood Apart* (New York: Basic Books, 1997), 255. Whybrow is a professor of psychiatry at the University of Pennsylvania.
2. Antonio R. Damasio, *Descartes' Error: Emotion, Reason, and the Human Brain* (New York: G. P. Putnam's Sons, 1994). For a more philosophical treatment, one could turn to the works of Gerald Edelman, Edwin Hutchins, or Mark Johnson, all of whom give accounts of the mind, accounts which take embodiment seriously and are nondualistic: Gerard M. Edelman's *Bright Air, Brilliant Fire: On the Matters of the Mind* (New York: Basic Books, 1992); Mark Johnson's *The Body in the Mind: The Bodily Basis of Meaning, Imagination, and Reason* (Chicago: University of Chicago Press, 1987); and Edwin Hutchins's *Cognition in the Wild* (Cambridge, Mass.: MIT Press, 1995) argue that embodiment is central to the process of knowing. These texts critique cognitive science as buying into a model of the mind that is disembodied and as holding onto objectivist assumptions about the fixed, external, measurable nature of reality. Hutchins argues that the physical operations we refer to as mind can only be understood in terms of the organism's—or even the community's—interaction with the environment. Hutchins's analysis of cognition as a dynamic, interactive event and his critique of cognitive science as adopting a model of the mind based on a disembodied brain are very much in accord with the nondualistic perspectives adopted here. Of the disembodied models of intelligence used in AI (artificial intelligence), Hutchins explains how AI understood the person in terms of a computer rather than a computer in

terms of a person (Hutchins, *Cognition*, xiv, 368). One might also consider Jane Gallop's *Thinking through the Body* (New York: Columbia University Press, 1988). Gallop, inspired by Adrienne Rich's *Of Woman Born* and works by the Marquis de Sade (particularly *Justine*), theorizes the body from feminist and poststructuralist perspectives.

3. Louis A. Sass, *Madness and Modernism: Insanity in the Light of Modern Art, Literature, and Thought* (New York: BasicBooks, 1992), 67.

4. Jean-Paul Sartre, *Nausea*, trans. Lloyd Alexander (New York: New Directions, 1964), 77 and 10.

5. Characteristics ascribed to chaos theory include attention to small and often unpredictable details, recognition of fluid boundaries, and attention to wholes rather than to parts and to discernible patterns with no exact repetition. Edward Lorentz at MIT discovered that small influences, assumed irrelevant by traditional mathematical sciences, make for completely different situations in complex systems. In the winter of 1961, Lorenz, wishing to repeat a computer simulation about weather, programmed the initial conditions from a printout, which—he had forgotten—rounded the data from six to three decimal places (.506 instead of .506127). The difference of one part in one thousand made for an entirely different weather schematic. Fuzzy mathematics was designed in part to help computers simulate the vagueness and uncertainty of daily life. Leading theoreticians include the Polish mathematician Jan Lukasiewicz in the 1920s, Lotfi Zadeh in the 1960s, and Bart Kosko in the 1980s, the latter two at the University of California, Berkeley. Once denounced as scientific heresy, fuzzy mathematics' founders and adherents describe it as the mathematics of Taoism or Zen Buddhism.

Fuzzy logic rejects the either-or categories of set theory as well as Aristotelian logic, particularly Aristotle's law of the excluded middle, which claims that every statement is either true or not true. By extrapolation, any existent either fits into a set or does not. However, fuzzy mathematics determines membership in a set according to degree (from .00 to 1 rather than either 0 or 1). Binary thinking is thereby eliminated, and shades of gray approximating actual embodied life are restored. (For example, in a set of tall men, a man who is six foot four inches might have a membership value of 0.70 while a man at seven feet two inches might be assigned a degree of 0.99.) "Fuzzy" refers to capturing realities like "somewhat hot" or "usually wrong." Kosko explains fuzzy sets by likening them to a Rubik's cube, with each set a point on the cube (qtd. in Sheldon Teitelbaum, "Making Everything Perfectly Fuzzy," *Los Angeles Times Magazine*, 1 April 1990, 41). Conventional sets would only occupy the corners (tall, not tall). All the rest are fuzzy, and at the midpoint the set equals its own opposite. The midpoint is where paradoxes reside—the yin-yang, the cup that is half empty and half full. The payoff for the technology of fuzzy mathematics is giving a subtlety to instruments so as better to meet environmental conditions, such as washing machines that adjust the level of water use to the amount of laundry one is washing. Fuzzy mathematics was initially dismissed in the United States as useless and imprecise; the Japanese were first to realize the potential of this math.

6. Carol Gilligan, *In a Different Voice: Psychological Theory and Women's Development* (Cambridge: Harvard University Press, 1982), 25–32. Gilligan has taken a lot of criticism for maintaining a position of essentialism with regard to gender. However, I am not entirely convinced that the criticism is warranted. She is not arguing that all boys see the world through an ethic of justice while all girls see the world through an ethic of care. Instead, she speculates, following Nancy Chodorow, that because women have been primarily responsible for childcare, female children have had the opportunity to create identities in relation to someone whom they do not need to regard as separate from themselves. By this same logic, male children have been forced to separate from the mother to define themselves as males. The theory is that girls are allowed the opportunity to develop selves with more fluid boundaries toward others, while the experience of separation leads to clearer ego boundaries for males. This would mean that males find intimacy more threatening while females find separation more threatening. We could add to this psychological theory the suggestion that evolution may have selected for empathy in females as primary caregivers of children. Of course, we all know women who think like Jake and men who think like Amy, but I still find the paradigm helpful to understandings of moral agency. For example, Jake's moral reasoning corresponds to a Kantian rule-based ethic, whereas Amy's corre-

sponds to the notion of the "fitting" in H. Richard Niebuhr's ethic of the responsible self. The helpfulness of the model in describing different approaches to morality is lost if the perspectives are essentialized.

7. John D. Barrow, *Pi in the Sky: Counting, Thinking, and Being* (Oxford: Clarendon Press, 1992), 15. Barrow finds Jain logic more sophisticated with regard to truth claims because its claims are tied to physical reality and because they are not as rigid as Aristotle's rules of logic. Beyond the law of the excluded middle (that every statement is either true or not true), Western logic has the law of identity, everything is what it is, and the law of non-contradiction, both A and not-A cannot be true. According to Barrow, Jain logic includes seven categories: "(1) maybe it is; (2) maybe it is not; (3) maybe it is, but it is not; (4) maybe it is indeterminate; (5) maybe it is but is indeterminate; (6) maybe it is not but is indeterminate; (7) maybe it is and it is not and is also indeterminate" (Barrow, *Pi*, 15). It is interesting that Aristotle's respect for the body never led him to acknowledge more fluid epistemological boundaries. One would imagine that the respect Aristotle held for the biological world would force his sense of logic away from pure mathematics. Aristotle is one of the few philosophers in the Western tradition to construe the sense of touch as important to our moral development, and he acknowledged the way the emotions, along with sensual pain and pleasure, can cause us to transform action, habits, and decisions. Unlike Plato, Aristotle did not want to transcend the emotions, but rather to train or discipline them through the use of reason. The problem with Aristotle's ethics, and the reason that his respect for the body never led to a more fluid epistemology, is that he essentializes the body completely. Different bodies have different souls with different faculties capable of different virtues. By the social hierarchy he followed, only Greek males over the age of eighteen had reason and were capable of moral virtue. Because slaves and women had inferior bodies with inferior souls and faculties, slavery was permitted, as was the ownership of women, who were regarded as "deformed" males.

8. Sara Ruddick, "From Maternal Thinking to Peace Politics," in *Explorations in Feminist Ethics: Theory and Practice*, ed. Eve Browning Cole and Susan Coultrap-McQuin (Bloomington: Indiana University Press, 1992), 145. Ruddick refers to all caregivers as "mothers" to express the experiential rather than biological sense of mothering.

9. Happé, "Autobiographical Writings," 216.

10. Williams, *Somebody Somewhere*, 118.

11. Grandin, "How People with Autism Think," 147.

12. Hans Asperger suggested parallels between the form of autism that bears his name and modern representations of scientific detachment, intellectual life, and traditional "male" thinking. In case histories, Asperger likened the mental life of his patients to "the caricature of a scholar, preoccupied with his own thoughts and out of touch with the real world." He wrote that "the autistic personality is an extreme variant of male intelligence" and, again, that "in the autistic individual the male pattern is exaggerated to the extreme" (Hans Asperger, "'Autistic Psychopathy' in Childhood," in *Autism and Asperger Syndrome*, ed. Frith, 40–41, 84, 85). I am assuming that Asperger was reading this association of science, autism, reason, and maleness in cultural rather than biological terms. His translator and interpreter Uta Frith supports such a reading when she remarks that "a dash of autism is not a bad way to characterize the apparent detachment and unworldliness of the scientist." She goes on to attribute to such "a dash" to herself, as Asperger did to himself (Frith, "Asperger and His Syndrome," 32).

13. Glen A. Mazis, *Emotion and Embodiment: Fragile Ontology* (New York: Peter Lang Publishing, 1993), 10.

14. Ibid., 10–11.

15. Robin May Schott, *Cognition and Eros: A Critique of the Kantian Paradigm* (Boston: Beacon Press, 1988), 96.

16. Ibid., 211–212.

17. Immanuel Kant, quoted in Schott, *Cognition and Eros*, 103.

18. Andrew Cutrofello, *Discipline and Critique: Kant, Poststructuralism, and the Problem of Resistance* (New York: State University of New York Press, 1994), 49.

19. Ibid., 53.

20. Ibid., 33.

21. See Donna Haraway, *Primate Visions: Gender, Race, and Nature in the World of Modern*

Science (New York: Routledge, 1989). Haraway calls this aesthetic posture realism and finds taxidermy an art most suited to it (Haraway, *Primate Visions*, 28). Her idea that taxidermy is most suited to the pursuit of realism is nicely complemented by Wittgenstein's insight in the *Tractatus Logico-Philosophicus* that solipsism, strictly understood, is pure realism (Ludwig Wittgenstein, *Tractatus Logico-Philosophicus* [New York: Harcourt, Brace and Co., 1922], 153). Sass calls this sense of realism narcissism without Narcissus because even the ghost in the machine has vanished (Louis A. Sass, *The Paradoxes of Delusion: Wittgenstein, Schreber, and the Schizophrenic Mind* [Ithaca: Cornell University Press, 1994], 69–71).

22. Peter Mack, ed., *A Bentham Reader* (New York: Pegasus, 1969).
23. Immanuel Kant quoted in Cutrofello, *Discipline and Critique*, 63.
24. Ibid., 39.
25. Emmanuel Chukwudi Eze, "The Color of Reason: the Idea of 'Race' in Kant's Anthropology," in *Postcolonial African Philosophy: A Critical Reader*, ed. Emmanuel Chukwudi Eze (Oxford: Blackwell Publishers, 1997), 115–116.
26. Schott, *Cognition and Eros*, 139–140.
27. Damasio, *Descartes' Error*, xii.
28. Ibid., 178.
29. Ibid., 4.
30. Ibid., 8.
31. Ibid.
32. Ibid., 44.
33. Ibid., 178.
34. Ibid., 211, emphasis added.
35. Mazis, *Emotion and Embodiment*, 87. To Mazis the errors that have been made in traditional philosophical discussions about emotion rest on not perceiving the circular nature of motion in emotion. Subjectivists have viewed the motion in emotion as a movement only of the self to the world, and therefore the self is seen as projecting private meanings onto the world. One is therefore just emoting or making a show. Yet the opposite is also true in that being open to emotion, the world is experienced as moving into us. This is the sense of emotion as being acted upon, the bewitchings of Plato. I take Mazis's point to be that the error made by each view taken alone is in reading the motion as unidirectional. In nondualism, both forms of motion are true at once, composing a circularity of emotion. (Mazis, *Emotion and Embodiment*, 29). Damasio's sense of emotion is similar. He understands emotions as judgments about what is happening to us and, therefore, as important intersections between self and world. Owen Lynch has likewise written, "The self is not merely a mind; it is a totality of mind and body. *Emotions affirm what they assert.* They assert an appraisal, and they affirm this by grounding it in the reality of the bodily self. In this way they are simultaneously body-mind as well as individual-social" (Owen M. Lynch, *Divine Passions: The Social Construction of Emotion in India* [Berkeley: University of California Press, 1990], 14).
36. Mazis, *Emotion and Embodiment*, 80–81 and 90–92.
37. Damasio, *Descartes' Error*, 212–217.
38. Ibid., 131–174.
39. Ibid., 174.
40. Ibid., xiii.
41. Ibid., 230, xvi.
42. Goleman, *Emotional Intelligence*, 10 and 12.
43. Damasio, *Descartes' Error*, 264.
44. Ibid.
45. Ibid., 182.
46. Ibid., 177.
47. Ibid., 178–79.
48. Maxine Sheets-Johnstone, "Charting the Interdisciplinary Course," in *Giving the Body Its Due*, ed. Maxine Sheets-Johnstone (Albany: State University of New York Press, 1992), 15.
49. Ibid., 3. See also Sheets-Johnstone, *The Roots of Thinking*.
50. Sass, *Madness and Modernism*, 75.
51. Ibid., 9–11.

52. See Philip C. Kendall and Constance Hammen, *Abnormal Psychology* (Boston: Houghton Mifflin Co., 1995), 294. An extremely complex and still mysterious disease, schizophrenia is an organic disorder but does appear to require social or environmental factors to become active. There are genetic propensities by which one can measure the degree of vulnerability to schizophrenia (diathesis). Genes that have been determined as making one vulnerable to schizophrenia are found in fewer numbers in persons with schizotypal personality (one to two genetic propensities) than in those with full-blown schizophrenia (nine to ten genetic propensities). Kendall and Hammen describe the prevailing theory as a diathesis-stress approach by which one takes account of both environmental determinants and biological factors. Biological factors include the reduced size of areas in the prefrontal cortex and the temporal lobe and possible abnormalities in the subcortical regions of the limbic system, such as the anterior hippocampus and the amygdala, all parts of the brain which attend to meaning and emotion. There is also reduced blood flow in the frontal regions, as viewed by PET scans. These structural abnormalities affect the ability of the brain to organize and process information as well as to regulate neurotransmitters. Current research focuses on neurotransmitters associated with emotional experience and information processing, in particular, dopamine, which supplies important pathways to the frontal lobe and limbic system. Any combination of these biological factors still seems to be unable to cause schizophrenia apart from environmental determinants. The biological features are necessary but not sufficient, and environmental factors may help account for the diversity of symptoms displayed. Stress, injury, physical pain, viral infections (particularly exposure in utero during the second trimester), psychological adversity, dysfunctional family relations, and negative life events affect the onset of this disease. Bacteria and viruses are also being studied as possible sources of infection. Even low income has been attached to the statistics, as contributing to environmental stress, lack of neonatal care, more frequent viral exposure, birth complications, and family disruptions.
53. Sass, *Madness and Modernism*, 4.
54. Ibid.
55. Ibid., 7–8.
56. Ibid., 168.
57. Ibid., 8.
58. Alexander Lowen, *The Betrayal of the Body* (New York: Macmillan Publishing Company, 1967), 32.
59. Renée, *Autobiography of a Schizophrenic Girl*, trans. Grace Rubin-Rabson, ed. with analysis by Margarite Sechehaye (New York: Grune and Stratton, 1951), 136.
60. Lowen, *Betrayal of the Body*, 67–68.
61. Lauren Slater, *Welcome to My Country* (New York: Random House, 1996), 147.
62. Ibid., 150.
63. Sass, *Madness and Modernism*, 310.
64. Ibid., 274.
65. Ibid., 326.
66. Ibid., 311.
67. Robert D. Romanyshyn, *Technology as Symptom and Dream* (New York: Routledge, 1989), 99.
68. Sass, *Madness and Modernism*, 168.
69. Ibid., 213, see also 445, nt. 82.
70. Mazis, *Emotion and Embodiment*, 40.
71. Ibid., 91.
72. Sass, *Madness and Modernism*, 445, 217–219.
73. Victor Tausk, "On the Origin of the 'Influencing Machine' in Schizophrenia," in *Sexuality, War, and Schizophrenia: Collected Psychoanalytic Papers*, ed. Paul Roazen (New Brunswick, N.J.: Transaction Publishers, 1991), 187. Victor Tausk, a student and member of Freud's original circle of friends, did some of the original research on the influencing machine, remarking that it produces effects of a "mystical nature." Sass explains that while Tausk saw the influencing machine as a projected image of the physical body, one might better read the machine as a projected image of "the subjective body—a lived body that is, so to speak, turned inside out and solidified, reified by the intensity of a self-directed gaze" (Sass, *Madness and Modernism*, 227).

74. Sass, *Madness and Modernism*, 213.
75. Blaise Pascal, *Pensées,* translated and introduced by H. F. Stewart (New York: Modern Library, 1967), 343.
76. Muller and Leary qtd. in Romanyshyn, *Technology as Symptom,* 19.
77. Romanyshyn, *Technology as Symptom,* 42. Romanyshyn dates the linear perspective to 1425, as found in the paintings of Alberti.
78. Romanyshyn, *Technology as Symptom,* 93. Walter Ong suggests that the printing press also worked toward a privatization of mental life. No longer required to listen and tell stories with others, the reader is allowed to sit quietly and enter a different and inner reality (Sass, *Madness and Modernism,* 93).
79. Romanyshyn, *Technology as Symptom,* 115. Romanyshyn dates modernity's conception of madness from 1656, the date the first clinic opened for the insane. He dates the astronaut by the atomic explosion. The suit of the astronaut is now being incorporated by the fashion industry as it seeks to provide clothing equipped with computer and cell-phone technology.
80. Schott, *Cognition and Eros,* 117.
81. Gail Faurschou, "Fashion and the Cultural Logic of Postmodernity," in *Body Invaders: Panic Sex in America,* ed. A. Kroker and M. Kroker (New York: St. Martin's Press, 1987), 82.
82. Susan Buck-Morss, "The Cinema Screen as Prosthesis of Perception: A Historical Account," in *The Senses Still: Perception and Memory as Material Culture in Modernity,* ed. C. Nadia Seremetakis (Boulder, Colo.: Westview Press, 1994), 48.
83. Allen Feldman, "From Desert Storm to Rodney King via ex-Yugoslavia: On Cultural Anaesthesia," in *The Senses Still,* ed. Seremetakis, 105–106.

CHAPTER 3: SADISTIC AND PORNOGRAPHIC TOUCH

1. Robert Kugelmann, "Life under Stress: From Management to Mourning," in *Giving the Body Its Due,* ed. Sheets-Johnstone, 122. See Maurice Merleau-Ponty, "The Child's Relations with Others," in *The Primacy of Perception and Other Essays on Phenomenological Psychology, the Philosophy of Art, History and Politics,* ed. James M. Edie (Evanston: Northwestern University Press, 1964).
2. Bessel A. van der Kolk and Alexander C. McFarlane, "The Black Hole of Trauma," in *Traumatic Stress: The Effects of Overwhelming Experience on Mind, Body, and Society,* ed. Alexander C. McFarlane, Bessel A. van der Kolk, and Lars Weisaeth (New York and London: Guilford Press, 1996), 12. In 1978, Henry Krystal was the first to suggest that trauma results in the "de-differentiation of affect," that is, the inability to identify appropriate emotions to serve as guides for behavior (Bessel A. van der Kolk, "The Complexity of Adaptation to Trauma and Self-Regulation, Stimulus Discrimination, and Characterological Development," in *Traumatic Stress,* ed. McFarlane, van der Kolk, and Weisaeth, 193).
3. Williams, *Somebody Somewhere,* 7–8.
4. Jennifer Manlowe, *Faith Born of Seduction: Sexual Trauma, Body Image, and Religion* (New York: New York University Press, 1995), 24. As we saw in the last chapter, given the right biological conditions, abuse can lead to forms of schizophrenia. As Joseph Berke said of his patient Mary Barnes's collapse into schizophrenia, "Long before I ever heard of Mary Barnes, I had begun to realize that what is commonly called 'mental illness' is . . . an example of emotional suffering brought about by a disturbance in a whole field of social relationships, in the first place, the family" (Mary Barnes and Joseph Berke, *Mary Barnes: Two Accounts of a Journey through Madness* [New York: Harcourt Brace Jovanovich, 1971], 77).
5. Barbara Kantrowitz, "Cradles to Coffins," *Newsweek,* 7 July 1997.
6. Alice Miller, *For Your Own Good: Hidden Cruelty in Child-Rearing and the Roots of Violence,* trans. Hildegarde Hannum and Hunter Hannum (New York: Farrar, Straus, Giroux, 1983), xvi.
7. Ibid., 85.
8. Ibid., 42.
9. Lowen, *Betrayal of the Body,* 264–268.
10. Miller, *For Your Own Good,* 85, emphasis added. Miller sounds here very much as if she were taking a page from the *Tao Te Ching:* from chapter 19, "Throw away morality and

justice, and people will do the right thing"; from chapter 38, "The moral man does something, and when no one responds he rolls up his sleeves and uses force. When the Tao is lost, there is goodness. When goodness is lost, there is morality. When morality is lost, there is ritual"; from chapter 57, "The more prohibitions you have, the less virtuous people will be" (Stephen Mitchell, trans., *Tao Te Ching* [New York: Harper and Row, 1988]).

11. Robert Jay Lifton and Eric Markusen, *The Genocidal Mentality: Nazi Holocaust and Nuclear Threat* (New York: Basic Books, 1990), 193.
12. Williams, *Somebody Somewhere*, 102.
13. Susan Bordo, *Unbearable Weight: Feminism, Western Culture, and the Body* (Berkeley: University of California Press, 1993), 146.
14. Ibid., 145.
15. Cutrofello, *Discipline and Critique*, 63.
16. David Shapiro, *Autonomy and Rigid Character* (New York: Basic Books, 1981), 127. Shapiro writes that sadomasochistic sexuality "is a highly ideational matter, far more a product of the imagination that the senses" (Shapiro, *Autonomy*, 128–129).
17. Susan Griffin, *Pornography and Silence: Culture's Revenge against Nature* (New York: Harper and Row, 1981), 36.
18. Felicity de Zulueta, *From Pain to Violence: The Traumatic Roots of Destructiveness* (Northvale, N.J.: Jason Aronson Inc., 1993), 275.
19. Charles Darwin, *Descent of Man, and Selection in Relation to Sex* (London: John Murray, 1871; facsimile edition, Princeton, N.J.: Princeton University Press, 1981), 71–72 (page citations are to the facsimile edition).
20. James Rachels, *Created from Animals: The Moral Implications of Darwinism* (Oxford, U.K.: Oxford University Press, 1991), 131.
21. Darwin, *Descent*, 71–72.
22. Rachels, *Created from Animals*, 136. Referring to Charles Darwin's *The Formation of Vegetable Mold, through the Action of Worms* (London: John Murray, 1881).
23. Linda Hogan, "Department of the Interior," in *Minding the Body: Women Writers on Body and Soul*, ed. Patricia Foster (New York: Doubleday, 1994), 160.
24. Stephen J. Gould, "Kropotkin Was No Crackpot," *Natural History* 97, 7 (1988): 12–21. Frans de Waal, *Good Natured: The Origins of Right and Wrong in Humans and Other Animals* (Cambridge, Mass.: Harvard University Press, 1996), 21–22.
25. Haraway, *Primate Visions*, 250.
26. Mary E. Clark, *Who Do We Think We Are?* (forthcoming).
27. De Zulueta, *From Pain to Violence*, 205.
28. C. Nadia Seremetakis, "The Memory of the Senses, Part II: Still Acts," in *The Senses Still*, ed. Seremetakis, 28.
29. Ibid., 27.
30. Ibid., 42 and 98.
31. Simon Baron-Cohen, *Mindblindness: An Essay on Autism and Theory of Mind* (Cambridge, Mass.: MIT Press, 1995), 42 and 37.
32. Clark, *Who Do We Think We Are?*
33. Baron-Cohen, *Mindblindness*, 119 and 99.
34. Frans de Waal, *Good Natured*, 84–85.
35. Jonathan Cole, *About Face* (Cambridge, Mass.: MIT Press, 1998), 4–6. Cole refers to research showing that as many as six facial expressions are now accepted by many researchers as universal or found in every human culture. This would place emotion squarely within the bounds of evolutionary development and confirm Darwin's speculations about the artificial borders between human and animal emotional life. Happiness, disgust, sadness, fear, anger, and surprise appear to be universally understood. Chimps and monkeys make many of these faces, including showing embarrassment, now under consideration as a seventh universal expression (Cole, *About Face*, 36).
36. McFarlane, van der Kolk, and Weisaeth, *Traumatic Stress*, 191; Goleman, *Emotional Intelligence*, 198. James Wilson explains that the guidance necessary to develop empathy toward others is particularly needed by males, who are known in every society to be "more likely than women to play roughly, drive recklessly, fight physically, and assault ruthlessly, and these differences appear early in life." Wilson argues that "compared to their sisters, men are born neurologically less advanced: they are four to six weeks less well developed and thus, corresponding, more in need of care. They are

more likely to be hyperactive, autistic, colorblind, left-handed, and prone to learning disorders." Males also appear to be harmed in more adverse ways by the drug use of their mothers and by domestic unrest than are females (James Wilson, *The Moral Sense* [New York: Free Press, 1993], 165–166).

37. See Rachels, *Created from Animals*, 218.
38. Ibid.
39. Haraway, *Primate Visions*, 231.
40. Ibid., 238.
41. Ibid.
42. Ibid.
43. Rachels, *Created from Animals*, 219.
44. Ibid., 220.
45. See Emmy Werner and Ruth Smith, *Overcoming the Odds* (New York: Cornell University Press, 1992).
46. Miller, *For Your Own Good*, 265.
47. Wilhelm Reich, *The Mass Psychology of Fascism* (New York: Farrar, Straus, and Geroux, 1971), 301.
48. Morton Schatzman, *Soul Murder: Persecution in the Family* (New York: Random House, 1973), 29–30.
49. Miller, *For Your Own Good*, 9.
50. Schatzman, *Soul Murder*, 177. James Wilson points out how strange it is to talk about teaching moral behavior as if it were the same thing as learning a skill like riding a bike. He points out the irony that Skinner used behaviorism with the intent of raising humans out of nature when "For all the difference it made, people might as well have been Labrador retrievers" (Wilson, *The Moral Sense*, 143).
51. Ibid., 41–42.
52. Ibid., 43–49.
53. Ibid., 67–122.
54. See Thomas S. Szasz, *The Manufacture of Madness: A Comparative Study of the Inquisition and the Mental Health Movement* (New York: Harper Torchbooks, 1970), 186.
55. Schatzman, *Soul Murder*, 119.
56. Ibid.
57. Ibid., 119–120.
58. Ibid., 169–171.
59. See Miller, *For Your Own Good*, 71.
60. Ibid., 165.
61. Hannah Arendt, *Eichmann in Jerusalem: A Report on the Banality of Evil* (New York: Viking Press, 1963), 121.
62. Haraway, *Primate Visions*, 59–68.
63. Sander Gilman, *Difference and Pathology* (Ithaca, N.Y.: Cornell University Press, 1985), 88; Sander Gilman, *The Jew's Body* (New York and London: Routledge, 1991), 64–79.
64. Gilman, *Difference*, 83.
65. G. S. Rousseau, "'A Strange Pathology': Hysteria in the Early Modern World, 1500–1800," in *Hysteria beyond Freud*, ed. Sander L. Gilman et al. (Berkeley: University of California Press, 1993), 100.
66. Schatzman, *Soul Murder*, 17. Little is known of Schreber's wife, but her daughter Anna portrays her as a supportive partner, eagerly reading galley proofs, busy helping to plan and live out her husband's agenda. Margaret Harlow called herself the "midwife" to Harry's rebirthing of their surrogate monkey children.
67. Adams, *The Sexual Politics of Meat*, 108.
68. Sass, *The Paradoxes of Delusion*, x and 1.
69. Schatzman, *Soul Murder*, 8–10.
70. Ibid., 51, see also 42–50.
71. Ibid., 77 and 161.
72. Shapiro, *Autonomy*, 148, see also 146–155.
73. Schatzman, *Soul Murder*, 94.
74. Shapiro, *Autonomy*, 150–155.
75. Ibid., 150.
76. Cutrofello, *Discipline and Critique*, 109.
77. Ibid., 115.

78. Barbara Ehrenreich and Dierdre English, *For Her Own Good: 150 Years of the Experts' Advice to Women* (New York: Anchor Books, Doubleday, 1978), 109.
79. David B. Morris, *The Culture of Pain* (Berkeley: University of California Press, 1991), 115.
80. Ehrenreich and English, *For Her Own Good*, 105.
81. Moore, introduction to *Building Bodies*, ed. Moore, 23.
82. Sandra Lee Bartky, *Femininity and Domination: Studies in the Phenomenology of Oppression* (New York: Routledge, 1990), 40.
83. Slater, *Welcome to My Country*, 50–51. Becky Thompson points out that one of the consequences of sexual abuse is the loss of a sense of an intact body. Instead of being "in one piece," sexually abused women describe their bodies as "a 'piece of swiss cheese,' as an 'eggshell that has been smashed into a thousand pieces,' as 'ashes thrown up in the air, no shape at all.'" Becky Thompson, *A Hunger So Wide and So Deep: American Women Speak Out on Eating Disorders* (Minneapolis: University of Minnesota Press, 1994) 47.
84. See Rousseau, "'A Strange Pathology,'" 131–132.
85. Griffin, *Pornography*, 172; Sander L. Gilman, "The Image of the Hysteric," in *Hysteria beyond Freud*, ed. Gilman et al., 389–391.
86. In "The Aetiology of Hysteria," published in 1896, Freud hypothesized that hysteria had its origins in premature sexual experience, that is, sexual experience in the earliest years of childhood. Freud and his colleague Joseph Breuer wrote of a "momentous discovery," that hysteria is a psychological state caused by "unbearable emotional reactions to traumatic events" leading to an altered state of consciousness. Bending under the weight of the prevailing cultural paradigm, Freud retracted the discovery, calling the original theory "my far-reaching blunder." Freud explained, in "The Theory of Infant Sexuality," that he had simply confused desire for reality. See Bessel A. van der Kolk, Lars Weisaeth, and Onno van der Hart, "History of Trauma in Psychiatry," in *Traumatic Stress*, ed. McFarlane, van der Kolk, and Weisaeth, 47–74; and Manlowe, *Faith Born of Seduction*, 11–14.
87. Van der Kolk, Weisaeth, and van der Hart, "History of Trauma in Psychiatry," 47–74; Manlowe, *Faith Born of Seduction*, 11–13. Recent research has begun to tie the pain of childbirth (and resulting postpartum depression) to PTSD.
88. McFarlane, van der Kolk, and Weisaeth, *Traumatic Stress*, 193.
89. Miller, *For Your Own Good*, 163.
90. Shapiro, *Autonomy*, 145.
91. Sigmund Freud, "On the Mechanism of Paranoia," 1911; reprinted in *Three Case Histories*, ed. and with an introduction by Philip Rieff (New York: Collier, 1963), 169.
92. Miller, *For Your Own Good*, 179.
93. Griffin, *A Chorus of Stones*, 136.
94. Miller, *For Your Own Good*, 81.
95. Arendt, *Eichmann in Jerusalem*, 93.
96. Eichmann in Miller, *For Your Own Good*, 87–89. See the discussion of Milgram's experiment in Felicity de Zulueta, *From Pain to Violence: The Traumatic Roots of Destructiveness* (Northvale, N.J.: Jason Aronson Inc., 1993), 249–261, and also in Wilson, *The Moral Sense*, 49–53. De Zulueta points out that societies based on violence exploit these tendencies by giving those who find the student's pain insignificant (or who enjoy it) the hands-on job of inflicting pain while others do the paperwork to make the violence happen. That description matches the dynamics in the slaughterhouse as described by Grandin.
97. Milgram in Wilson, *The Moral Sense*, 49–53.
98. Arendt quoted in Judith Halberstam, *Skin Shows: Gothic Horror and the Technology of Monsters*, (Durham, N.C.: Duke University Press), 161.
99. Griffin, *Pornography*, 86.
100. Ibid., 22.
101. Jacques Lacan, "Kant with Sade," *October* 55 (winter 1989): 74.
102. Miller, *For Your Own Good*, 113; Griffin, *Pornography*, 177 and 193.
103. Morris, *Culture of Pain*, 242.
104. Sonia Johnson, *Going out of Our Minds: The Metaphysics of Liberation* (Freedom, Calif.: Crossing Press, 1987), 252–253.
105. Griffin, *Pornography*, 219–228.

106. Ibid., 219.
107. Ibid., 222. Carol Adams recognizes parallels between equipment used to control farm animals and bondage equipment in pornography and sadomasochism, such as chains, prods, collars, and ropes. (Adams, *The Sexual Politics of Meat*, 40).
108. Griffin, *Pornography*, 25.
109. Adams, *The Sexual Politics of Meat*, 58. Adams also explicitly ties the liberation of animals with the liberation of women. Speaking of Mary Daly's suggestion that feminists raid the *Playboy*'s playground to let out "the bunnies, the bitches, the beavers, the squirrels, the pussycats, the cows, the nags, the foxy ladies, the old bats and biddies, so that they can at last begin naming themselves," Adams says, "We, her readers, know that she is talking about women and not about actual bunnies . . . but, I argue she should be" (Adams, *The Sexual Politics of Meat*, 61).
110. Johnson, *Going out of Our Minds*, 253.
111. Lionel Dahmer, *A Father's Story* (New York: William Morrow and Company, 1994), 62, 76, and 186. Jeffrey Dahmer's mother, Joyce, was extremely ill during the time she was pregnant. As she was portrayed by Dahmer's father, every noise and smell became unbearable to her. Joyce suffered from sleep deprivation, uncontrolled muscle spasms, forms of rigidity such as locked legs, and seizures that caused her to foam at the mouth. She was given barbiturates, morphine, and "various" other pills, up to twenty-six a day. She hated nursing and gave it up after several days. In addition, Jeffrey was born with a double hernia, for which he had surgery in the spring of 1964 when he was four years old. He awoke in great pain and asked doctors if they had cut off his penis (Dahmer, *Father's Story*, 31–36 and 58–59).
112. Halberstam, *Skin Shows*, 34–35.
113. Rousseau, "'A Strange Pathology,'" 100.
114. Morris, *Culture of Pain*, 242.

CHAPTER 4: MASOCHISTIC AND ASCETIC TOUCH

1. Arthur Kroker and Marilouise Kroker, "Theses on the Disappearing Body in the Hyper-Modern Condition," in *Body Invaders*, ed. Kroker and Kroker, 20.
2. See Susana Herrera, *Mango Elephants in the Sun: How Life in an African Village Let Me Be in My Skin* (Boston and London: Shambhala, 1999).
3. Ibid., 192.
4. Richard Sennett, *The Fall of Public Man* (New York: Alfred A. Knopf, 1977), 9.
5. Margaret Miles, "Textual Harassment: Desire and the Female Body," in *The Good Body: Asceticism in Contemporary Culture*, ed. Mary G. Winkler and Letha B. Cole (New Haven: Yale University Press, 1994), 49–63.
6. Belden C. Lane, *The Solace of Fierce Landscapes: Exploring Desert and Mountain Spirituality* (New York and Oxford, U.K.: Oxford University Press, 1998), 188.
7. Lorde, "Uses of the Erotic," 210.
8. Christian Wertenbaker, "Awakening the Emotions: The Transformation of the Emotional Life," *Parabola* 23 (fall 1998): 79–82.
9. Miles, "Textual Harassment," 54.
10. Joseph Campbell, quoted in Peter Levine, "The Body as Healer: A Revisioning of Trauma and Anxiety," in *Giving the Body Its Due*, ed. Sheets-Johnstone, 106.
11. Debra Niehoff, *The Biology of Violence: How Understanding the Brain, Behavior, and Environment Can Break the Vicious Circle of Aggression* (New York: Free Press, 1999), 245–246.
12. Ibid., 202, see 200–202.
13. Goleman, *Emotional Intelligence*, 110.
14. Niehoff, *The Biology of Violence*, 101 and 130.
15. Robert M. Sapolsky, *Why Zebras Don't Get Ulcers: A Guide to Stress, Stress-Related Diseases, and Coping* (New York: W. H. Freeman and Company, 1994), 13–14 and 7.
16. Kugelmann, "Life under Stress," 110 and 117.
17. Niehoff, *The Biology of Violence*, 187
18. Sapolsky, *Why Zebras Don't Get Ulcers*, 211.
19. Ibid., 217–221.
20. Niehoff, *The Biology of Violence*, 185.
21. Ibid.

22. See Thompson, *A Hunger So Wide and So Deep*, 47–60, 96–102.

23. Linda Hess, "Craving," in *Being Bodies*, ed. Friedman and Moon, 200.

24. Ibid.

25. Thompson, *A Hunger So Wide and So Deep*, 109.

26. Manlowe, *Faith Born of Seduction*, 56.

27. Karen Conterio and Wendy Lader, *Bodily Harm: The Breakthrough Program for Self-Injurers* (New York: Hyperion, 1998), 56 and 64–65.

28. Niehoff, *The Biology of Violence*, 209.

29. Juliet B. Schor, *The Overspent American: Upscaling, Downshifting, and the New Consumer* (New York: Basic Books, 1998), 158.

30. Ibid.,15–21.

31. Ibid., 6–28.

32. Mazis, *Emotion and Embodiment*, 269–270. Schor found that people with the most debt said that they watch too much television: "Each additional hour of television watched per week reduces annual saving by $208" (Schor, *The Overspent American*, 78). This doesn't sound like much until you consider that the average American watches twenty-eight hours of television a week (two months a year, nine years by the age of sixty-five). The American Academy of Pediatricians recently advised parents not to let children under two years old watch television at all and not to allow older children to have a television in their bedroom because the resulting physical and mental isolation are suspected as taking a toll on human relations.

33. Susan Bordo, *Twilight Zones: The Hidden Life of Cultural Images from Plato to O. J.* (Berkeley: University of California Press, 1997), 112–113.

34. Ibid., 128.

35. Bordo, *Unbearable Weight*, 151.

36. Jenefer Shute, "Life-Size," in *Minding the Body*, ed. Foster, 254 and 256.

37. Ibid., 258.

38. Angelyn Spignesi, *Starving Women: A Psychology of Anorexia Nervosa* (Dallas, Tex.: Spring Publications, 1993), 18–19 and 35. Spignesi is referring to the work of Hilda Bruch and quotes one of Bruch's patients as saying, "It's not that I fear food as much as I do fear the irrational feeling that somehow the food almost has the power over me that a person would—it is almost as if it [the food] could make me eat it" (Spignesi, *Starving Women*, 21).

39. Stephen D. Moore, *God's Gym: Divine Male Bodies of the Bible* (New York: Routledge, 1996), 76.

40. Alan M. Klein, *Little Big Men: Bodybuilding Subculture and Gender Construction* (Albany: State University of New York Press, 1993), 27.

41. Maria R. Lowe, *Women of Steel: Female Bodybuilders and the Struggle for Self-Definition* (New York and London: New York University Press, 1998), 124–126.

42. Klein, *Little Big Men*, 214; Moore, *God's Gym*, 100.

43. Lowe, *Women of Steel*, 141.

44. Klein, *Little Big Men*, 177–178.

45. Moore, introduction to *Building Bodies*, ed. Moore, 2.

46. Novid Parsi, "Don't Worry, Sam, You're Not Alone: Bodybuilding Is So Queer," in *Building Bodies*, ed. Moore, 128.

47. Ibid., 123.

48. Ibid., 129 and 133.

49. Roy F. Baumeister, *Masochism and the Self* (Hillsdale, N.J.: I. Erlbaum Associates, 1989).

50. Lynda Hart, *Between the Body and the Flesh* (New York: Columbia University Press, 1998), 81.

51. Robert Stoller, *Pain and Passion: A Psychoanalyst Explores the World of S&M* (New York: Plenum Publishing, 1991), 26. Stoller believes that consensual sadomasochism may be able to reach a level of therapy unavailable to the traditional therapist by reconstruction of the earlier trauma "in the theater of pain" (Stoller, *Pain and Passion*, 290).

52. Hart, *Between the Body and the Flesh*, 81.

53. Ibid., 161.

54. See Barbara Rose, "Is It Art? Orlan and the Transgressive Act," *Art in America* 81 (February 1993): 82–87; and Miriam Sas, "The Doyenne of Divasection," *Mondo 2000* 13 (1995): 106–111.

55. Sas, "The Doyenne of Divasection."

56. William Harris, "Demonized and Struggling with Demons," *New York Times*, 23 October 1994, 31–35.
57. The juxtaposition of the anorexic to the astronaut is Romanyshyn's interpretation in *Technology as Symptom and Dream*, 170–173.
58. Fakir Musafar, "Body Play: States of Grace or Illness?" epilogue to *Bodies under Siege: Self-Mutilation and Body Modification in Culture and Psychiatry*, by Armando R. Favazza, 2nd ed. (Baltimore and London: The Johns Hopkins University Press, 1996), 328, see also 325–327.
59. Ibid., 333.
60. Miller, *For Your Own Good*, 113.
61. Kim Power, *Veiled Desire: Augustine on Women* (New York: Continuum, 1996), 98.
62. Schott, *Cognition and Eros*, 51.
63. Peter Brown, *The Body and Society: Men, Women, and Sexual Renunciation in Early Christianity* (New York: Columbia University Press, 1988), 408.
64. Schott, *Cognition and Eros*, 47.
65. Brown, *The Body and Society*, 415. Power argues that Saint Augustine's harshness toward his own body not only was consistent with his aim for perfection in everything that he did, but also was due to the fact that, within a span of four years, he lost his lover of nine years, their son, his mother, and two close friends. Filled with pain himself, he came to associate relationships and sexuality with grief and freedom from them with transcendence (see Power, *Veiled Desire*, 100–101).
66. Seremetakis, "The Memory of the Senses," 5.
67. Logan Jenkins, "39 Bodies: In God's Name, Why?" *San Diego Union Tribune*, 28 March 1997.
68. Thanks to my colleague, Dr. Alan Sparks, for this reference to the Sayings Source Q as found in Luke 7:31–35.
69. Lane, *The Solace of Fierce Landscapes*, 192.
70. Thomas Merton, quoted in Lane, *The Solace of Fierce Landscapes*, 50.
71. Kallistos Ware, "The Way of the Ascetics: Negative or Affirmative?" in *Asceticism*, ed. Vincent L. Wimbush et al. (New York: Oxford University Press, 1995), 9.
72. Lane, *The Solace of Fierce Landscapes*, 165 and 188.
73. Henry Nelson Wiemer, quoted in Bernard Lee, "The Appetite of God," in *Religious Experience and Process Theology: The Pastoral Implications of a Major Modern Movement*, ed. Harry James Carges and Bernard Lee (New York: Paulist Press, 1976), 378.
74. Miranda Shaw, *Passionate Enlightenment: Women in Tantric Buddhism* (New Jersey: Princeton University Press, 1994), 20–21 and 70.
75. Ibid., 168. These are public gatherings, with the goal of restoring people to their senses by releasing their negative, habitual, and narcissistic responses to life. When we are released from these things, the transient and interwoven nature of reality becomes evident; this is difficult to generate in solitary meditation and completely unavailable in the mode of fixity (Shaw, *Passionate Enlightenment*, 21). One finds similar practices in some of Judaism's meditation exercises, in which sexual partners become "aware of the spark of the Divine in the pleasure itself and elevate it to its source" (Roger Kamenetz, *The Jew in the Lotus: A Poet's Rediscovery of Jewish Identity in Buddhist India* (San Francisco: HarperSanFrancisco, 1994), 205.
76. Shaw, *Passionate Enlightenment*, 24.
77. See Morris, *Culture of Pain*, 131.
78. See Teresa M. Shaw, *The Burden of the Flesh: Fasting and Sexuality in Early Christianity* (Minneapolis, Minn.: Fortress Press, 1998), 236.
79. Maureen Flynn, "The Spiritual Uses of Pain," *Journal of the American Academy of Religion* 54 (summer 1996): 272. There were some exceptions. For example, Margaret of Oingt had a vision of a dead tree (herself) coming back to life when flooded by a great river. On the tree's branches were written—touch, taste, smell, hearing, sight (Caroline Walker Bynum, *Holy Feast and Holy Fast: The Religious Significance of Food to Medieval Women* [Berkeley: University of California Press, 1987], 219).
80. Bynum, *Holy Feast and Holy Fast*, 213.
81. Ibid., 114 and 210.
82. Ibid., 246.
83. Edith Wyschogrod, *Saints and Postmodernism: Revisioning Moral Philosophy* (Chicago: University of Chicago Press, 1990).

84. Bynum, *Holy Feast and Holy Fast*, 250.
85. Ibid., 122.
86. See Cristina Mazzoni, *Saint Hysteria: Neurosis, Mysticism, and Gender in European Culture* (Ithaca, N.Y.: Cornell University Press, 1996), 211.
87. Mark Taylor, *About Religion: Economies of Faith in Virtual Culture* (Chicago and London: University of Chicago Press, 1999), 151 and 154.
88. Michele Martin, "On the Other Side of Attachment," in *Being Bodies*, ed. Friedman and Moon, 153–162; Tsultrim Allione, *Women of Wisdom* (London and Boston: Routledge and Kegan Paul, 1984), 143–149. Allione explains that the Chod kills four "demons," including the demon that blocks the senses by means of control and objectification, the demon that attracts us in obsessional ways, the demon that presents the self as separate from others, and the demon of unawareness (Allione, *Women of Wisdom*, 147).
89. Lee, "The Appetite of God," 383.
90. Mazzoni, *Saint Hysteria*, 205–206.
91. Ibid., 51.
92. Michel Foucault, quoted in Dana Becker, *Through the Looking Glass: Women and Borderline Personality Disorder* (Boulder, Colo.: Westview Press, 1997), 3.

CHAPTER 5: MINDFUL TOUCH

1. Audre Lorde, *A Burst of Light* (Ithaca, N.Y.: Firebrand Books, 1988), 117.
2. Trungpa, *Myth of Freedom*, 75.
3. James H. Austin, *Zen and the Brain: Toward an Understanding of Meditation and Consciousness* (Cambridge, Mass.: MIT Press, 1998), 18 and 58.
4. Ibid., 82.
5. Anne C. Klein, "Grounding and Opening," in *Being Bodies*, ed. Friedman and Moon, 141.
6. Trungpa, *Myth of Freedom*, 49. It should be said that meditation can also be used to self-medicate, as psychologist Mark Epstein thinks happens when people who are depressed seek relief in meditation. In a fascinating essay, "Prozac and Enlightened Mind," Epstein makes this remark to Judith Hooper as she attempts to sort out the differences between facing individual psychological depression and facing the human condition. The dharma, like the pedagogy of pain, is about the latter. One cannot face the human condition adequately from a state of depression, according to Epstein, because most of the energy in the meditation goes to fighting depression. Thus, many Buddhist practitioners report that their use of Prozac gives them the strength to face life as it is (Judith Hooper, "Prozac and the Enlightened Mind," *Tricycle: The Buddhist Review* 8, 4 (summer 1999): 38–41). Loren Slater records the opposite problem in her book *Prozac Diary*. Slater's medication left her no longer interested in Viktor Frankl or Kierkegaard. Instead, she found herself reading *Glamour* magazine and going shopping (Loren Slater, *Prozac Diary* [New York: Random House, 1998], 7–8).
7. Klein, "Grounding and Opening," 143.
8. John Kabat-Zinn quoted in *Healing Emotions*, ed. Goleman, 128.
9. Sandy Boucher, *Turning the Wheel: American Women Creating the New Buddhism* (Boston: Beacon Press, 1988), 14.
10. Thich Nhat Hanh, *The Sun My Heart* (Berkeley, Calif.: Parallax Press, 1988), 65. Epstein points out that the deepening of subjectivity that comes with the force of eros is so strong that eros is referred to in traditional Buddhist literature as "pseudo-nirvana" (Mark Epstein, *Thoughts without a Thinker: Psychotherapy from a Buddhist Perspective* [New York: BasicBooks, 1995], 150). However, in moral terms, eros as pseudo-nirvana may be at least as important as nirvana understood as the transcendence of subjectivity. Amadeo Solé-Leris explains that absorptive forms of meditation were traditionally taught in monasteries along with vipassana. However, this was done with the explicit recognition that while complete withdrawal from physical and mental stimuli can lead to "highly rarefied states of pure, unrestricted consciousness," it cannot lead to the "insight" or "clear seeing" which is vipassana (Amadeo Solé-Leris, *Tranquillity and Insight: An Introduction to the Oldest Form of Buddhist Meditation* [London: Rider, 1986], 22–23). Vipassana is arguably the better choice for the novice, the laity, and for erotic morality because of its practical nature and because of the difficulty spiritual novices

have translating experiences of rarefied consciousness into everyday life. By stressing the virtues of vipassana, I do not mean to imply that wisdom cannot be had in forms of transcendence that go beyond the senses. Sandra Boucher writes about her recent struggle with colon cancer, saying that even though vipassana helped sustain her throughout surgery and recovery, she finally learned its limits. After five days of chemotherapy that left her unable to quit vomiting, she was lying on a gurney in the hall of a hospital, with a ten-inch open incision in her belly, surrounded by people enduring their own agonies. Finding herself left without protections, the pain of everyone there entered her directly and became so severe that she passed over into a space that entailed neither sensation or solidity, space captured by a Buddhist sutra: "in emptiness no form, no feelings, no perceptions, no impulses, no consciousness." This was not the vibrating energy Boucher had experienced during vipassana at Denison's: "No, this is something else, as if all of me has been lifted out into a vast space that is both inside me and outside me. A space that encompasses every person and object, sound and smell, holding all in exquisite pleasurable suspension" (Sandy Boucher, "Thirteen Hours," in *Tricycle: The Buddhist Review* 9, 3 [spring 2000]: 65). Perhaps such a state is available to and awaiting all of us in our most painful moments. But the first task of erotic morality is the practical task of finding the inner ground and stillness that comes with awareness of feeling in doing.

11. Thich Nhat Hanh, *Being Peace*, ed. Arnold Kotler (Berkeley, Calif.: Parallax Press, 1987), 46–47.
12. Mazis, *Emotion and Embodiment*, 243.
13. Mary Kay Blakely, "Psyched Out," *Los Angeles Times Magazine*, 3 October 1993, 48.
14. Ibid., 28.
15. Ibid.
16. Ibid.
17. Sutherland, "Body of Radiant Knots," 3–4.
18. Klein, "Grounding and Opening," 143.
19. Nhat Hanh, *Being Peace*, 26.
20. Ibid.
21. Sandy Boucher, *Opening the Lotus: A Women's Guide to Buddhism* (Boston: Beacon Press, 1997), 12.
22. Williams, *Nobody Nowhere*, 206.
23. Pema Chödrön, *When Things Fall Apart: Heart Advice for Difficult Times* (Boston and London: Shambhala, 1997), 12 and 118.
24. Lorde, "Uses of the Erotic," 209.
25. Chödrön, *When Things Fall Apart*, 95.
26. Alice Walker and Pema Chödrön, "Good Medicine for This World," *Shambhala Sun* 7, 3 (January 1999): 34.
27. Pema Chödrön, "Three Methods for Working with Chaos," in *Being Bodies*, ed. Friedman and Moon, 164; Pema Chödrön, *Awakening Compassion: Meditation Practice for Difficult Times* (Boulder, Colo.: Sounds True Audio), audiocassette 1; Lane, *The Solace of Fierce Landscapes*, 194.
28. Chödrön, *Awakening Compassion*, audiocassette 1.
29. Audre Lorde, *The Cancer Journals* (San Francisco: Aunt Lute Books, 1980), 60.
30. Epstein, *Thoughts without a Thinker*, 86.
31. Solé-Leris, *Tranquillity and Insight*, 94.
32. Chödrön, *Awakening Compassion*, audiocassette 4.
33. Austin, *Zen and the Brain*, 522.
34. Niehoff, *The Biology of Violence*, 254.
35. Francisco Verela, in *The Embodied Mind: Cognitive Science and Human Experience*, ed. Evan Thompson, Francisco J. Varela, and Eleanor Rosch (Cambridge, Mass.: MIT Press, 1991), 122–123.
36. Kenneth S. Cohen, *The Way of Qigong: The Art and Science of Energy Healing* (New York: Ballantine Books, 1997), 11.
37. Philip Smith, "Moving Zen," *Tricycle: The Buddhist Review* 9 (spring 2000), 58.
38. Cohen, *The Way of Qigong*, 13. In a way similar to Reich's critique of the Prussian military, Cohen compares the instability of the posture of the soldier standing at attention to the stability of the rooted T'ai Chi posture. The military posture places the chest out, stomach in, knees locked—a position from which one is easily pushed over. Cohen

speculates that this is because the posture is designed to leave soldiers cut off and ready to accept external orders. In qigong the chest sinks, knees are bent, feet rooted, leaving one balanced and very difficult to push over (Cohen, *The Way of Qigong*, 95–96).

39. John Dewey, introduction to *The Use of the Self: Its Conscious Direction in Relation to Diagnosis, Functioning, and the Control of Reaction*, by F. Matthias Alexander (Downey, Calif.: Centerline Press, 1984).

40. Yuasa Yasuo, *The Body, Self-Cultivation, and Ki-Energy*, trans. Shigenori Nagatomo and Monte S. Hull (New York: State University of New York Press, 1993), 210–212.

41. See the work of contemporary neuroscientists as presented in Bill Moyer's series *Healing the Mind*, part 2, "The Mind Body Connection"; also Niehoff, *The Biology of Violence*, 149; and Goleman, *Healing Emotions*, 34–43.

42. Cohen, *The Way of Qigong*, 45–46.

43. Herbert Benson et al. "Body Temperature Changes during the Practice of g Tum-mo Yoga," *Nature* 295, 21 January 1982, 234–235.

44. Julie Henderson, "Tulku," in *Being Bodies*, ed. Friedman and Moon, 217 and 218.

45. Austin, *Zen and the Brain*, 142 and 305.

46. Ibid., 665.

47. Dalai Lama, in *Healing Emotions*, ed. Goleman, 90.

48. Austin, *Zen and the Brain*, 296–298.

49. Ibid., 78.

50. Ibid., 182.

51. Winnie Tomm, *Bodied Mindfulness: Women's Spirits, Bodies, and Places* (Waterloo, Ont.: Wilfrid Laurier University Press, 1995), 310–317.

52. Casey Hayden, "Body on the Line," in *Being Bodies*, ed. Friedman and Moon, 148 and 151.

53. Tomm, *Bodied Mindfulness*, 23.

54. Nhat Hanh, *Being Peace*, 115.

55. Austin, *Zen and the Brain*, 633.

56. Epstein, *Thoughts without a Thinker*, 187.

57. Austin, *Zen and the Brain*, 76.

58. Epstein, *Thoughts without a Thinker*, 65.

59. Austin, *Zen and the Brain*, 567.

60. David Foster, "On the Inside," *San Diego Union Tribune*, 8 April 1998.

61. Mark Epstein, *Going to Pieces without Falling Apart: A Buddhist Perspective on Wholeness* (New York: Broadway Books, 1998), 75.

62. Yasuo, *The Body*, 58.

63. Austin, *Zen and the Brain*, 75.

64. Cohen, *The Way of Qigong*, 117.

65. Austin, *Zen and the Brain*, 94–95 and 98.

66. See, for example, Arthur I. Waskow, *Down-to-Earth Judaism: Food, Money, Sex, and the Rest of Life* (New York: W. Morrow, 1995).

67. Stephen Mitchell, trans., *Tao Te Ching*, chapter 12.

68. Lorde, *Cancer Journals*, 52.

69. Robert F. Kennedy Jr., "I Don't Like Green Eggs and Ham!" *Newsweek*, 26 April 1999, 12.

70. Roshi Philip Kapleau, *To Cherish All Life: A Buddhist Case for Becoming Vegetarian*, 2nd ed. (San Francisco: Harper and Row, 1982), 12. The U.S. Department of Agriculture gives statistics on the slaughter of cattle in this country at approximately 1,117,650,000, sheep and lambs at 6,487,000, and poultry at 8,006,980,000 for 1999. Department of Agriculture, *Agricultural Statistics 2000* (Washington, D.C.: U.S. Government Printing Office, 2000).

71. William E. Thompson, "Hanging Tongues: A Sociological Encounter with the Assembly Line," *Qualitative Sociology* 6 (fall 1983): 215–237.

72. Kapleau, *To Cherish All Life*, 75–78; Daniel C. Maguire and Larry L. Rasmussen, *Ethics for a Small Planet: New Horizons on Population, Consumption, Ecology* (Albany: State University of New York Press, 1998), 6.

73. Kapleau, *To Cherish All Life*, 78.

74. Kennedy, "I Don't Like Green Eggs and Ham!" 12.

75. Rita M. Gross, *Soaring and Settling: Buddhist Perspectives on Contemporary Social and Religious Issues* (New York: Continuum Publishing Company, 1998), 84–85.

76. Ronna Kabatznick, "The Zen of Eating," *Inquiring Mind: A Semi-Annual Journal of the Vipassana Community* 14 (spring 1998): 16–17. The Worldwatch report by Brian Halwell and Gary Gardner found that for the first time in history the number of overweight people is approximately the same as the number of the underfed—1.1 billion. Worldwatch proposes taxing food based on nutritional value per calorie; therefore, fast foods would have the highest tax, fruit and vegetables the lowest (Associated Press, *San Diego Union Tribune,* 5 March 2000, A-10).

77. David Kligman, "The Edible Schoolyard," *San Diego Union Tribune,* 24 May 1998.

78. See the Heifer Project International homepage at http://www.heifer.org or write to Heifer Project International—World Headquarters, P. O. Box 8058, Little Rock, Arkansas, 72203; tel. 501-907-2600.

79. Robert Sardello, quoted in Romanyshyn, *Technology as Symptom,* 197.

80. Schor, *The Overspent American,* 146–154.

81. Ibid., 137.

82. Maguire and Rasmussen, *Ethics for a Small Planet,* 8, 18.

83. Karl Marx, "Theses on Feuerbach," in *Basic Writings on Politics and Philosophy: Karl Marx and Friedrich Engels,* ed. Lewis S. Feuer (Garden City, N.Y.: Doubleday and Company, 1959), 243.

84. Elaine Scarry, *The Body in Pain: The Making and Unmaking of the World* (Oxford: Oxford University Press, 1985), 263, see 255 and 261–263.

85. Wyschogrod, *Saints and Postmodernism,* 194.

86. Peter Van Ness, "Practices and Meanings of Asceticism in Contemporary Religious Life," in *Asceticism,* ed. Wimbush et al., 593.

87. See Epstein, *Thoughts without a Thinker,* 22–24; Trungpa, *Myth of Freedom,* 35–37.

88. Austin, *Zen and the Brain,* 127.

89. Tomm, *Bodied Mindfulness,* 67–68.

Index

Cutrofello, Andrew, 67, 69, 96, 116
Cuvier, Georges, 112

Dahmer, Jeffrey, 126, 126n111
Dahmer, Lionel, 126n111
Dalai Lama, 189, 190
Daly, Mary, 126n109
Damasio, Antonio, 61, 70–79, 74n35
damping apparatus, 178–181
Darwin, Charles, 97–98
de Beauvoir, Simone, 96, 165, 167
Deism, 87
Denison, Ruth, 171
deontology, 62, 64, 64n6, 95, 111; and
    autistics, 44, 64–65, 76; and habits,
    67, 121
dependent co-arising, 172, 184
depression, 136–137, 170n6; see also
    learned helplessness
de Sade, Marquis. See Sade, Marquis de
DeSalvo, Albert, 54
Descartes, René, 5, 61–62, 85–86, 91
desire, in American economy 204–205;
    and desirelessness 143–144; and disci-
    pline, 123–124; forces of, in Bud-
    dhism, 173–174, 185–186, 202–203,
    206–207; as illness, 111–123,
    155–156, 182; see also addiction; con-
    ditioning; consumerism
de Waal, Frans, 99, 102
Dewey, John, 188
de Zulueta, Felicity, 97, 101, 122n96
dharma, 170n6, 177
Diamond, Marion Cleaves, 30
Dieters Feed the Hungry, 203
discipline, in bodybuilding, 146; and
    character, 69, 106–107, 110–111,
    143–146; in child-rearing, 103–104,
    106–107; and desire, 123–124; over
    nature, 95–96; obsessive-compulsive,
    154; and punishment, in Foucault, 68,
    in Kant and Sade, 69; and weakness,
    144–145; see also asceticism; condi-
    tioning
dissociation, 82, 92–97, 154 182; in
    Janet and Freud, 119; of the ego, 43,
    60, 129, 140
Dogon, 11
drugs, effect on brain, 33, 38–39,
    57n124; see also substance abuse
dualism, 66–70, 90, 207; Cartesian, 61,
    61n2, 80; as control, 96; culture-na-
    ture, 55–56, 58, 98–99, 111, 125, 187;
    mind-body 60–76, 86, 154–156; in

autism, 24; in individuals and soci-
    eties, 83–97; modern 88
Dunagan, Dianna, 33, 50
duty, cultivation of, 95, 110–111; and
    obedience 107, 121–122

eating, compulsive, 138–139, 155; ha-
    bitual 82, 107, 121; as measure of
    worth, 69, 145; mindful, 198–204; as
    sacrament, 162–166
eating disorders. See anorexia; bulimia;
    compulsive eating; food intolerances
Edelman, Gerald, 61n2
Edible Schoolyard, 203
ego, boundaries of 64n6, cultivation of,
    185; dissociated, 60, 129, 140; and
    false identities, 43, 46, 182; freedom
    from, 159
Ehrenreich, Barbara, 116
Eichmann, Adolf, 70, 111, 121–122
emotional: awareness, 60; connection,
    and sexuality, 123; development,
    31–32, 100; disorder, 24; experience,
    78–79; memory, 136, 150; protec-
    tions, 176–179; responses to the envi-
    ronment, 100, 134; and sensory
    systems, 34
emotional intelligence (Goleman), 3,
    77–79, 195
emotions, 5; and adaptation, 60–61,
    73–79, 91, 188; and autism, 24; bio-
    chemistry of, 73, 189, 197; and cogni-
    tion, 60–77, 80; and culture, 79,
    92–97; in Damasio, 73, 74n35, 76;
    and practical reason 70–79, 121; in
    Descartes, 85–86; as illnesses, 94,
    111–123; and intelligence, 31; in
    Kant, 66; in Lynch 74n35; in Mazis,
    73–74, 74n35; in Plato, 66; and mus-
    cular rigidity 83, 107; and sensations,
    58, 73, 78, 82, 134, 183, 186, 189–190;
    and situatedness 78, 128, 133–134;
    and somatic markers 76–79, 179, 194;
    in Tantric practice, 159; see also "ani-
    mal spirits"; "mattering"
empathy, 6, 19, 50–53, 55–58; capacity
    for, 92, 97–100, 101–104, 104n36;
    and equanimity, 176; erosion of,
    54n135, 55; see also compassion;
    squeeze machine
emptiness, in Buddhism, 13, 171–172,
    192
endorphins, 42
English, Deirdre, 116

About the Author

Linda Holler is associate professor and chair of the religious studies department at San Diego State University.